Praise for *Counselling Pathways: Developing your career*

Rick Hughes and his contributing authors offer an accessible, rich and thought-provoking introduction to the main contexts in which UK counsellors are currently building their careers. Each chapter provides the opportunity to hear from a range of experienced practitioners who are both passionate about their work and realistic about the challenges it poses. This book is gold dust for counsellors embarking on their careers, as well as those considering a change in direction.
Dr Susan Stephen, Lecturer in Counselling, University of Strathclyde

This is a handy pocket mentor offering essential guidance, information and a steadying influence during and post qualification in what can seem like a mystifying maze of options (hidden and in plain sight) in the counselling profession. Your training will teach you about the healing and transformative effect of counselling and the costs and benefits to you and clients. In this book, you will learn what counsellor/psychotherapy practitioners continually do to ensure effective safe and ethical practice of what goes on 'in the counselling space/s' with clients, including the important components of creativity and spirituality in those relationships.
Val Watson, independent coach, counsellor, psychotherapist and supervisor, formerly head of Nottingham University counselling service

As counselling students approach the end of their training, the conversation in the classroom turns to what next. My thanks to Rick Hughes – this book is very welcome and will be a most valuable resource for those conversations. Contributors speak about their careers and experiences in healthcare, education, workplaces and private practice. Offering insights, advice and guidance for those embarking on their careers and for those seeking new directions, this book will be key reading.
Professor Stephen Joseph, University of Nottingham, author of *Think Like a Therapist*

Rick Hughes' book on counselling careers pathways should be essential reading for students and counselling practitioners considering their future career development. It's packed with information about online counselling, counselling in the private practice, workplace counselling, counselling and coaching. It is extremely well organised,and provides readers with a variety of options for future career development. A must-read for all in the counselling field.
Professor Sir Cary Cooper, CBE, University of Manchester, Chair of the National Forum for Health & Wellbeing at Work

An essential aspect of doing good work as a counsellor or psychotherapist involves finding a role or niche within the profession that makes it possible to put one's skills and experience to best use. *Counselling Pathways* is an invaluable resource both for students of counselling and psychotherapy and for more experienced practitioners to learn more about the options and what it is like to work in different therapeutic settings. This book offers a series of vivid and authentic snapshots of the realities of being a therapist in the UK at the present time and how colleagues in the varied branches of the profession handle the distinctive challenges with which they are faced. This is an accessible, consistently informative, hopeful and unique book that is highly recommended for anyone with an interest in the diversity of contemporary therapeutic practice.
Julia McLeod, Lecturer in Counselling, University of Aberdeen

This unique text provides a straightforward and engaging map of the diverse landscape of employment in counselling and psychotherapy. The contributors offer a wealth of personal insights gained from real-world experience in the field, showing clearly how to succeed in a range of therapy settings. Inspiring, thorough and accessible, this book is a goldmine of information for everyone training as a therapist and planning their future career, as well as qualified therapists wanting to understand and break into a new sector of work.
Nicola Blunden, Programme Leader for the MA in Counselling and Psychotherapy at UWE Bristol, co-author of *Next Steps in Counselling Practice*

COUNSELLING PATHWAYS

DEVELOPING YOUR CAREER

Edited by
Rick Hughes

Foreword by
Professor Andrew Reeves

First published 2024

PCCS Books Ltd
Wyastone Business Park
Wyastone Leys
Monmouth
NP25 3SR
United Kingdom

contact@pccs-books.co.uk
www.pccs-books.co.uk

This collection © Rick Hughes, 2024
The individual chapters © the contributors, 2024

All rights reserved.

No part of this publication may be reproduced, stored in a retrieval system, transmitted or utilised in any form by any means, electronic, mechanical, photocopying or recording or otherwise, without permission in writing from the publishers.

The authors have asserted their right to be identified as the authors of this work in accordance with the Copyright, Designs and Patents Act 1988.

Counselling Pathways: Developing your career

British Library Cataloguing in Publication data: a catalogue record for this book is available from the British Library.

ISBNs   paperback – 978 1 915220 43 1
               epub – 978 1 915220 44 8

Cover design by Jason Anscomb
Typeset in-house using Minion Pro and Myriad Pro
Printed in the UK by 4Edge, Hockley, Essex

CONTENTS

	Foreword *Professor Andrew Reeves*	*ix*
	Introduction *Rick Hughes*	*1*
1	Counselling in NHS primary care settings *Vicki Palmer*	*11*
2	Counselling in private practice *Rick Hughes*	*29*
3	Online counselling *Sarah Worley-James*	*48*
4	Workplace counselling *Vianna Boring Renaud*	*69*
5	Counsellors who coach *Lucy Myers*	*90*
6	Counselling in higher and further education settings *Géraldine Dufour*	*112*
7	Counselling in the third sector *Jeremy Bacon*	*130*
8	Counselling in hospice settings *John Wilson*	*147*
9	Counselling children, young people and families *Sarah Watson*	*168*
10	Spirituality in counselling practice *Alistair Ross*	*186*
	About the contributors	*207*
	Appendix: Professional bodies	*219*
	Name index	*227*
	Subject index	*231*

About the editor

Rick Hughes is currently editor of *BACP University & College Counselling* journal, having also been editor of *BACP Workplace* journal, when he was Deputy Chair of the Association for Counselling at Work (now BACP Workplace). Latterly, he was Head of Service at the University of Aberdeen Counselling Service, after eight years as BACP's Lead Advisor: Workplace. He completed his initial counselling training at the University of Strathclyde in the 1990s, under Professor Dave Mearns, who awarded him an Honorary Research Fellowship for his MPhil.

His portfolio counselling career has involved working in a range of sectors, including private practice, workplace, NHS primary care, NHS secondary care, and higher education. In the workplace sector, he was a case manager, account manager and business development consultant for one of the world's largest (at the time) EAP providers. As well as working as an affiliate counsellor for several EAP providers, he has also been the nominated lead counsellor, in a privately contracted capacity, for a host of organisations, including regional counsellor for a global pharmaceutical corporation.

He has published widely, including books on stress, trauma, people support and wellbeing, and continues to work as a freelance writer, BACP-accredited counsellor, coach and wellbeing consultant.

Acknowledgements

This book would not have come to life without the fantastic efforts of the great and the good from the counselling world, to whom I am eternally grateful.

First, to the talented team at PCCS Books for their support, encouragement and professionalism – a big thank you. A three-gun salute to commissioning editor Catherine Jackson, who kept me on the straight and narrow when I felt I was losing the plot.

An equally massive thank you to the wonderful contributors who have come together to share their therapeutic journeys, insights, learnings and personal life experiences so that you can get a real sense of what it's like to work as a counsellor from those who have been there and done it.

In no particular order, a loud round of applause to all the contributors to this book: Sarah Watson, Jo Holmes, Sarah Houghton, Alison Roy, Lorna Birrell, Rhona Kenny, Alex.Arthur, Lindsay Gardner, Paul Carslake, Lucy Myers, Joanne Wright, Shane Buckeridge, Veronica Lysaght, Yvonne Inglis, Carolyn Mumby, John Wilson, Paul Parsons, Vicki Palmer, Catherine Jackson, Alistair Ross, Sukhi Sian, Keith Duckett, Amy McCormack, Salma Khalid, Delroy Hall, Lesley Ludlow, Géraldine Dufour, Desmond Channer, Mark Fudge, Jane Harris, Dominic McLoughlin, Allie Scott, Stella Sookun, Stefan Wilson, Jeremy Bacon, Sabrina Bailey, Sarah Worley-James, Matthew Leavesley, Tasha Gibbard, Ellie Fretwell, Eleanor Brown, Cloie Parfitt, Rachael Klug, Jennifer Hamilton, Vianna Boring Renaud, Nick Wood, Julie Hughes, Eugene Farrell and Andrew Kinder.

I'm also indebted to Professor Andrew Reeves for his foreword, setting the scene for what follows. Thank you, Andrew.

And last but not least, grateful appreciation to my wife, Kirsty, for her ceaseless encouragement.

Foreword

Professor Andrew Reeves

Haven't we come a long way? I mean, really, haven't we? Reading this book, I am in awe at the range of practice, the richness of perspective and how we, as a profession, are really working hard to respond to, and meet the needs of, the diversity of peoples and communities we aim to support. It has left me feeling proud that I am a small part of this vast community, but also very aware of what we haven't yet tackled and where we might go next – and there is still an awful lot to do.

But why do I begin with looking back at our professional journey, suggesting much has changed?

You could look back in history and determine that, right across our development as humans in contact with each other, that relationship – the being with, the listening to and the supporting of the 'other' – has been fundamental to our growth and development. Also, that the failure to do that has led to the most bloody and devastating conflicts, which sadly is still part of our experience. If relationship is the beating heart of humanity, counselling is just one dimension of that. This, of course, would be true.

Or you could reflect on the early analysts, such as Freud, Jung and others, who, in the late 1800s and early 1900s, prepared the ground for the diversity of practice that is now contemporary therapy. Along the way, of course, we can identify critical figures who, in response to or in reaction against the analytic position, developed different ways of thinking about human experience and shaped what we understand through humanistic, cognitive and behavioural lenses. You could argue that these developments have literally spanned more than a century – plenty long enough for us to get to where we are now. Perhaps my question about 'coming a long way' is not so much an accurate reflection of the reality and more my own falling into the narcissistic trap of seeing the world only through my lens and experience.

I am sure that the latter point is almost certainly true, for it is one of the dangers we face as a profession today (more of that later). But I still hold faith in the validity of my original assertion about the extent and depth of change we are witnessing in counselling, psychotherapy and mental health. When I trained as a counsellor (and I remain proud to call myself a counsellor), we, as a profession, still sat on the fringes of mental health and comparatively few clients were able to access counselling as a positive choice for help. Indeed, in the late 1980s when I began my counselling training and approached the local GP surgery to ask if they would consider me for a placement, they responded as if I had suggested something slightly indecent. I ended up on placement in a therapeutic community for young men with drug-related problems, but I suspect that was possibly more because of my social work background rather than my counselling training.

Things then began to change, however; over the following years, slowly, counselling began to find its place in an ever-increasing range of settings and working with a broader set of client groups and experiences. From the fringes, we began to move into the mainstream. The third sector, often at the leading edge of innovation, really began to develop the counselling 'offer', and important work around bereavement counselling was built into other areas. University counselling, a long-established sector, increasingly became seen as a critical part of the student support service, as opposed to a 'nice thing to do' for some. Almost all universities in the UK developed their own counselling service, embedded in the institution. Workplace counselling, again sometimes built into the organisation itself and at other times offered through third-party organisations (such as Employee Assistance Programmes (EAPs)) began to thrive as employers either saw the benefit of supporting employee mental health or, having found themselves taken to court, began to see the dangers of not supporting employee mental health. Counselling in schools, an early innovation, found a new momentum, and provision for young people was greatly improved. Indeed, in some nations of the UK, it is now a requirement that all schools have counselling in place. Independent practice, always the cornerstone of counselling, began to thrive, with many practitioners seeing it as either an opportunity for paid work or a space where they could create their own preferred way of working, or both.

In parallel with this was the growth of the professional associations, with more becoming available, offering a choice of professional 'home' to the practitioner. And more and more people are opting to train and work as counsellors, whether independently or for the NHS or in the voluntary and independent sectors. As a measure of this expansion, when I was Chair of the British Association for Counselling and Psychotherapy (BACP), from 2014–2019, membership rose from 42,000 to 62,000. And it is still rising.

While counselling and psychotherapy are, at the time of writing, not a statutory regulated profession (that is, anyone can use the title 'counsellor' or 'psychotherapist', unlike in, say, social work or clinical psychology, where only those registered with a relevant professional body can use the title to describe what they offer), they are regulated through the Professional Standards Authority. The various professional bodies still have their own ethical codes and frameworks, as well as professional conduct processes, but they operate to the same high standards of quality and its assurance. Research is blossoming in academia and practice settings, and we now know so much more about how people can be helped most effectively. We have also a huge range of ways of working with our clients (modalities), with more and more coming on stream, as well as innovations in how they can all be used in conjunction with each other, in the form of integration and pluralism.

Beyond this, however, and for me the most powerful and important change, is how counselling has moved into the parlance of social discourse – people now talk routinely about 'therapy' and 'counselling' and know more or less what it means. Counselling features regularly on social media, in other media and in our everyday conversations. This means that the stigma of going to see a counsellor is arguably less that it has ever been. Surely, that can only be a wonderful thing, when people can take their own decision to find their own preferred kinds of support without having to go through the medicalisation of traditional psychiatric services, which used to be the case. That is not to dismiss the importance of mental health services, for they are essential and often save lives, but people need different things at different times, and they have more choice than ever before.

So, this remarkable book speaks not only to contemporary practice across a broad range of settings, but also of innovation, risk-taking, boundary-pushing, imagination and of so many practitioners who have wanted things to be different and gone ahead and changed them. As I said at the start, there is much more to do and much more to change. In my view, we have perhaps become overly narcissistic as a profession – we are perhaps spending too much time reflecting on our own image rather than looking outwards and seeing where we might be needed and what we can learn from others in other settings and other client groups. Social media too, is an area where we are still trying to find an appropriate professional voice. But, having read this book, I remain very optimistic about our future and hope to continue to be part of that journey.

Professor Andrew Reeves
Chester, UK

Introduction

My aim with this book is to give you, the counselling trainee/student/practitioner, an idea of what it's like to work as a counsellor in the range of different settings and contexts that is, currently and broadly, available to you. Counselling training may equip you with the skills to be a counsellor, but once you've finished your training, where next? Would you like, say, to set up in private practice, or work with students in higher or further education, or specialise and take further training to work with children and young people and their families? These are just some of many counselling pathways on offer, and all have their own histories, environments, cultures, skills requirements and idiosyncrasies of policy, procedure and practice.

Whether you're starting out on your counselling career or considering a change in your career trajectory to work in a different environment, this book seeks to give you a taster of what's out there. Purposefully, it's not 'academic'; rather, it draws on the real-life experience of people who have been there and done it themselves – the experts. Hopefully their experiences and insights will give you useful information and, importantly, inspiration to explore further the potential paths that lie ahead of you.

The work of a counsellor is always a journey of continual professional and personal learning and development. That is its beauty. And it has the huge advantage as a profession that the skills are highly transferable; we can carry our basic toolkit with us from one context to another, adding specialist knowledge and adaptations as we go. And it shows in the breadth of experience we can claim – the stickers on our luggage, if you like. Few of us will have followed a closely curated career pathway as we reach the end of our professional journey, and the contributors to this book illustrate that.

So, as an opener to how the book is presented, here's the itinerary for my own professional journey.

I left school in the mid-1980s with a set of abysmal qualifications. School bored me. I didn't really know what to do next, but managed to get onto a BA (Hons) Business Studies degree, which I hoped would be sufficiently broadly based to help me eventually find a purpose and meaning in life. I enjoyed two subject areas in particular – marketing and organisational psychology. Marketing initially triumphed, and I subsequently found a job with an advertising agency.

But, after a few years, I started to question my suitability for advertising. While I enjoyed the creative side, to me it seemed to be all about persuading people to buy something they often didn't need; it was all about the exchange of money and conspicuous consumption. I felt the 'people' side was missing in my life. The only account I really enjoyed working on was Guide Dogs for the Blind Scotland, mainly because I'd make up excuses to visit their Scottish training HQ, where I would go and play with the puppies. The writing was on the wall. I was definitely a people person – and a puppy person.

One constant for me during my first university degree and beyond was that I always seemed to be the person folk would seek out, albeit usually in a pub, to talk about the struggles in their lives – relationship issues, losses, stresses, worries, anxieties and so on. I enjoyed being able to help. When my partner of the time raised the idea of me training to be a counsellor, it was a eureka moment… and the planets started to align.

I 'tested the water' with a certificate in counselling skills, then completed a full-time diploma in counselling. Both gave me the skills and competences to start my new career. During the diploma, I completed two placements to build up my practice hours with clients – one at a GP practice and the other at a private therapy centre. They were very different environments, and that is when I realised that I could be a counsellor in different contexts – that counselling training is where you learn the therapeutic skills that you can then carry with you into a wide range of practice contexts.

But my diploma course provided very little information and guidance about these varied, different environments and what it's like to work in them. And when I was researching for my first book, *Experiences of Person-Centred Counselling Training* (Buchanan & Hughes, 2000), I realised this lack of preparation for a counselling career and teaching about the different options ahead was common throughout the UK.

Fast-forward to 2022, and my nephew began to show an interest in training to be a counsellor. 'What's it like?' he asked. I gave him some pointers and a few books that I felt would provide him with a broad picture. Then he asked, 'But where could I work?' So I talked about my own experience of working as a counsellor in private practice, in primary and secondary care, in the workplace, employee assistance programmes (EAPs) and universities, plus a foray into coaching and mentoring. I didn't give him any books to read about the different counselling contexts because I couldn't find any.

So, welcome to this book! My aim here is to provide that vital information about career development pathways and the different sectors where you can work.

Choices, choices...

Do you choose your preferred sector or does it choose you? Much can depend on the work opportunities in your local area. When I was a workplace counsellor, I found many colleagues had had previous experience in other roles and organisations before training to be a counsellor, so they were already familiar with industrial, commercial and business settings.

A major component of the ethical frameworks produced by our professional bodies is the commitment to ensure we are competent to practise safely and effectively, as well as ethically. While ultimately the work is all about the client you see in front of you, the context can have a massive impact. Understanding the environment in which you work is crucial to your therapeutic competence needed to work there.

Before I introduce the book chapters, it's relevant to offer an idea of what the wider workplace landscape is like out there and where counsellors actually practise.

Every year, the British Association for Counselling and Psychotherapy (BACP, the largest professional body of counsellors in the UK, with more than 67,000 members at the time of writing) conducts a workplace mapping survey to fill out a picture of the working practices of their members. Here is a quick summary of the relevant highlights of the 2021–2022 survey results – the most recent available as this book went to print (BACP, 2023) – and I thank BACP for permission to quote from its findings.

The largest majority of members worked in private practice (nearly 70%); nearly one third (32%) worked in the third, charitable and voluntary sector, and after that the numbers drop sharply in relation to the other main settings and contexts. Table 1 summarises these findings and the data on other roles such as supervisors, tutors and service managers.

The United Kingdom Council for Psychotherapy (UKCP) conducted a similar mapping survey of its members in 2020. UKCP tends to represent mainly psychodynamic therapists, rather than counsellors. Specifically, of the 2,180 members who completed the survey, 80% were working in private practice,

Table 1: Top 15 professional roles of BACP members

Professional roles (many respondents held more than one role)	%
Practitioner in private practice	69.26%
Practitioner in the third sector/charity sector/voluntary sector	31.37%
Supervisor	25.14%
Practitioner in an Employee Assistance Programme/workplace setting	9.18%
Practitioner in a healthcare setting	8.61%
Trainer/tutor	8.13%
Trainee/student	7.50%
Practitioner in a secondary school	7.29%
Practitioner in NHS IAPT (England)	5.80%
Other non-counselling/psychotherapy role	5.23%
Practitioner in a primary school	4.82%
Service manager/clinical lead	4.44%
Practitioner in private group practice	4.36%
Practitioner in a university/higher education institution	4.12%
Coach	3.74%

education or the charity/volunteer sector; 163 worked in an EAP; 67 worked for an organisation funded by their local authority; 1,850 worked in private or independent practice; 107 worked for a non-NHS health service provider; 487 were based in the charity/volunteer sector; 208 worked in further or higher education and 130 worked in schools. Of the 20% working in the NHS, the majority were paid at Band 7 or Band 8a – that is, at the more experienced, senior end of the NHS pay scales for psychological practitioners (UKCP, 2020).

The voices of those who know

A key objective of this book is to present real-life experiences of what it's like to practise as a counsellor or therapist in a range of sectors. It has been an enthralling experience to seek out, make contact with and solicit contributions from some of the leading practitioners in the counselling world.

Each chapter presents several personal perspectives on a particular workplace context. This means the chapters are all slightly different in format and focus. This diversity deliberately reflects both the realities of the various environments, where different issues are likely to be more prominent, and the breadth of diversity among practitioners. We come from all backgrounds and bring a wide array of experience, views, values and priorities of concern.

I'm delighted and humbled by the quality and calibre of the contributions from those who have joined me in putting this book together. Again and again, contributors told me they wished they had had a book like this to guide them when they started out, and that this had fuelled their enthusiasm to contribute. Indeed, one of the questions I put to all authors was, 'What do you know now that you wish you had known when you began your counselling career?'

The contributors willingly and graciously share their own professional experiences and insights. The hope is that, by following their journeys, you the reader will be inspired to take the next step into developing your own counselling career.

The book doesn't cover every conceivable counselling working context as it would be impossible to examine the nuances of every opportunity out there. That said, there are some specialist areas worth mentioning. Within the health sector, fertility counselling, for instance, has its own professional membership body, the British Infertility Counselling Association (BICA), which provides guidelines, training and accreditation. Similarly, genetic counsellors have their professional body, the Association of Genetic Nurses and Counsellors (AGNC), and specialist training requirements. In some NHS trusts, there are oncology counsellors, although oncology departments may refer patients to fertility counsellors where the cancer impacts fertility issues. There are also cancer counsellors, though in many areas this support is contracted from third sector organisations, such as Marie Curie and Macmillan, and the roles may be performed by clinical psychologists and/or mental health nurses.

BACP, like other professional bodies, includes a number of specialist divisions that represent, campaign for and champion specific areas of practice, and I have largely adopted these as the framework for this book. BACP members can join any of these divisions for a modest fee. They each have their own journal, networking groups, events, online communities and, in most cases, competence frameworks.

I have been a member of BACP all my professional life, so the contacts I have made – and many of the contributors to this book – are associated with BACP in some form or another. I am also very grateful for the help, assistance and support provided by BACP in putting this book together. That said, there are other professional membership bodies available for counsellors, and I have listed these in the Appendix at the end of the book.

The chapters

We begin with the world of counselling in primary care settings, largely exploring the training and career development opportunities offered by what was previously known as Improving Access to Psychological Therapies (IAPT) and is now called NHS Talking Therapies. As someone who has worked in this sector for many years and successfully bid for and delivered IAPT contracts across the south west of England, Vicki Palmer is well placed to tease out the intricacies of this complex environment and offer a dispassionate view of the very real benefits as well as the challenges. She also offers some excellent guidance regarding work opportunities and how to prepare for interviews. She is joined by Shane Buckeridge, Tasha Gibbard and Matthew Leavesley, who provide snapshots of frontline practice (respectively) in Scotland and in NHS Talking Therapies services in England.

As BACP's and UKCP's workplace mapping surveys suggest, private practice is where most counselling and psychotherapy practitioners work. In Chapter 2, I draw on my experience to address what it's like to follow this popular counselling pathway. I have had many varied experiences of working in private practice over the years. In my experience, and that of other practitioners who have helped me write the chapter, private practice is a big step for recently qualified practitioners, although not impossible. You're very much on your own as you take on the responsibility for your own policies and procedures and the welfare of your clients, and you'll find it perhaps a bit isolating after being so very much part of a group during your training. All counsellors need to assess for, manage and mitigate risk, for client and self, and if you are employed in an organisation, it should give you a safety net and support that you won't have as an independent practitioner. The peer support and learning and mentoring from more experienced colleagues in an organisation are also invaluable as you build your knowledge and confidence, as well as skills. Having said that, if you prepare and plan for this, it can be a very fulfilling experience, and for some these days, it may be their only way to get work. Grateful thanks to private practitioners Alex.Arthur, Paul Carslake and Lindsay Gardner, who provide their insightful perspectives on working in this environment.

The Covid-19 pandemic also forced many of us to work in different ways. Before Covid, virtual and online counselling was very much a side-shoot from mainstream in-person counselling. Few practitioners felt confident to pursue and offer it, and it was widely regarded with suspicion, bordering on hostility. Yet, as Sarah Worley-James illustrates in Chapter 3, online counselling in all its myriad forms (emails, instant messaging, video, audio…) has not only entered the mainstream but, in many settings, has become the preferred delivery platform for counselling. Supported by Ellie Fretwell, Eleanor Brown, Cloie Parfitt, Rachael Klug and Jennifer Hamilton, Sarah explains what online counselling is about, the challenges and opportunities in practising in this way, and the opportunities offered by the new delivery platforms that are emerging.

Counselling in the workplace is the focus in Chapter 4, with contributions from a highly experienced team led by Vianna Boring Renaud, Chair of BACP's Workplace division. She is joined by Nick Wood, Julie Hughes, Eugene Farrell and Andrew Kinder.

Drawing on their experience of offering counselling in various workplace settings over the years, including through EAPs, the contributors brilliantly capture the different components, variables and idiosyncrasies of this sector. Many counsellors who practise in workplace settings have had some prior experience as an employee themselves in a range of organisations. Indeed, as the chapter's contributors reflect, it is really very helpful for counsellors to have a working understanding and appreciation of the intricacies and imperatives of organisations and negotiating the complexities of corporate cultures, policies and procedures, to say nothing of the relational issues involved. And throughout this work runs a constant dynamic – when you are, or work for, the organisation that is paying you to provide the counselling, who is your client? The employer or the employee?

In Chapter 5, we enter into the world of counsellors who coach. This is a relatively new work area; for a long time coaching has been seen as very separate from counselling and a distinctly different discipline. Yet, while there are clear demarcations and differences between the training and approach of the counsellor and the coach, counsellors who coach have found it brings an added dimension to their work and it has evolved into a distinct area of very fruitful practice. We have a great line-up of contributors here, headed by Lucy Myers, who chairs BACP's Coaching division, and supported by Joanne Wright, Veronica Lysaght, Yvonne Inglis and Carolyn Mumby.

BACP has recently published a coaching competence framework (BACP, 2022), which maps out the competences required of qualified counsellors/ therapists who wish to develop the scope of their practice to include coaching. What emerges from this, and Lucy's chapter, is that integrating coaching into your practice is more suited to experienced counsellors – it is perhaps not an entry-level option, although there are some excellent courses offering this at master's level. Those interested in pursuing coaching as a main area of practice or to complement their counselling toolkit might want to check out the Association for Coaching and its competency framework (Association for Coaching, 2012), and the International Coaching Federation (see Appendix for details of both of these organisations).

Chapter 6 delves into the realm of counselling in universities and further education colleges. Géraldine Dufour previously led the University of Cambridge's counselling service and here she heads up a group of highly experienced colleagues from both higher (university) and further (college) education settings: Desmond Channer, Mark Fudge, Jane Harris, Dominic McLoughlin, Allie Scott, Stella Sookun and Stefan Wilson. They bring massive enthusiasm for the work they do in their roles.

With increasing demand from students for counselling and often limited funding, this can be a challenging sector to work in. There may be pressures in some work environments to adapt the counselling models you have only recently learned. For example, some settings have introduced single-session counselling in order to reduce waiting lists, and most are now offering guided self-help and online groups for the same reason. But it's exciting work and trying out different ways of working can only broaden your horizons and hone your skills. Post-qualification, we need always to be receptive to change and new developments. And, as the contributors illustrate, working with young people at such a pivotal and influential stage in their lives provides immeasurable work satisfaction.

In Chapter 7, Jeremy Bacon, BACP's Third Sector Lead, guides us through the myriad opportunities offered in the charitable and voluntary sector. As BACP's workplace mapping survey showed, this sector is the second most common source of employment opportunities for counsellors. Indeed, many trainees will be benefiting from and engaging with this sector when they complete their placement requirement. As Jeremy explains, employment opportunities often emerge from these placements or volunteering.

Jeremy also includes a fascinating contribution from Sabrina Bailey, who talks about her experience of working at Bedfordshire Open Door, an award-winning charity offering free and confidential counselling to young people aged 13 to 25. Sabrina Bailey completed her student placement with Open Door and found it a career-defining experience that shaped her counselling practice. Jeremy also writes about the growing opportunities to provide counselling for older people – an age group that is much more embracing of counselling as its demographic profile changes but is still too often sidelined.

Next, John Wilson, who is director of the bereavement service at York St John University Counselling and Mental Health Clinic and an honorary research fellow of the university, provides a fascinating account of working in hospice settings. In Chapter 8, he outlines some of the therapeutic models that practitioners need to be familiar with and gives some guidance on how to get work in these settings. He also provides a historical overview to demonstrate how hospice and bereavement care have changed. John has spent his whole professional career working with the dying and bereaved and can offer an informed insight into the very varied demands and rewards of this sector. He is joined by Paul Parsons, who offers a vivid first-person account of his own role.

And finally, in terms of the specialist sectors, in Chapter 9 we turn to children, young people and families (CYPF). Grateful thanks to Sarah Watson for her absorbing examination of this sector. Sarah is a BACP senior accredited CYPF psychotherapist and a cognitive behavioural therapist. As well as running a private practice, she works at BACP as its CYPF Ethics Consultant.

What strikes me most about Sarah's chapter are the sheer complexities of issues that a counsellor working with children, young people and families needs to be aware of. As a CYPF adviser to BACP members, she gets lots of enquiries about people wanting to specialise in this sector, yet she finds many either don't have the necessary qualifications and skills or don't appreciate the importance of the ethical issues and safeguarding factors that can impact the work. Thanks also to Jo Holmes, BACP's Lead for Children, Young People and Families, for her feedback on this chapter, and to Sarah Houghton, Alison Roy, Lorna Birrell and Rhona Kenny for their contributions.

We close with a chapter on spirituality in counselling practice. This is not a 'sector' as such – these days, few counselling roles are specific to a particular faith or faith setting, although there are, of course, opportunities to use counselling skills in other roles within faith organisations, and Islamic counselling (for example) is an area of specialist practice within the profession.

However, many clients connect deeply with a religion, belief system or spirituality, and counsellors, of course, follow many different faith traditions and hold varied spiritual beliefs. Being able to see a counsellor who understands and appreciates the significance of religious and spirituality issues can make it easier for clients to bring and engage with their own values and beliefs within the counselling relationship.

As lead author, Alistair Ross brings vast knowledge from a long career pioneering the appreciation of spirituality in the counselling context. Here he knits together contributions from practitioners with a wide span of spiritual and religious beliefs and practices: Sukhi Sian, Keith Duckett, Amy McCormack, Salma Khalid and Delroy Hall. Collectively they demonstrate some of the opportunities to provide counselling in a range of faith environments and bring a faith perspective to working environments.

So, to sum up, all of us involved in this book hope what we offer here will give the newly qualified counsellor and those contemplating a change of direction or shift into a specialist arena some insight into the fascinating career opportunities that lie before you. We hope you find information, guidance and encouragement in these pages. And, perhaps above all, we really hope this inspires you as you develop your own career pathway as a counsellor.

Best wishes and good luck!

Rick Hughes
January 2024

References

Association for Coaching. (2012). *AC coaching competency framework.* https://cdn.ymaws.com/www.associationforcoaching.com/resource/resmgr/Accreditation/Accred_General/Coaching_Competency_Framewor.pdf

BACP. (2022). *Coaching competence framework.* www.bacp.co.uk/media/17866/bacp-coaching-competence-framework-2022.pdf

BACP. (2023). *2021–2022 workplace mapping survey.* www.bacp.co.uk/about-us/about-bacp/2021-2022-workplace-mapping-survey

Buchanan, L. & Hughes, R. (2000). *Experiences of person-centred counselling training: A compendium of case studies to assist prospective applicants.* PCCS Books.

UKCP. (2020). *A snapshot of how our members work.* UKCP. www.psychotherapy.org.uk/news/a-snapshot-of-how-our-members-work

Chapter 1

Counselling in NHS primary care settings

Vicki Palmer
with Shane Buckeridge, Tasha Gibbard, Catherine Jackson, and Matthew Leavesley

Working in the NHS is highly rewarding, highly demanding and one of the best training grounds a counsellor can have. You will gain experience, knowledge and skills through access to a wide diversity of clients in age, background, race, sexuality, culture and presentation. Moreover, NHS services are generally well supervised, well managed, well supported, and offer additional training.

In this chapter, I will briefly summarise the history of counselling in NHS primary care over the past 30 years. Much of my focus is on England and its Improving Access to Psychological Therapies (IAPT) programme, now called NHS Talking Therapies for Anxiety and Depression. The chapter will mainly cover employment opportunities in England, but it will also look briefly at how NHS primary care counselling is accessed and provided in the other three UK nations. While IAPT was only rolled out in England, it has influenced the development of talking therapy services elsewhere in the world, including as far afield as Australia. I will also explain how to prepare for an interview for NHS employment as a trainee or a fully qualified counsellor.

My counselling career in the NHS

I will start with a brief resumé of my own career to demonstrate the varied routes a counsellor may take in their working life.

Throughout my 30-plus years in counselling, I have been passionate about achieving equal access to counselling for all, not just for those who can afford to pay for it.

Like many counsellors, I began my career in the voluntary sector, starting out as a volunteer counsellor in a young people's service in Cambridge, before moving into paid roles that were not always counselling jobs but where I used my counselling skills, knowledge and experience. Once I was fully qualified, I worked towards becoming accredited, which led to paid roles teaching on certificate and diploma courses in counselling. Alongside, I continued my own counselling practice, which became a combination of working in the NHS and private practice. In the NHS, I set up the counselling practices for two GP surgeries in Edinburgh, where my colleague and I pioneered one of the earliest pieces of research evaluating counselling in the NHS. This research led directly to the development of CORE (Barkham et al., 2016), which became a widely used tool for evaluation in other sectors as well as the NHS.

I trained and qualified as a counselling supervisor early in my career, as it was necessary in order to be a trainer and also for supervising volunteer counsellors and others in private practice. My love of counselling supervision led to collaborating with a colleague to design and teach an accredited counselling supervision diploma, which continues to run under the auspices of Severn Talking Therapies.

I have always been passionate about the NHS because it offers physical and mental health free at the point of delivery, making healthcare accessible to all. Early on, I became aware that, if you had money and education, you could afford the most experienced counsellors and psychotherapists in private practice, and that this was not accessible to the majority of people. I also became aware that in England only 50% of GP surgeries had counsellors on site, and there were even fewer in Scotland, Wales and Northern Ireland. So, talking therapy via the NHS was not accessible to all. In addition, counselling delivered by charities varied in quality because of their reliance on volunteers, who were often in training or newly qualified. So much depended on the volunteers having experience in other roles, in addition to their counselling training, and on the amount and quality of the supervision the charity was able to provide.

The profession became dominated by white, middle-class women who were in a financial position to be able to cover the costs of training and to work for little or no pay. Access to counselling was also limited by the postcode lottery of whether or not your GP surgery had a counsellor. The launch of IAPT – the first ever universal primary care counselling service within the NHS – was a significant step towards reducing these inequalities, in that it would ensure that everyone in England could access talking therapy through their GP and that therapists working in the service could get fully funded training through the NHS.

My involvement with IAPT dates back to 2005, when I was consultant to the South Gloucestershire NHS commissioners, who needed help to set up a counselling service for 28 GP surgeries as quickly as possible, to fit their funding timetable. As I had previously set up GP counselling services elsewhere, I knew what needed to be in place, and I also knew the importance of evaluation, good quality supervision and ongoing CPD, so was able to ensure these were available too.

Within six months, the commissioners had all the data they needed to report on the effectiveness of the service to their CEO, so they were able to get funding to expand the service. This iterative process happened every year until 2009 and the introduction of what was then called IAPT. As we were part of the NHS Mental Health Expert Reference group for South-West England, the commissioners and I were aware of the early IAPT pilots in Doncaster and Newham in 2006. We were keen to learn from the pilots and welcomed the increased access to counselling for all surgeries across England. But when IAPT was rolled out across England, sadly many counsellors working in GP surgeries lost their jobs because the programme was initially primarily geared to the provision of just CBT, and counsellors working for GPs were considered superfluous if there was local IAPT provision.

In South Gloucestershire, however, the commissioners were totally convinced of the efficacy and cost-effectiveness of counselling in the NHS. So, instead of decommissioning the counselling, they asked me to help integrate an IAPT service with the existing counselling services that we had implemented in all surgeries over the preceding years. Our practitioners had established relationships with GPs, nurses, social care and children's services that were essential to the effectiveness of the primary care mental health service. So, we kept our counselling service until 2012, when the then Coalition Government introduced 'Any Qualified Provider' commissioning, opening up IAPT to competitive tendering from any bidders. To preserve the successful services and our therapists' jobs, I set up the Oasis-Talk community interest company (CIC), which meant we could tender to provide the new IAPT services in both South Gloucestershire and Bristol. This became a successful main IAPT provider of counselling and CBT through until 2019, when the commissioners awarded the contract to a company in the private, commercial sector.

The IAPT programme was intended to make psychological therapies freely accessible and available to all. It was also intended to be the largest quantitative evaluation of psychological therapy services in the world. It was rolled out across England and was successful in both of these ambitions. People wanting talking therapy from the NHS are no longer subject to a postcode lottery; access to primary care psychological therapies is universal across England, although waiting lists can be long in some areas. All the services are fully evaluated on an ongoing basis, with IAPT practitioners required to assess and report their clients' progress at every session.

In South Gloucestershire, we were able to reach out to marginalised groups and others that traditionally do not engage with counselling services, such as Black and other racialised minority groups (Rhead et al., 2021; Harwood et al., 2023). User groups told us that services often felt complicated and non-user friendly to access, that there were language and cultural barriers, and often a lack of trust in mainstream statutory provision. IAPT provided us with a platform and vehicle to highlight and address all of these.

It also provided a route to address a particular concern of mine – the failure of mental and physical health services to work collaboratively and seamlessly together, recognising the links, especially for people with long-term conditions (Seaton et al., 2022).

A range of talking therapies – not just CBT but counselling, couples counselling, dynamic interpersonal therapy (DIT, brief psychodynamic therapy) and short forms of psychodynamic psychotherapy – are all widely available, and there is a national training programme for CBT practitioners and, since September 2022, also for counsellors. This is a major step forward as, while accredited counsellors have been employed in IAPT and have been able to access specialist training in a manualised form of counselling known as counselling for depression (more recently renamed person-centred experiential counselling for depression (PCE-CfD)) for almost a decade, there was up until the launch of this pilot no fully NHS-funded high-intensity training for them on a par with that available to CBT practitioners.

There are drawbacks, which have been consistently highlighted throughout IAPT's history. These are, summarised very briefly:

- its emphasis on CBT and the lack of choice for clients – which is finally being addressed and was largely due to lack of evidence of therapeutic effectiveness for other modalities and the restrictions this imposed on the recommendations of NICE, the national guidelines authority
- the reliance on randomised controlled trials (RCT) evidence to inform NICE guidelines and non-acceptance of evidence-based practice and qualitative research
- the limitations of using standard questionnaire-type assessments

delivered by psychological wellbeing practitioners (PWPs, who have no counselling qualifications) at point of entry to meet the high demand
- the stepped care model, which means clients have to be progressed through lower levels of intervention before getting to talk with a qualified CBT practitioner or counsellor
- the limits on the number of sessions offered to clients in many services.

That said, it cannot be denied that many more people have been seen and helped by what is now NHS Talking Therapies than ever were before IAPT was introduced, when the most you could hope for was that your local GP employed a counsellor in their surgery or you could access low-cost counselling from the voluntary sector.

Working in NHS Talking Therapies
The stepped care model

All NHS Talking Therapies services follow the stepped-care model, as recommended by NICE for treatment of mild-to-moderate and severe anxiety and depression. Stepped care is designed to ensure that patients/clients receive the level of care and treatment that is most clinically effective and cost-effective for their problems. This is decided when they first contact the service and receive an initial assessment. If the level of care offered does not achieve improvement, they can then be stepped up to the next level. The four steps in NHS primary mental health care are:

Step 1: Assessment and triage (delivered by PWPs).

Step 2: Psychoeducation, groupwork and guided one-to-one self-help for mild-to-moderate depression and anxiety (delivered by PWPs, often by phone or video).

Step 3: One-to-one high-intensity therapy, such as counselling or CBT, for mild- to-moderate and moderate-to-severe depression and anxiety (delivered by qualified therapists including counsellors).

Step 4: Specialist high-intensity therapy for chronic depression, anxiety and personality disorders (delivered by high-intensity practitioners with additional training).

Step 5: Referral to secondary mental healthcare services (delivered by mental health nurses and psychologists in hospital and community mental health centres) if a patient/client is assessed to need more intensive treatment and possibly hospital admission.

Practitioner/therapist roles

There are two main practitioner roles in NHS Talking Therapies services: the psychological wellbeing practitioner (PWP) and the high-intensity therapist (HIT), who may be trained in delivering any or several of the therapies on offer in that particular service.

The psychological wellbeing practitioner (PWP)

The main job of the PWP is to deliver the standardised assessments at Step 1 of the stepped care programme. The rest of their time is spent on delivery of Step 2 interventions, such as guided self-help.

The PWP follows a standardised script for the assessments, which are carried out over the phone. When they are unclear about anything, they refer to a senior PWP, who will have at least two years' experience and will also be responsible for weekly supervision of and supporting the PWPs. The PWP will have a high weekly caseload of 50 or more appointments, which will include delivering assessments, Step 2 interventions, webinars and online group work.

The Step 2 one-to-one PWP delivery consists of up to six sessions of 30–40-minute psychoeducational interventions for:

- mild-to-moderate generalised and social anxiety
- mild-to-moderate depression
- sleep hygiene
- panic
- identification and challenge of negative automatic thoughts
- self-help
- problem-solving.

They may also offer support for computerised CBT, and signposting to other services and resources.

The psychological wellbeing practitioner experience

(*The writer chose to be anonymous, but worked as a PWP in the south-west region*)

The psychological wellbeing practitioner role involves a wide range of duties, including being the first point of contact the patient has with the service after their referral has been received. I assess their suitability for treatment and triage them to the most suitable treatment pathway, in line with NICE guidelines. During the assessment, I conduct a thorough risk assessment, identify their main difficulty, ascertain their goals for treatment and give an outline and rationale for treatment. I have a caseload of patients with mild-to-moderate mental health difficulties and offer low intensity CBT interventions. I particularly enjoy one-to-one sessions, both face-to-face and via the telephone. The number of sessions is limited – typically between four and six, sometimes more and sometimes less, depending on need. The sessions last between 30 and 45 minutes.

Alongside offering assessments and treatment, I also act as a supporter for patients completing a disorder-specific online guided self-help programme called Silver Cloud, and I co-facilitate psychoeducation groups with another practitioner. I receive weekly case management supervision and clinical skills and CPD training to support my practice and enable me to grow as a practitioner.

I have completed additional training to work with patients with long-term health conditions and medically unexplained symptoms. The role itself brings opportunities to progress into more senior positions as supervisor, line manager and trainer for other PWPs. It also allows the opportunity to undertake further training to become a high-intensity CBT practitioner (this is the route I have since taken). I can if I wish then progress to senior management positions within NHS Talking Therapies services.

The PWP role is a demanding one and involves carrying a high caseload of clients, requiring the practitioner to be very organised. It provides the opportunity to work with a range of disorders using a guided self-help approach. As well as working with a diverse range of people from all walks of life, the role involves offering sessions with an interpreter to people whose first language is not English. I personally have found it very rewarding to be part of a patient's mental health journey, hearing from them how they have integrated the treatment strategies into their life and made progress in overcoming the difficulties and accomplishing their goals.

The high-intensity role in all modalities

High-intensity practitioners work with moderate-to-severe anxiety and depression at Step 3. Regardless of their modality, practitioners deliver

50–60-minute therapy sessions and carry a full-time caseload of some 20–25 clients a week.

Counsellors work with depression, anxiety, bereavement, relationship issues, trauma and other issues. CBT practitioners work primarily with obsessive compulsive disorder (OCD), anxiety, depression, specific phobias, health and social anxiety, intrusive thoughts and post-traumatic stress disorder.

At Step 4, the more experienced senior therapists work with greater complexity, especially where previous treatment has not been successful. Their clients will be presenting mainly with severe and recurrent depression and anxiety, complex trauma and personality disorders. These practitioners will also offer supervision to other therapists. They may have undertaken additional training in eye movement desensitisation and reprocessing (EMDR), dialectical behaviour therapy, DIT and interpersonal psychotherapy to support their work.

There is a career pathway in the NHS, with the possibility of management/leadership roles for more experienced therapists, such as team leaders and service managers.

The high-intensity therapist

Matthew Leavesley is an accredited high-intensity counselling specialist working for an NHS Talking Therapies service. He currently offers person-centred experiential therapy (PCE-CfD) to clients with a diagnosis of long Covid. Here he describes the benefits and challenges of this role.

Since joining the NHS as a high-intensity therapist, I feel that my competence and confidence in providing person-centred therapy has flourished. That statement may seem at odds with the perception out there about NHS Talking Therapies services. But in my experience, although working within the medical model can be challenging, I've been able to uphold my humanistic principles while meeting the needs of the service.

Counsellors who work at high-intensity level typically work with clients who have been assessed as having symptoms of depression. However, within 'depression' there are myriad different components that can contribute to a person's low mood. This means that I work with a wide range of presentations. As a counsellor, I believe in the importance of working with the individual and not putting my clients into any 'box'. This, for me, is what makes the work worthwhile and rewarding – working with clients to enable them to take that one step closer towards self-actualisation.

As a qualified PCE-CfD therapist, I work with my client's emotions and feelings. My role is to facilitate an introspective process for the client to become more self-aware. Bearing witness to this process is a real honour and privilege and one that can be very rewarding. Working in an unstructured way is one of the main strengths of my modality, but there is always that tension and fear that I may not be able to complete the work before the time-limited course of therapy runs out. That said, in all the time that I've been working for the NHS, the vast majority of my clients have mostly got what they needed from their therapy before it ended.

The benefits of working in the NHS include the opportunities for progression and training. I have trained and qualified in PCE-CfD and have also started training in EMDR. Alongside this funded training, there are other opportunities that you can apply for. Last year, I was successful in securing a secondment to work as part of a long Covid multi-disciplinary team. Having a team of multi-disciplinary professionals around me has been hugely beneficial. Like any chronic illness, long Covid can have a severe impact on a client's quality of life, so having a specialist service dedicated to helping them adjust to their new reality can make a huge difference. It is through this kind of work that the counselling profession can make a real impact and I am very proud to be a part of it.

Counselling in any setting can be emotionally draining, and the service I work for makes sure I receive appropriate supervision. Yes, there are certain things we need to cover that may mean there are some constraints on what I can bring, but in the main I get what I need from supervision and it fuels me to keep doing this work. I also value having a team of therapists around me that I can call upon for advice and guidance, and to offload too.

Working for the NHS is hard work and change is constant. But its benefits do outweigh the negatives, in my opinion, and you have a lot to gain and nothing to lose if you decide this is a career path for you.

The high-intensity CBT practitioner

Tasha Gibbard is team lead and a CBT therapist with DHC Talking Therapies, which provides an NHS Talking Therapies service to people in Surrey. She describes her experience of the role.

Being a CBT therapist is a privilege. An opportunity to sit with someone in their darkest hour when they feel most vulnerable, and to see them transform in a short space of time. I think it is important to acknowledge that the role of a CBT therapist is challenging, but all the most rewarding things have some form of challenge to them.

The training year is demanding, no matter what background you come from, due to the amount covered in a relatively short space of time. The training involves three days in service and two in university. Working while training is a fantastic opportunity to put learning straight into practice and have ample support in university and in service.

For a qualified therapist, no two days are the same. A typical day as a CBT therapist involves five clinical hours, which can be made up of treatment sessions, clinical supervision, groups or assessments. CBT therapists typically work with depression, generalised anxiety disorder (GAD), obsessive compulsive disorder (OCD), social anxiety, health anxiety, phobias, panic disorder and post-traumatic stress disorder.

The CBT treatment approach involves following disorder-specific protocols. A formulation is developed with each client to help make sense of how their difficulty started, their current symptoms, maintenance factors and the key areas to address in treatment.

Cognitive and behavioural interventions are used with all clients but how you apply them varies greatly, depending on each individual's formulation. You may start the day working with a client with longstanding depression who has disengaged with their world. Your role is to support them to gradually build in meaningful activities and review the impact of the changes. You may then have a client with generalised anxiety whom you are supporting to embrace uncertainty. Here, you will be supporting them with behavioural experiments to test out their fears. You may next see someone with a needle phobia, where you may be offering them a graded exposure to needles. And your next client may have suffered a traumatic event, and you will be supporting them to process the experience and update their beliefs about what happened.

Clinical supervision is fundamental to being a therapist. It's your safe space to reflect, learn, ask questions, manage risk, practise techniques and develop treatment plans. My service offers both one-to-one supervision and group supervision, which gives the opportunity for a range of perspectives and the closeness to one person who knows you well.

I have had the opportunity to do supervisor training. Supervising trainees has been such a valuable learning opportunity for me and a chance to sharpen up on some of the basics. Watching sessions and providing feedback has allowed me to see how different therapists bring their own perspectives and experience.

Working in the Talking Therapies team means you are collaborating closely with a range of experienced clinicians who come together to share our wealth of experience and consider how we can best support clients and their diverse needs.

There are also lots of opportunities to develop areas of interest. Since working in Talking Therapies, I have had the opportunity to develop from the PWP role into a CBT therapist and attend top-up trainings in acceptance and commitment therapy (ACT), long-term conditions training and EMDR.

The short-term therapy model in NHS Talking Therapies can at times leave you wanting to offer more. However, the joy of seeing a client feeling empowered to face their fears, achieve their goals and embrace their life again is one of the most rewarding experiences. Working as a therapist, your focus is supporting clients, but the experience also enables you to grow, teaching you invaluable things about yourself, your beliefs and your vulnerabilities.

Training in NHS Talking Therapies

Psychological wellbeing practitioners are required to complete a full-time, salaried, six-month training at a university. This comprises two days a week in class and three days in supervised practice. They receive a basic CBT training that does not offer a qualification as a counsellor/therapist and is not transferable to the independent sector. Having completed the NHS-funded training, there is normally a requirement to work in the NHS as a PWP for a minimum of two years. This position can provide a good starting point for a career in the NHS, especially for those who cannot afford to pay for counselling training themselves.

High-intensity CBT therapists complete a full-time, salaried training for one year in high-intensity CBT. This consists of three days a week in practice and the rest in study days, leading to a CBT therapist qualification that is recognised outside of the NHS. Qualified accredited counsellors can apply for the training, as can PWPs who have been practising for at least two years.

Counsellor training placements are also offered. This is an unpaid part-time position, although supervision and line management support are provided. This is another excellent opportunity as a starting point for a career in the NHS or elsewhere. It offers a well-supported grounding in the variety and diversity of NHS work. It is easy to accumulate hours for accreditation and it places the counsellor in a strong position to apply for a paid position if one comes up.

Counselling for Depression (PCE-CfD) is a specific person-centred experiential therapy training for accredited counsellors to equip them to work in NHS Talking Therapies. It can usually only be accessed by counsellors already employed in an NHS Talking Therapies team. However, since September 2022, a pilot three-year, salaried high-intensity counselling training has been available through Health Education England. The programme will be evaluated and reviewed at the end of three years. Applicants must have completed an introduction to counselling training at Level 2 as an entry requirement. The training leads to a permanent post in NHS Talking Therapies as a band 7, high intensity counsellor. It is a full-time training combining practice and study, paid at band 5 in the first year and band 6 in years two and three. Personal therapy in the first year is also paid for as part of the training. The trainee identifies at the start which modality they wish to train in: PCE-CfD, DIT, interpersonal therapy (IPT) or couples therapy for depression.

With all of these trainings, specialised supervision is provided in addition to usual supervision, and both supervision and training are paid for by the NHS.

Finding employment in NHS Talking Therapies

Competition for employment and salaried training places in the NHS is high. To find out where these opportunities are available, you have to register your interest on the NHS Jobs website[1] and regularly check for when and where positions are advertised. The key to getting an interview is to take time with your application. Ensure that your answers follow the requirements of the post in the job description in an organised way. This will help the application to stand out for the recruiter when they do an initial assessment of the high volume of applications. Highlight any prior experience in the voluntary sector, as this is considered to be good preparation for working in NHS Talking Therapies, especially where you have no prior experience of working in the NHS.

At interview, you should anticipate questions about:

- **Equality and diversity**: All public services have a mandate to be inclusive and your employer will therefore want to know about your knowledge, attitude and experience of working with equality and diversity. Equality is about ensuring everybody has an equal opportunity to access services

---

1. www.jobs.nhs.uk/candidate

and is not treated differently or discriminated against because of their race, culture, education, gender, sexuality, identity, age or ability. Diversity is about taking account of the differences between people and groups of people and placing a positive value on those differences.

- **Safeguarding of children and vulnerable adults**: All practising and registered therapists are required to update their training in these areas every three years as safeguarding practice is continually changed and updated to incorporate new learning. If you have had training or experience in either of these areas in previous roles, it will be helpful to speak about what you learned, the policies and procedures you followed, and how you dealt with any incidents in practice and to whom and how you reported them.

- **Your modality**: Be able to describe your modality clearly, as if you were talking to a client. If applying for a trainee role, you are likely to be asked about your understanding of the modality.

- **Your experience, attitude and knowledge of data collection**: How it can be of value to clients, therapists, services and commissioners.

- **Self-care**: It is important not to take our work home with us, so the interviewer will want to know how you switch off from work, and if you have other fulfilling activities in your life.

- **What attracts you to working in this sector in particular**: Some of the issues I discuss in this article around diversity, challenge and teamworking may be relevant here.

Remember, the interview is your chance to find out more about the role and what it requires, as well as your interviewer's opportunity to find out more about you. You may want to ask:

1. **Supervision**: Will your employer pay for individual and/or group supervision with a qualified practitioner? What will be the modality of the supervisor? How much supervision will you receive and does that meet the requirements of your professional body?

2. **Reflective practice**: Not all services provide this. It is of great benefit if they do, because it provides a space to reflect on practice with colleagues and is often a space for additional in-house training.

3. **Team meetings**: When and how often?

4. **Number of sessions to be delivered per day/per week?**

5. **Line management**: Who with and how often?

Most services provide and pay for:

- individual and/or group supervision to BACP requirements for counsellors while in training and after training. For high-intensity trainees, this is one hour of fortnightly supervision per eight client sessions. For full-time high-intensity counsellors, it is one hour of weekly supervision per 24 clients a week. It is different for a PWP role, which is usually supported by senior PWPs
- regular line management that provides support and guidance about NHS requirements, and a connection to your team. Your line manager will support you in considering your CPD needs, your role in the service and your wellbeing. Usually, line management takes place monthly
- reflective practice opportunities with colleagues where there is learning and collaboration with therapists of different modalities and training in safeguarding of children and vulnerable adults. It also offers support and exchange of ideas about how to work safely and ensure self-care within a demanding, full practice
- sometimes additional peer group supervision, which provides further opportunities to learn from colleagues
- internal and external further training and CPD opportunities, which are likely to be free or low cost.

Clients in NHS Talking Therapies

While many clients will present with anxiety and/or depression, other issues are likely to feature, such as bereavement, change, relationships, employment and work issues, abuse and many other complexities. People presenting with addiction or eating disorders are usually referred to specialist agencies, but you may also see clients with these issues.

Your working day will be intense – as a full-time high-intensity practitioner, you may see up to six clients a day. PWPs will see more because their sessions are shorter and at less depth.

A day can include support and training activities. Self-care and self-management help to relieve the pressure. Being well organised is key to self-care, as is asking for help when you need it. It will best suit people who like to work as part of a team. This is one of the greatest joys of working in this sector: you are always learning, sharing and growing together. You can't get stuck in your own echo chamber!

The challenges of working in NHS Talking Therapies

It is a government-led programme and is therefore accountable to national policy constraints, budgets and statutory requirements. If you prefer autonomy, this sector is not for you. If you like challenge, collaboration, teamwork, stimulation, support and encouragement to grow as a therapist, you can thrive in this sector. The main challenge is that you will always be busy! The other main challenge is that you will be required to collect data at every session with every client. You will be trained how to do this therapeutically so the client feels well supported, seen and heard, and encouraged to see how their sessions are working (or not working), which can lead to a conversation about what else is needed.

Scotland, Wales and Northern Ireland

There is no equivalent to England's NHS Talking Therapies service in the other three UK nations. Each has developed its own way of providing counselling in primary care, but self-referral is generally not possible. There is considerable reliance on online self-help to meet needs at step one of the stepped care approaches, and use of one-to-one counselling commissioned from third sector providers at step two, supporting people with mild to moderate depression and anxiety.

Paid employment as an NHS primary care counsellor is therefore less readily available in Scotland, Northern Ireland and Wales, with no clear career path into more senior, practitioner roles on higher pay bands, as there is in England.

In Scotland

In Scotland, a few GP practices continue to directly employ qualified counsellors to work with their patients (see Shane Buckeridge's description of a day in his working life below). This tends to be in areas of high deprivation, where GPs can get NHS funding to employ their own practice staff. Otherwise, GPs will refer patients presenting with mild-to-moderate mental health problems either to a range of online self-help courses, support groups, befriending schemes and self-help books or to any local NHS-funded or third-sector (charity) counselling organisations, or to the local community mental health team.

Mostly, as in England, what is offered and available on the ground in terms of counselling is led by decisions higher up that are in turn influenced by what is considered to be evidence of proven effectiveness. Health boards have to commission the recommended therapies, which are primarily CBT-based, from any external providers.

Health boards may offer CBT-based skills training to existing healthcare staff in other roles, but there is no national funding scheme for primary care counsellors.

> *Shane Buckeridge works as a counsellor employed in a GP practice in Scotland. Here he describes his typical working day.*
>
> In my experience in a primary care setting, I have had to become an ambassador for counselling in that I see it as part of my role to educate and inform the other healthcare professionals about what I do and how I work. It's important that I don't appear precious about sharing information about clients I'm working with – I need to balance what the client feels okay with me sharing and what information the other healthcare professionals involved in their care may need to know.
>
> Different practices may have a more structured approach with clear line management. In my experience, as the only employed counsellor in the practice, it is often the practice manager who is my key contact.
>
> Supervision is an important part of my support, as a lone practitioner. Also, I offer placements to trainee counsellors, and I appreciate the opportunity to engage with them and see this as a form of mutual support.
>
> The great thing about NHS work is the diverse client population – I see people aged from 18 to 100+, with a wide range of presenting issues. Also, because I am part of the practice team, clients tend to see me as trustworthy as they are likely to have a longstanding, cradle-to-present-day relationship with their GP. It's also important to me that I am delivering a service that is free at the point of delivery and that I am not working in isolation – I am in constant communication with GPs and other practice staff concerning my clients. I also get paid holidays and pension, of course!
>
> My advice to anyone considering this role (or students on placement, as often practices offer these to counsellors in training) is to make sure you spend time building your relationship with the administrative staff, as they are the gatekeepers for other services for your clients. If they think you're a bit precious or standoffish, they won't necessarily go out of their way for your clients!

In Wales

In Wales, the situation is broadly similar to Scotland's set-up: there is no NHS Talking Therapies service, and each health board or trust does its own thing to make counselling available in the community, depending on local need and resources. If someone needs counselling, they generally start with their GP, who refers them on to the local primary mental health team, where the patient is assessed and referred on again, using the stepped care approach, either to online self-help or, if that doesn't help, to face-to-face counselling, which is currently, for the most part, commissioned from the third or independent sectors and often means a long wait.

Lack of trained counsellors at primary care level has prompted health boards to start training up other community mental health professionals, such as nurses, in an attempt to reduce the pressure of demand on the secondary psychology services. But there is no government-funded counselling training scheme, nor likely to be one. Counsellors with a nursing qualification may be able to find employment within the primary mental health care service in an assessment/gatekeeping or team management role, where their counselling skills may be regarded as a useful add-on but not an essential qualification.

In Northern Ireland

In Northern Ireland the situation is similar. GPs can get funding from their local NHS trust to employ counsellors directly, as part of their practice team. But GPs are not always willing to take on the responsibility of direct employment, and some enterprising counsellors have responded to this by setting up small enterprises and social firms that contract with local GPs to provide counselling in their practices. However, this is the exception. Northern Ireland has a network of 'wellbeing hubs' run by the health trusts, to which GPs can refer patients with mild-to-moderate mental health issues. Here, patients will be assessed and maybe signposted to other services or referred on to online counselling or CBT and one-to-one counselling with local charities.

Conclusion

A career in counselling can take you in many directions, and I feel very fortunate to have had such a varied career that took me from trainee volunteer to CEO of an organisation providing 75% of the high-intensity therapies in Bristol and South Gloucestershire and 50% of the guided self-help provision.

My counselling in the NHS has been significant in providing breadth and depth to my own counselling practice. It extended my ability to work with complexity and diversity. It taught me that context is everything and that I need to pay as much attention to my clients' many and varying contexts as to the content of what they are telling me. It is their context that provides the meaning for them and their therapy journey. It also helped me to see the relevance of race and class and social background to the therapy, making me very aware of my unconscious bias and assumptions from my own background of class and culture.

References

Barkham, M., Mellor-Clark, J., Connell, J. & Cahill, J. (2006). A core approach to practice based evidence: a brief history of the origins and applications of the CORE-OM and CORE system. *Counselling and Psychotherapy Research,* 6(1), 3–15. https://doi.org/10.1080/14733140600581218

Harwood, H., Rhead, R., Chui, Z., Bakolis, I., Connor, L., Gazard, B., Hall, J., MacCrimmon, S., Rimes, K.A., Woodhead, C. & Hatch, S.L. (2023). Variations by ethnicity in referral and treatment pathways for IAPT service users in South London. *Psychological Medicine,* 53, 1084–1095. https://doi.org/10.1017/S0033291721002518

Rhead, R. & the TIDES team. (2021). *Barriers to accessing talking therapies for ethnic and minority groups.* Kings College London. https://www.kcl.ac.uk/barriers-to-accessing-talking-therapies-for-service-users-from-racial-and-ethnic-minority-groups

Seaton, N., Morris, R., Norton, S., Holm, K., & Hudson, J. (2022). Mental health outcomes in patients with long-term health conditions: Analysis of an IAPT service. *British Journal of Health Psychology,* 26(2), 307–324. https://bpspsychub.onlinelibrary.wiley.com/doi/full/10.1111/bjhp.12475

Chapter 2

Counselling in private practice

Rick Hughes
with Lindsay Gardner, Alex.Arthur
and Paul Carslake

This chapter seeks to give you a taster of what it's like to work in private practice. It's not a complete 'to do' list or 'how to' guide, and it might not answer all your questions, but I hope my own experiences and those of others can give you enough of the flavour of private practice as a possible counselling career choice.[1]

Setting up in private practice

Is private practice right for you? It's a big question and taking time to consider it thoroughly can help you avoid problems later down the line. Here are some of the main points to think about.

If you were working as a counsellor employed by an organisation, you'd usually have guidance, mentoring and support in place, together with a plethora of systems, policies and procedures all written up for you to follow. In private practice, this largely becomes your responsibility.

How will you find clients? How will you manage your diary and workload? How do clients contact you and how and when do you respond?

---

1. This chapter draws substantially on contributors from fellow private practitioners and on the highly recommended *Private Practice Toolkit* published by BACP (BACP, 2023). My thanks to my colleagues and to BACP and Caz Binstead, one of the main contributors to the toolkit, for their assistance, input and support. The toolkit is free online to BACP members (see references).

What paperwork do you have in place, including contracts? Are you compliant with all the necessary business requirements and regulations, including tax returns (and paying tax), registering with the Information Commissioner's Office, having appropriate insurances in place and following GDPR (data protection) best practice guidelines? How do you market yourself and promote your practice? Do you need a website and how can you best present yourself and what you offer? How do you deal with finances, payments and invoicing? What will you do if a client doesn't pay you? If you are impacted by particularly emotionally draining work, what support is available to you? Does your supervisor have sufficient understanding of private practice to give you the support you need?

There are some good books out there, and numerous journal articles. I can only touch on these topics.

When I started in private practice after qualifying, several issues emerged that I had not expected. For instance, I found it quite lonely and isolating – I didn't have colleagues I could debrief with after a difficult session or a tiring day. My supervisor was excellent but sometimes supervision wasn't enough.

I had one client who would test my boundaries, phoning me at night in crisis, another who gave me concerns about my own physical safety and another who said they had fallen in love with me. And I was living alone and working alone, from home. When you're counselling in an organisation, you have greater protections in place and colleagues for support; in private practice, you need to plan and prepare for this yourself.

So, again, is private practice right for you? Caz Binstead sums it up nicely in the following list of 'known knowns':

> I know myself, I know who I am, I know what kind of business I run, I know how I want to present myself, I know how I run my practice, I know my worries, I know the things that could crop up, I know how I am with boundaries. (Binstead, 2021)

Where to practise

Most people in private practice either work from home or rent a room elsewhere. Post-Covid, many are also working online, so can potentially be based anywhere that offers the necessary basics. The main benefit of working from home is that you're not paying rent for a counselling room (which may stand empty a lot of the time). However, this is your home and your living space. Is it convenient, safe and appropriate for you *and* your clients? There are different considerations for both parties. How might you both feel meeting in your home?

You'll need to inform your house insurance company that you are using your home as a business premises, so your premiums may go up. Think about the client experience: from entering the door, how do they get to your counselling room in a way that is safe for them and maintains your privacy and personal boundaries?

Even things like the layout, décor and furnishings can be important. Initially, I furnished my counselling room with two large, matching leather swivel chairs, which reclined slightly. Most clients loved that they could recline slightly or swivel round gently. But a few larger clients found them unstable, so I introduced a sofa (which could seat a larger client and also gave clients space for handbags, laptop cases, jackets etc.), and a matching chair for me, which seemed to work better.

I chose the pictures carefully and ensured I had no personal photos on display. I put my qualifications and insurance certificates into clip frames and hung them on the wall. Again, most clients seemed to find this reassuring, although one thought I was being smug.

I had to consider the state of my bathroom, in case clients needed to use it. What was on show? What did my choice of shampoo and deodorant say about me? It became the least cluttered and certainly the cleanest room in my house.

And at one stage, I had a large, illuminated fish tank in my counselling room, quietly bubbling away in the background. All but one client seemed to like this and felt it created a relaxing atmosphere. One client arrived for a session and said they wanted to use the space just to sit quietly, watch the fish and use this as a time to reflect, think and contemplate. It was the longest silence I ever experienced. But another client berated me for keeping fish in an aquarium, saying they should be free and not kept as pets or treated as toys.

You can't always win! But it's useful to think about the consequences of your choices and how your clients might react. This is where supervision can be really helpful, giving you a chance to reflect on client feedback – the good and not so good.

Based at home, I worked as an affiliate for several employee assistance programme (EAP) providers (see Chapter 4). Each wanted to inspect my premises, either in person or from photos I was asked to provide. It was a bit unnerving to be 'inspected'; it made me realise clients might be consciously or subconsciously doing the same. And I should point out that working for an EAP affiliate is not an entry-level occupation; normally providers require you to be accredited and have several years' post-qualification experience.

Online counselling is now commonplace in private practice and means that you can potentially provide counselling from anywhere to anywhere. However, there's much to consider here and Sarah Worley-James has given us an excellent overview in Chapter 3, so I won't add more here.

Practice management

The counselling contract between you and your client is a crucial document, setting out your terms and conditions for providing counselling. It formalises your boundaries and sets out your mutual obligations and responsibilities (yours, as counsellor, and those of your client). It's worth spending time reflecting on this and devising one that works for you, and certainly consult your supervisor. Some practitioners upload their contract to their website, so potential clients can read it in advance. Whether you're seeing a client online or face-to-face, you need to check they have read, understood and agreed to the terms of the contract. If you're working as an affiliate for an external organisation, such as an EAP provider, they will have their own terms and conditions for you to use with their clients.

How will you begin your therapeutic journey with a client? Many private practitioners offer a free initial assessment, whether in person, online or on the phone, to clarify what is required and check that you have the experience to offer what they want. This could be a first session 'assessment' or an 'exploratory' discussion. Clients need to have the opportunity to decide if you are right for them, and you need to feel you can work with them.

You'll need to have systems in place to safely and securely store your case notes (if you take them), and any other client data. How much detail will you write? You'll need to comply with the General Data Protection Regulations (GDPR) and, where relevant, register with the Information Commissioner's Office (ICO). Bear in mind too that your notes could be requested by the police or courts and used as evidence if a client is involved in any relevant legal process, which is most likely to be to do with safeguarding and child custody and protection issues. You should also make a 'clinical will'. This sets out who you have nominated (with their agreement) to act on your behalf, contact your clients and access and deal with your confidential records in the event of your death or long-term incapacity.

How often will you see clients and how long for? What hours will you work? I tended to see clients weekly and, unless specified otherwise by a referring organisation, review this after six sessions. But some clients may want (or only be able to afford) to attend fortnightly or monthly, or wish to come more frequently than once a week. Managing your diary can be tricky – not every client will attend weekly, so you're going to have gaps in your calendar where you aren't earning. As you build up your practice, you may consider offering evening and weekend appointments, which can considerably expand your availability to clients who might have work or childcare commitments during working hours, but it will eat into your 'me time'.

In my first experience of private practice, I offered five one-hour appointments a day, and worked a five-day week. But, even though this equated to five 'therapeutic hours' in an eight-hour working day, it still didn't give me the time I needed for breaks and writing up my notes. So I changed my workweek pattern to four or five clients, Monday to Thursday, keeping Friday as my administration and marketing day. I'd always aim to clock off at noon on Friday, so I had some time off too. When you don't have a boss or colleagues keeping an eye on you, it's important to be mindful of and factor in a healthy work-life balance (Hughes, 2020).

There are numerous practice management software packages now available specifically designed for counsellors, and they are increasingly popular. They will manage your diary, store your records safely and according to GDPR standards, produce client progress reports, analyse your business activity and client throughput and outcomes, invoice clients, record payments – pretty much everything to do with your business admin, leaving you with more time to focus on your clinical practice. They come at a price but are worth investigating and could be an invaluable investment.

Show me the money

Many counsellors feel uncomfortable about the payment side of private practice. For them, asking for money seems inappropriate within a therapeutic relationship. But a private practice is a business; you need to be paid something for all the investment you have made in your training, supervision and development, as well as maintaining your practice. Think how much it's cost you to get through training – course fees, years without income, supervision fees, living costs and so forth. Your expertise has a value; that is what your clients are paying you for. From a client's point of view, counselling is an investment in themselves, and paying you is an acknowledgement that they recognise your expertise and are committed to engage in the process.

Will you provide concessions or reduced fees for those on a low wage, and do you ask for proof? I tended to allocate four 'low-cost' sessions out of a standard 16–20 session week. If all the spaces were allocated, anyone else would have to wait until one of those slots became available. I chose not to ask for proof of income – I needed to trust my low-cost clients. And I genuinely believe it was not abused.

How will you ask for and receive your fees from clients? This is something you should agree in advance with clients and include in your contract. Some practitioners prefer their clients to pay them at the end of each session, whether in cash, online or using a card payment machine (these days, they are readily available and accessible, but at a cost). Some ask for payment upfront for a block of sessions. Consider how this might make you and your client feel. Might they feel you don't trust them? Might it impact on your therapeutic relationship, and in what ways? Some therapists think it does, others don't. I used to ask for payment at the end of a session but now I invoice clients at the end of each month. This is more because I find it easier to manage my finances this way, and with the majority paying via bank transfer, it cuts out all the business associated with cash, paying in cheques and paying fees for card machines. You'll need to find the format and system that suits you, financially and therapeutically.

You may wish to consider including a clause in your contract about non-payment. How might you manage non-payment professionally and sensitively, and when and how might you end a counselling contract for non-payment of fees, if at all?

Marketing and promotion

Who are you? To establish your practice, you will need to create an identity and branding. Are you going to set up under your own name or create a brand name to work under? I chose 'Edinburgh Counselling & Coaching' (ECC). I wanted to give the impression that I wasn't a sole operator and that the organisation was a larger enterprise. I considered 'New Town Therapy', as I lived in Edinburgh's New Town, but it's an affluent part of the city and I decided it might put off people from less affluent areas coming to see me. So think carefully – try your ideas out on friends, to make sure you haven't missed an accidental blooper. How will it abbreviate? Once you've chosen a name, and it's on your stationery, website, and bank account, it can be costly to change it later.

What sort of image are you wanting to convey: experienced, personable, empathic, corporate, professional…? I called another of my private practices 'PCT Glasgow', as I wanted to reinforce that I offered person-centred therapy to the Glasgow community. But would a client new to counselling understand what 'PCT' stands for? And it doesn't say anything about me personally or my way of counselling. If you want to adopt a brand name, you'll need to check on the Companies House website that a company of the same name doesn't already exist.[2]

I can't tell you what will work best for you, and in your part of the country. You'll need to research this and also consider what suits you too. Are there many other counsellors in your locality? How will you distinguish yourself and your offer from them? I've seen business cards for private practitioners posted up in local supermarkets, post offices, hospitality venues and even chip shops.

---

2. Companies House is the government body responsible for regulating private companies. If you set up a limited company, you'll need to register it with them. There's a free online 'company name checker' facility on the website at https://find-and-update.company-information.service.gov.uk/company-name-availability

There are several online directories that, for an annual fee, will post your details and credentials. I've noticed that clients search and find counsellors via a range of filters – usually by locality and area of specialism, but with the expansion and growing acceptance of online counselling, where you live could be immaterial, so long as you are qualified and insured to work in the countries where your clients live (see Chapter 3 on counselling online).

Several social media platforms allow you to advertise your business and, increasingly, you can pay to promote yourself as 'sponsored advertising' to a niche audience or geographical area. This can be more cost-effective and means the 'cost-per-click' rates should better reflect the clients you seek and where they live.

What about a website, and do you really need one? You can certainly create a custom platform from the many online website template companies on the internet, and some organisations design and host websites specifically for counsellors. It's worth learning about search engine optimisation (and how this works) and how you'll get found on the internet. I've tended to regard my website as a 'shop window' – I refer potential clients to it for more information; I don't rely on it so much to bring me new clients. Some practitioners write blogs where they discuss a particular issue, and this can create a following – internet search engines like this too. It also keeps your website looking fresh and current. But if you're listed on counselling directories and find your clients come this way, then do you need a website? I know several private practitioners who don't have a website and just advertise via social media – it can be cheaper and much more interactive. But you need to ensure your on-site presence is professional and appropriate, and keep it well separated from any personal accounts – and be very mindful of what you post on your personal accounts – you have to assume clients will go searching online for more information about you, and act accordingly.

Once you have selected a range of marketing tools and techniques, the key is to make sure these are monitored, reviewed and regularly updated or reassessed. I've seen so many websites with blogs or news sections that haven't been updated for years.

New platforms

In what might feel like a consumerist approach to therapy, new platforms have emerged to offer 'instant access' counselling by video, telephone or text-based therapy – a concept pioneered by Talkspace in New York in 2012. Potentially it sounds like a win-win – the client gets counselling when they want it, and the counsellor gets the referrals. (You'll find this is also covered in Sarah Worley-James' Chapter 3.) I have concerns, as do others: for the client, it might not be helpful to have this level of instant access to their counsellor – how then do they learn to manage their own emotional states? Might they not benefit more from the containment and security provided by a more boundaried structure? And it may not be the attractive offer it first appears to the counsellor. Some of these platforms are promoted heavily on social media and via internet influencers and can be quite persistent when recruiting counsellors, making promises of very attractive returns, when this is not always the case (Brown, 2022). The challenge for the counsellor is to decide if the recruitment, therapeutic and business model aligns with your professional ethics, including data protection. These are commercial operations, focused on profit and delivering what the creators believe the clients want – instant access to support – without necessarily understanding how therapy works. So, investigate the platform, talk to other counsellors who work for them, and take an informed decision as to whether this type of counselling fits with your model, values and ethics.

Making connections

A lot of people don't like the word 'networking', so I've called this section 'making connections'. Connecting with others not only allows us to develop business and therapeutic relationships with other, like-minded practitioners; it's also important for how you promote yourself and your practice. I've always regarded networking as a two-way process – you help me and I'll help you. It might not be reciprocal at the same time, or for the same reasons, but it's essentially about looking out for others in the knowledge (but never the expectation) that they may help you too. Personal connections and recommendations aren't always a bad thing!

Conferences and events are a great way to make and renew connections, hear what others are doing and share what you're up to, as well as essential to your continuing professional development.

You'll also find that your professional membership organisation offers volunteering opportunities – whether that's sitting on committees or getting involved on a consultancy basis with certain projects. You won't be paid but you'll get travel expenses. It's also a way of keeping in touch with what's really going on out there at policy-making levels, getting known, and influencing your profession for the better. I joined the executive committee of what is now called BACP Workplace division many years ago, and later became its deputy chair. It was a big time commitment and I wasn't earning much at the time, but I thoroughly enjoyed the experience and got to know many great people, some of whom became friends, work colleagues and co-editors – several of the books I've published have been collaborations with people I got to know then (Hughes, 2004; Kinder et al., 2008, 2022; Hughes et al., 2012, 2017, 2019).

Making connections can build life-long professional relationships (and friendships) and you never know where they might lead and the opportunities that could emerge.

Self-care

While self-care applies in any counsellor role, I think it's particularly relevant when you are a sole practitioner. As I've said, I found private practice initially isolating. The only people I really engaged with were clients; I missed the connection and banter of work colleagues. What helped me was to focus on my work-life balance and to build a 'dream team' of people I could connect with, professionally and socially, to help me take a psychological break from client work.

I've arranged with several private practitioner colleagues over the years to have a regular mutual 'check-in' with them. It wasn't supervision, and we didn't talk about client work; we used it to monitor each other's wellbeing. A former boss called them 'Keep-In-Touch meetings' (KITs), and I've used this tactic in several contexts ever since.

It's important that we know our limits too. In my first private practice scenario, I initially focused on getting as many clients as I could to make it financially viable. But I soon ditched this financial priority and resolved to attend more to my wellbeing. By reducing my working week and caseload, I felt able to deliver a better counselling service to my clients. I was lucky that I could afford to do this; I think initially my concern to earn as much as I could distracted me from my whole *raison d'etre*: to be a skilled, ethical and competent counsellor.

I have heard, and I discovered it to be the case, that it can take a year or two to get yourself established and find a work pattern that fits. It doesn't happen overnight.

Self-care is also about recognising signs of stress, fatigue and burnout. Life events can also impact our practice, and we need to react accordingly. When my dad died in quite a tragic way, I knew I needed some time out from working with clients who had suffered bereavement, loss and/or trauma, as I worked through my personal grief. But it's not just life events; you need to be monitoring your client workload and their presenting issues. For instance, it can be very draining to have a number of clients who present with depression.

Personal safety is another important consideration. There are many potential variables, so I won't try to cover them all – I will just stress the point that we need to be mindful of the risks and potential dangers of lone-working, and we need to be similarly mindful of the risks and threats to clients too.

Ideally, your supervisor will understand and appreciate factors relevant to working in private practice. But it's important that you can bring these issues to supervision too. Yes, supervision is about your client work, but it's about the big picture too, all of which ultimately impacts your clients. When I've brought anxieties about lone working to supervision, my supervisor has helped me to identify ways to mitigate the risks for me and clients and has given attention to how I might be subconsciously reflecting my anxiety back onto my clients.

A jack of all trades?

Each counsellor is unique and so what we offer should be similarly unique. I'm often amazed to see the massive list of 'specialist areas' in which therapists claim to be competent in their listings in counselling directories. While you don't necessarily need to be an 'expert' for a particular presenting issue, you do need to have an understanding and experience, and clients will expect this too.

A newly qualified counsellor really needs to know the extent of their competence and their limitations. It can be tempting to take on every client who contacts you. But there is a risk that you don't have the experience of dealing with particularly complex issues, and you may potentially do more harm than good. It's okay to say no – in my mind, that's a mark of professionalism and conscious competence. Many of the private practitioners I spoke to while researching and writing this chapter highlighted the importance of thorough assessments, sometimes over two sessions. This diligence also helps you determine whether you can or should proceed to work further with this client.

A number of years ago, I had a friend who was desperately trying to find an appropriately experienced counsellor to support their daughter who, they suspected, had autism spectrum condition (ASC). The daughter met with several counsellors, all experienced, but apparently with limited understanding of ASC. They just didn't know enough of the condition for the daughter to feel understood.

This example, however, does shed light on the opportunity private practice presents to specialise in a particular area and to become experienced and competent (or an 'expert') in that field. Often events in our own life can introduce us to issues we might not have otherwise experienced and can present opportunities for specialism.

When I started out, I went on a couples-counselling course, hoping this would equip me with the skills to offer couples' work. It was, I think, a good course, and we had plenty of time dedicated to role playing and putting theory into practice. After this, I added 'couples counselling' to my own list of 'skills'. But I found the work incredibly challenging and I'm not sure I fully mastered the multiple relationships and dynamics at play. The first six couples I counselled all split up. This was probably inevitable, and they were likely using counselling to give themselves permission to do what was right for them. But it challenged my confidence and, with the help of my supervisor, I came to the conclusion that either I needed much more training or it wasn't an area in which I was cut out to practise. Ultimately, I chose to remove couples counselling from my therapeutic repertoire.

Managing risk

When I have been employed as a counsellor by an organisation, I've had policies and procedures to mitigate risk, colleagues to support or advise me, and a physical environment that has been risk assessed. All of this provided a safety net for me and the client.

But in private practice, we need to conduct our own client risk assessments. We have an ethical and legal duty of care to our clients and a human responsibility, and that's particularly relevant when dealing with risk. We need to understand the scope and the limits of our responsibility (BACP, 2018). Over the years, I've learnt to consider risk ultimately from a legal perspective – if something terrible happened to one of my clients and I needed to testify in court, would my actions (and omissions) be deemed reasonable, appropriate and sufficient?

Risk needs to be assessed at all stages of the client's journey with us. Many private practitioners' websites highlight their confidentiality and privacy policies, including the limits of confidentiality and the circumstances under which this might be broken. These policies need to be clarified with and understood by a client at the start, and, where and when relevant, during the therapeutic journey.

Our professional bodies all have guidance and advice about risk management for their members, so whichever organisation you are registered/accredited with, please do become very familiar with their frameworks and policies. And put them into practice.

As a private practitioner, you should have in place a series of escalation procedures in case this is required. What would you do if a client collapses or suffers a psychotic episode? What would you do if a client states as they leave the session that they are considering ending their life? What would you do if a client reveals they have committed a criminal offence? What would you do if a client admits they've harmed or threatens to harm a child or other vulnerable person?

Such events are rare, but we need to be prepared to act. Once, a client admitted they had committed a serious criminal offence and they had, so far, evaded the police. I think I managed the situation okay. I can't go into detail, for confidentiality reasons. But suffice to say, supervision was crucial here – I saw my supervisor a lot at that time to help me manage this situation as best I could.

I have got into a habit of becoming a hoarder of self-help leaflets, advice guides and information resources. Some of these are related to risk. But much also depends on circumstances. You need to consider the client's context, home environment and state of mind too, and any inadvertent consequences. For instance, if a client talks about being at risk of domestic abuse, you need to be careful about giving them leaflets and other support materials, in case they are found by the abuser.

I've had very few experiences of a client telling me they intend to end their life just as they leave the counselling room, but I have experienced countless situations when I was sufficiently concerned to decide it was necessary and appropriate to facilitate an emergency appointment with a client's GP. This is a scenario you really do need to prepare for – it will happen.

As part of your risk management process, you need also to explain in your contract, initial discussions and information materials that you are not an emergency or drop-in service, where clients can just turn up if they are in crisis. This reflects the clear and firm boundaries you'll need to have in place.

Professor Andrew Reeves has written and spoken extensively about risk, and his seminal book on this is well worth reading (Reeves, 2015).

Professional development

When you work for an established counselling service, you are likely to be offered and are more likely to hear about useful continual professional development (CPD) and training opportunities. In private practice, we need to be proactive and seek out the CPD that's right for us. The challenge is that often we don't know what we need to know. Supervision can help us identify areas for professional development, as indicated by particular client issues that emerge.

Most of the mainstream professional bodies offer a range of CPD resources, platforms and modules for their members, all of which give us the opportunity to develop, learn and grow, and with others, not just through personal study.

Your professional body is also likely to expect you to record and track your learning, and to evidence it when you renew your membership/registration. You might also consider progressing from registration to accreditation – taking your professional status to a higher, deeper level of expertise – with your professional body. Many people I know who have gone down the accreditation route tell me it has given them a sense of professional value and enhanced competence. Accredited status does not, in my view, necessarily make you a better counsellor, but – speaking personally – I found it a positive challenge that made me really reflect on my practice and sharpened my therapeutic radar in all my client work thereafter.

Unplanned endings

One of the greatest frustrations I've had in private practice are the clients who don't turn up (DNAs – did not attend) and unplanned endings. They are, I realised quite early on in my counselling career, just one of those things that happen in counselling, irrespective of the sector. But they do raise many issues that need consideration.

Whether we offer clients a set number of sessions or our work is more open-ended, we don't always get a 'clean' ending when a client wraps up their therapeutic journey with us. The client may just decide they've had what they need and stop coming. Or they may feel you are not the right counsellor for them, or that they're not getting what they think they need, or the counselling with you is doing more harm than good, or now is not the right time – or they may no longer be able to afford sessions.

We don't ever know what happens with unplanned endings, yet we'll inevitably wonder what happened. Is it something about us, what we said, or did? It can be difficult to let this one go. Obviously, and ideally, we want our work with clients to be helpful and a positive experience for the client, but we're not always going to get that. But be careful about contacting the client to check this out. It could be our stuff, not theirs. We need to trust the client and empower them to make their choices, whether they inform us about them or not. The very few clients I have contacted as a 'follow-up check-in' involved risk. Again, discussing this in supervision helped me determine when it was ethical and appropriate and when it perhaps wasn't.

DNAs can be tricky to manage too. If a client doesn't turn up to a prearranged appointment, how do you deal with that? It can be useful to discuss this with new clients and include your policy in the contract. If you are worried for their safety, have you agreed that you can seek to contact them? Are you going to charge them for appointments they don't attend? If you do charge, what impact might this have on them and their decision to return? If you don't charge, what might be the impact on your workload and income? As I said, it raises lots of considerations that you may need to discuss in supervision before jumping to any conclusions about your practice and your clients' behaviours.

Enough from me… let's hear what other counsellors in private practice have to say.

Perspectives from others in private practice

Lindsay Gardner – What I love about private practice

I am an accredited person-centred counsellor and supervisor. I have my own counselling practice and work with children, young people and adults, as well as supervising groups and individuals. My areas of special interest include bereavement and working with young adults, many of whom are neurodiverse.

Private practice was something I fell into, rather than planned. My initial intention was to continue volunteering as a counsellor after graduating, but an opportunity came along that was risk-free. I was approached to work in a podiatry clinic where the owner was looking to expand to provide for the whole body, mind included. We agreed I would pay for the room hire, but only if the client attended the session, which meant I wasn't out of pocket if clients cancelled or didn't turn up. For me, this felt too good an opportunity to be turned down, and so I took my first tentative steps into private practice.

Of course, this meant I needed to get insurance and to think about pricing. What would I charge? Would I ask clients to pay upfront for their session? What means of payment would I accept? Would I give discounts or charge on a sliding scale? Would I offer online sessions or simply face-to-face? Would I have a cancellation policy? What platform would I use if offering online sessions? This was way before Covid and lockdowns, before online therapy became mainstream. Would I have a website? How would I advertise? I needed to draw up policies and procedures. What other paperwork did I need? Luckily, I had experience of working in residential care and creating pop-up respite units from scratch, so some of these things I could tackle easily.

I still had all the doubts running through my head: Do I have enough experience? Will people come? Will they like what I offer? One of the biggest issues for me was around asking for payment. I tried prepayment and I tried charging for missed appointments, none of which sat well with me. So, I opted for a simple solution: I just asked people to pay at the end of their sessions. At the beginning this was cash, cheque or bank transfer; these days it includes card payments, due to the ease of the new point-of-sale machines. I have got better at asking for payment and try to bring it up when clients first contact me, but it is still the most awkward part of private practice for me, even after all these years.

What I love about working for myself is having my space and the ability to focus on my clients' unique needs. I don't have to work to a set number of sessions; I don't have to prove change has occurred; I don't have to fit in with anyone else's way of working. I do have to be responsible to my clients, ensuring I am giving them the highest quality service I can. This means keeping up with my CPD and thinking outside the box. Of particular importance to me is being flexible around the needs of my clients. Obviously, there are boundaries to this as I do have a life of my own but, as much as I can, I try to fit around my clients regarding timing, duration and frequency of appointments. This means that I need to have a strong sense of how flexible I am going to be. Yes, I work late; yes, I work weekends; yes, I can see clients twice a week; yes, they can have appointments that are more than an hour. These are all possible, but I have to feel able to be present and authentic with clients to maintain this flexibility. I always have an eye on my capacity meter. It often runs very close to full capacity and at those times I readjust the balance a little – maybe start a little later, not have as many evening appointments, have a weekend off, but these are all my choices. After all, if I'm not fully present, my clients aren't getting the level of service they deserve.

I cannot emphasise enough the need for good supervision when working in private practice. If you don't have a supervisor with whom you can be genuine and authentic, to whom you can bring your whole self, then you need to find someone else. When working for an organisation, you have policies and procedures laid down for you, and other people to keep you accountable, but when working on your own, it is simply you. Therefore, you need to be grounded in your practice, know your professional body's guidelines and be able to explain your reasons for any actions or omissions in your client work, which at times can feel exposing. Private practice isn't for everyone, and you have to see how it fits for you, but remember, you and you alone are accountable, and that's what I love about it.

Alex.Arthur – Practising in a partnership

I am a person-centred counsellor working in private practice with my partner. I spent my childhood in Southern Ontario and Easter Ross, Scotland. I studied philosophy as an undergraduate at the University of Aberdeen and returned to complete a research degree in the same subject at a later date. I worked most of my life as a chartered accountant and as a business academic. I came to counselling training fairly late in life, when I took early retirement in 2011, but I'd previously had a long involvement with a counselling charity and a lot of experience with pastoral support roles (student advice and trade union personal casework). My life has included a significant episode of debilitating emotional dysfunction.

My partner and I have had some advantages. I was able to devote a retirement lump sum to our training, and we were able to set up our domestic arrangements so that we could practise from home. We have also been able to provide each other with informal peer supervision, and we spend quite a lot of time discussing counselling and related issues. I count our periodic disagreements and confusions among our advantages!

We work almost entirely with self-referred clients, who most frequently find us on public directories. We do relatively little work for referring agencies. Our experience with these is that the framework they provide constrains the counselling relationship in an unhelpful way, and that the associated administrative and billing arrangements are onerous.

I have a workplace pension, which helps financially. We took an early decision to price our services at the middle-to-upper end of the rates charged by other counsellors, but to offer reduced rates to clients who might not be able to access counselling otherwise. We both think of our counselling engagements in terms of clinical commitment – we have never stopped seeing a client because they could no longer afford to pay us. In a small handful of cases, we have deferred our fees indefinitely. We don't think we could work ethically otherwise.

We have found that there is enough demand for counselling to completely fill the time we can give to it. We never planned to become rich, but the practice is financially viable and gives us an opportunity to spend this part of our lives in a deeply satisfying and creative way.

It is also difficult, emotionally demanding and intrinsically risky. If it were not, I would wonder whether we were doing it with integrity.

Person-centred practice depends on forming a counsellor-client relationship that allows the client to develop awareness in a safe environment. Human beings are meant to talk to one another – we live in relational groups. Conversation – real conversation – is to us what hunting Thomson's gazelle is to the cheetah, or exploring the deep ocean is to the sperm whale. Using a communicative relationship with another to build our congruence is a core human activity. Indeed, we are barely human without it – however little this is recognised by the institutions and interests that dominate our lives.

Real conversations change all those who are party to them. In supervision, I often find myself exploring ways in which a client engagement has deeply changed the way I think about something – not just my opinions but also the frameworks within which my opinions are formed.

We sometimes make mistakes. Studiously avoiding error is a sure route to incongruence and relationship failure. We can expect an aeroplane pilot to make safety a priority, but not to the point where they never get past the pre-flight checks.

As well as being professionally, practically and financially prepared, a counselling practitioner needs an emotional support network for these moments of free fall – moments when we wonder about our own preconceptions, or about whether we might have handled a situation 'better'. They come with the territory.

Sharing a practice with someone and having supportive supervision are also useful when it comes to managing one of the significant benefits of working in private practice: the freedom to structure client engagements in a way that suits the client's needs. We can see people as many, or as few, times as they feel would be productive. We don't have a sessions limit, or even a time-based review policy. We review when the counselling process indicates it, and we take difficult cases to supervision.

Whatever rules you might choose to follow, you will find yourself in circumstances that challenge them. For me, part of being person-centred is to develop my capacity to handle the particular, unique circumstances that arise in the context of particular unique relationships. Private practice has proved to be the right context for this.

Paul Carslake – How I got started

I am a psychodynamic therapist working in private practice in London.

I launched my practice just before the 2020 Covid lockdown began, with a couple of clients at the start, referred to me via a local counselling centre where I had – speculatively – rented rooms for two hours a week. I was also advertising with two online directories, but with little success. So, I spent time writing and rewriting my profile, trying to convey my approach to therapy in a voice that felt distinct from the others. Finally, a family member advised me to try a different portrait photo, and after this, I saw an uptick in contacts. By the autumn of 2020, my schedule was beginning to fill up – mostly with online sessions, as we were still in lockdown, and later with in-person bookings. I can't deny that the pandemic helped me to launch my practice: it removed the financial risk of paying for block room bookings with no guaranteed clients and allowed me to offer online sessions at an affordable price.

During the three months between finishing my degree and getting my certification to practise, I put together a fairly extensive website (www.talkplace.co.uk) and thought a lot about marketing and advertising. For a while I wondered if my website had the potential to become a 'platform' for a small number of therapists but decided against this: my focus had to be therapy, not a small business, and it felt like mission creep. In fact, the website functions as a kind of calling card: it has a certain kind of look and feel that is, perhaps, attractive to some clients but not others. So it is communicating something about me.

I looked at more traditional means of advertising my services too. At the very start, I had little sense of how successful or otherwise the online directories would be. So, I got business cards printed up, bought some perspex card racks and took them round to local cafés and shops, some of whom agreed to display them. Shortly after, all those businesses closed during the Covid pandemic.

Without question, the online directories have been the most important source of new clients during my start-up phase and beyond. After two full years of private practice, I am typically signing up around 40 new clients each year, of whom 90% have found me on a directory. To throw in a few more statistics: my average cost of acquiring each new customer (ie. total marketing spend divided by new clients starting in the year) is fairly stable at around £25–£30 – so for a client engagement of, say, 12 weeks, these marketing costs would count for less than 5% of a £60 hourly fee (and obviously even less for longer contracts).

Another aspect that has been crucial in setting up in private practice has been offering a generous amount of time (30–40 minutes) for a free introductory call. The concept of comparing therapists is gaining traction in the market, and especially, it seems, with clients in their 20s and 30s. I use these sessions as the initial part of an assessment, and currently around two thirds lead to a new client contract.

Our fees have to be competitive; there is a prevailing market price and we ignore it at our peril. I started working exclusively via an online platform during the Covid lockdown, without the overhead costs of consulting rooms, and my initial fees reflected that. I added a higher 'face-to-face' fee when the lockdown ended. I have increased my fees slightly each year for existing and new clients, usually at a time when the schedule is fairly full and I want to slow things down a little. I feel it is important that no current client finds themselves paying more than my 'advertised' rate on the directories, so prices go up but not down. It is also important to check what local competitors are charging; a quick directory search provides an instant answer.

I conduct part of my therapy work from rented therapy rooms at two local locations (each offering five rooms). These are popular with therapists and have created a thriving therapy grouping, with its own WhatsApp group, social evenings and peer supervision opportunities. Notably, all of the rooms are rented by the hour using a scheduling app, with free cancellation up to 24 hours before the booked session. This removes the financial burden of paying for unused room space – a particular problem when starting up.

And a final note on fees: I bill clients after each session and send an invoice and online payment link via an accounting software that has a 'bank feed' from my business account. This is well worth the £90 annual subscription, as it minimises my admin time and provides a convenient dashboard listing paid and outstanding invoices.

All these factors may look a bit commercial, but it's in a good cause: reducing the amount of time and money spent on unnecessary costs and admin means less pressure to raise fees, and more time to spend thinking about our clients.

Conclusion

Setting up in private practice and developing and maintaining it requires us to explore, tease out and answer multiple considerations.

This sector context can be hugely rewarding. You're your own boss, you can pick and choose how often you work and, potentially, with whom and for how long.

If you're thinking of private practice as a career path, I wish you the very best. You'll join tens of thousands of fellow private practitioners and, hopefully, make a powerful, positive and purposeful impact on the clients you meet.

Good luck!

Acknowledgements

With grateful thanks to Lesley Ludlow, BACP senior accredited counsellor, supervisor in private practice in south London and past chair of the BACP Private Practice division executive committee, for additional material, input and insight.

References

BACP. (2018). *Ethical framework for the counselling professions*. BACP.

BACP. (2023). *Private practice toolkit*. BACP. www.bacp.co.uk/bacp-divisions/bacp-private-practice/private-practice-toolkit/setting-up-your-private-practice (available to members only).

Binstead, C. (2021). *Student to private practice – use of the BACP toolkit*. Presented at the BACP student conference. Recording is available in the *BACP Private Practice Toolkit* (free to members).

Brown, S. (2022). On the right platform? *Therapy Today, 33*(7), 18–22.

Hughes, R. (Ed.). (2004). *An anthology of counselling at work II*. Association for Counselling at Work.

Hughes, R. (2020). *Get a life! Creating a successful work-life balance*. Kogan Page.

Hughes, R., Kinder, A. & Cooper, C. (Eds.). (2012). *International handbook of workplace trauma support*. Wiley.

Hughes, R., Kinder, A. & Cooper, C. (2017). *The crisis book: Overcoming and surviving work-life challenges*. LID Publishing.

Hughes, R., Kinder, A. & Cooper, C. (2019). *The wellbeing workout: How to manage stress and develop resilience*. Palgrave MacMillan.

Kinder, A., Hughes, R. & Cooper, C. (Eds.). (2008). *Employee well-being support: A workplace resource*. Wiley.

Kinder, A., Hughes, R. & Cooper, C. (Eds.). (2022). *Occupational health and wellbeing: Challenges and opportunities in theory and practice*. Routledge.

Reeves, A. (2015). *Working with risk in counselling and psychotherapy*. Sage Publications.

Chapter 3

Online counselling

Sarah Worley-James
with Ellie Fretwell, Eleanor Brown, Cloie Parfitt, Rachael Klug and Jennifer Hamilton

In this chapter, I am going to introduce you to online counselling and the many ways it can open up your practice to clients who might otherwise not be able to access counselling. There are contributions from several counsellors working online in a range of different settings, including private practice, university counselling, the third sector, services for young people and people with eating disorders, and services specialising in neurodiversity. Their reasons for training to work online are varied: some were responding to the changes enforced by the Covid pandemic; others had already chosen to enter the online world many years ago.

This chapter, like Chapter 10 on spirituality, differs from the others in that its focus is applicable to all the sectors covered in the book. However, it can be argued that it is an area of specialist practice: many organisations, such as employee assistance programmes (EAPs) and some third sector providers, offer only online counselling, and a growing number now offer a hybrid approach.

Let's start with a definition of online counselling, as it incorporates several different forms, and the particular benefits it offers our clients.

What is online counselling?

Online counselling simply refers to the process of conducting counselling via online communication. This is through a secure internet communication platform using video, webcam, audio (voice only), instant messaging (IM), live chat (LC), email or the telephone. Some of the terms used are pretty much interchangeable (such as video and webcam, instant messaging and live chat) or relate to the same form of communication using different technology (audio and telephone).

What are the benefits of online counselling and therapy for the client?

1. Environment. Rather than enter the counsellor's formal, professional world, the client can choose the room and chair they feel most comfortable in at home, and even the drink they have beside them. They may choose a room they associate with feeling safe, where it's easier to discuss and disclose painful or distressing experiences and issues. They are also free to move around if this is helpful, whether for physical reasons or to manage strong emotions in the moment.

Simpson and colleagues have reviewed the benefits of videotherapy (2020) and list several such environmental advantages. These include clients with post-traumatic stress disorder, who may feel safer exploring and working through the trauma from their own home; the calming and grounding effect of stroking the family pet during sessions, and clients who have been confined to their home by agoraphobia or obsessive compulsive disorder, for example (or, indeed, the Covid pandemic), who can show their online counsellor around their living space as part of an exploration into taking steps beyond that space.

2. Medium. The client can choose which medium to use for counselling. Although not all counsellors work in all the online media, the client can choose one who specialises in their preferred medium. It is also worth noting that moving between different media can prove beneficial to the therapy – for example, a client might ask if they can turn off the video and just use audio when disclosing something they feel shame or embarrassment about.

3. Control. Online disinhibition (Suler, 2004) is a well-researched aspect of online therapy that can be beneficial but needs to be managed by the counsellor. Briefly, it refers to the client finding it easier to disclose information and share vulnerabilities online than they would in person. This may be due to the anonymity that the non-visual media offer and the physical distance from the counsellor. Online disinhibition can lead to the pace of counselling being swifter for both client and counsellor. Online counselling gives the client control over the pace and depth of disclosure.

Ellie Fretwell is a BACP senior accredited counsellor and qualified online therapist who specialises in working with clients with eating disorders. She has worked for Stockport NHS Adult Community Eating Disorder Service since 2012. Recently she has developed a specialist interest in clients with neurodiversity who experience eating disorders. She believes:

> Online CBT for eating disorders works really well online. There are so many useful online resources. I use an app with clients called Recovery Record – it's a food diary that can be shared with me. Many clients with eating disorders have comorbidities such as social anxiety and they find it easier to attend online rather than coming to the clinic in person. Clients with eating disorders who have body image issues might prefer to work online as they can be in control of how much of them is seen. As long as the client's GP is willing to liaise and monitor their medical health, I work confidently online with many clients who have eating disorders like bulimia and binge eating disorder.

4. Convenience and flexibility. Having a variety of ways to connect with a counsellor online allows the client to choose the medium that best suits their lifestyle and availability. The client can access sessions more easily without having to travel to the counsellor's place of work at a set time. They can even choose a counsellor from almost anywhere in the world to get the best fit for them (subject to that counsellor being insured and legally eligible to provide counselling within the client's country of residence).

As mentioned earlier, the potential to move between media, if necessary or useful, is a further example of the flexibility of counselling online and the control and choice it gives to clients. As Ellie points out, it gives clients the option to communicate by audio alone if they don't feel comfortable being seen, and they can switch to using video as they become more confident about being in their body and about their appearance.

Eleanor Brown, a counsellor at Cardiff University, works both in person and online. She says:

> From a personal perspective, I love the flexibility of online working and the immediacy of support from my team if I put a query or concern on our Teams feed. Used effectively within a counselling team, you can remain highly connected and involved in the day-to-day of being part of a service.

Cloie Parfitt is an integrative psychotherapist who works with adults and young people online and in-person from her office in Norwich. She takes a trauma-informed, collaborative and compassionate approach to her therapeutic work in an effort to foster connection, healing and personal growth. She works entirely online in private practice and values the flexibility that online working gives her to manage her workload and reduce stress:

> Throughout my psychotherapy career I have worked in a variety of different settings – including schools, charitable organisations and private practice – and each of these settings has provided invaluable learning opportunities that have strengthened my therapeutic practice. Currently, I operate a small private practice, working with adults and young people online. This way of working allows me to manage my hours and work from the comfort of my home, both of which I find beneficial for my own emotional wellbeing.

5. **Accessibility.** The geographical flexibility of working online makes it much easier for clients to receive counselling. According to the World Health Organization (2019), between 44% and 70% of people in developing countries who need mental health treatment are unable to access it.

Common barriers to accessing counselling include geography, physical disability and mental health problems that make it difficult for someone to travel or meet strangers face-to-face. Clients who are in an abusive relationship may not be able to go to a counsellor's premises because their movements are being closely monitored.

People in some cultures and countries have a different concept of and attitude to mental health to those that predominate in the Western industrialised world. In some cultures and families, there is a belief that personal problems should never be shared outside the immediate family, for fear of stigma, shame and judgement. In others, it's expected that you would talk to your priest or spiritual leader or adviser about mental/emotional and relationship problems, but never to a mental health professional, lest you are seen to be 'mad'. Being able to access the different forms of online counselling, such as asynchronous email and IM, can be hugely beneficial to people who don't feel able to share with their partner or family their need for privacy while they have counselling.

Online counselling can also offer a way through the barriers to counselling created by various social and cultural norms and expectations. For example, men are expected to 'man up' – not to have emotions or show them and to be able to deal silently and stoically with their problems. Many men are raised to think it is not acceptable to talk openly about their struggles or mental health. Such deep-rooted cultural values can take generations to change, and so it is positive to see proactive campaigns and influential people focusing on challenging this, such as the Movember men's mental health campaign.[1] Being able to access counselling privately and anonymously online has, arguably, made it easier for men to seek and find help and support.

Rachael Klug works in private practice with a range of ages, from children up to adults. She has trained to work with neurodiverse clients and has both personal and professional experience of neurodiversity. Rachael is also Director for Children and Young People at the Association for Counselling and Therapy Online (ACTO). She only works online, and explains:

> Developing an online therapy practice has not only opened up my world, but it has also provided me with so many resources and ways to connect with my clients. Many of my clients are so traumatised that when they first come to me for therapy, they are stuck in their bedrooms, unable to leave their homes. Online therapy has not only given me a way to work; it's also meant I can reach clients who would not even consider going out the house, let alone going to a therapist's room. Perhaps my feeling stuck and unable to work enabled me to deeply empathise with many of my clients who mirror these feelings at the start of therapy.

6. Anonymity. A huge draw for many clients is the anonymity that text-based communication gives them. People from cultures with a long history of being discriminated against are likely to have a high mistrust of authority and professionals and may be wary of or reluctant to access mental health support. These include people from Black, Asian and other racially minoritised backgrounds and LGBTQI+ communities. The anonymity that online counselling provides can be especially beneficial to clients who experience multiple discrimination (such as racism, sexism and disability discrimination). Such 'intersectionality' (the interaction of multiple forms of discrimination) can create a multiplying or layering of barriers that prevent them seeking counselling.

7. Engage differently. Reynolds and colleagues (2013) have coined the phrase 'online calming hypothesis' to describe how online counselling can feel less threatening than in-person sessions for both client and counsellor. They point out that this is particularly so for clients experiencing anxiety-based disorders such as social phobia, agoraphobia and obsessive-compulsive disorder, and also for clients with autistic spectrum condition (ASC).

Online counselling can also enable the client to express aspects or configurations of their self (Cooper et al., 2004) that they feel would not be

---

1. See https://uk.movember.com

accepted or valued if they were to show them in person. As Suler writes (2015, p.111):

> The self expressed in one place is not necessarily deeper, more real, or more authentic than any other. Each environment allows us to see the different perspectives of that complex thing we call 'self'.

Personal experiences of moving into the online world

I first began counselling online in 2011, when it was very much a niche mode of practice and was regarded with huge suspicion by much of the counselling and therapy profession. It remained this way until spring 2020, when the Covid pandemic forced everyone to start working online almost overnight.

My interest in online counselling began when I joined the counselling service at Cardiff University in 2009. I immediately saw the potential for using forms of communication with which students were familiar and in which they were already proficient in order to make our services more accessible – most students are 'digital natives', born and brought up in a digital age. Alongside this, it seemed obvious that online counselling would enable students to access support outside term time or when they weren't in Cardiff. So, I embarked on my training with Jane Evans, who, as a founder member of ACTO, introduced me to the organisation, where my enthusiasm and growing skills in online counselling soon led me to join its board and subsequently become chair for a number of years.

Over the years, I have worked with an interesting mix of clients who want exclusively online counselling, exclusively face-to-face or a mix of both. Some ask for an occasional email session when they are away or too busy to commit to a set time and day for a session but still want to meet regularly. These clients value the flexibility I can offer, and I think we both find it useful and illuminating to experience relating to each other in a different medium. I have also found this mix of communication allows both therapist and client to experience different aspects of each other and so gain a deeper understanding and connection. With clients who value the space to talk, I am conscious of remaining a quieter presence in the face-to-face sessions, but in emails I feel able to share more of my reflections and ask more questions.

When the Covid pandemic led to the first national lockdown in the spring of 2020, I offered all my face-to face clients the opportunity to move to work online. Most of them readily agreed (only one declined, for technological reasons – they did not have adequate broadband). With each, we used the first online session to re-contract and discuss how this new form of communicating might change the nature of our relationship and the counselling process. This was when I first heard the expression 'car therapy' and experienced it myself. One client was visibly inhibited and quieter than usual in our first video session and, when I noted this, shared that they were worried about their partner overhearing our conversation from the next room. I offered IM for the remainder of that session. At the end, the client suggested conducting future sessions from their car (parked up), as they felt it was a safe and private space. A useful point here is the importance of discussing with the client self-care and access to support immediately after the session, as well as between sessions. For example, if a client has driven somewhere for the session and the therapy has been particularly emotional or challenging, they might need some time to ground themselves before being safe to drive home.

Jennifer Hamilton is a clinical supervisor and psychotherapist/counsellor accredited with IACP and BACP. She uses a humanistic person-centred approach with a body-mind perspective that emphasises the importance of the body and 'bodywork' in achieving, holding and maintaining emotional, mental, physical and spiritual wellbeing. Even so, she says:

> Transforming my face-to-face work online was not as challenging as I had imagined. I found I could use most of my bodywork techniques online to help clients and could still help them connect with their bodies through art therapy and other methods. The only part of the body therapy I could not offer was the hands-on body massage and some energetic interventions that required physical presence to help the client. However, I continued using different body exercise techniques. The client could still do these with my direction through video and phone calls.
>
> Cognitive behavioural therapy techniques and expressive art therapy interventions were possible while using PTSD and trauma therapy with traumatised clients. In my work as a therapist/supervisor with supervisees, it was similar; I used all my body training techniques except the hands-on ones.
>
> My main reason for training in online work was to know and understand the legal requirements of working online. I was not sure about working with people in other countries. I needed to understand the language of the online world. With more profound knowledge of contracting, I felt safer and created safety for my clients by having a more substantial contract and proper training for online work. Self-care in online work was significant for me as I intended to work with supervisees online, and I wanted that knowledge to pass on. Training and competence in self-care is as important as all other aspects of the therapy work.

Ellie had a different motivation:

> I was inspired to train as an online therapist after attending my first OCTIA (Online Counselling and Therapy in Action) conference in 2013, where I heard Sarah Worley-James speak about how she had developed an online counselling service. She made online work sound exciting, creative and relevant to my clients and me.
>
> I live with a health condition (multiple sclerosis), hence I am a wheelchair user and experience extreme fatigue. Working online suits me very well because of this; I can work from home in an environment that is as comfortable as possible; there is no commute; I can work out a schedule with regular comfort breaks to suit me. The therapeutic relationship feels very liberating in terms of my disability; it is my choice whether I disclose to the client that I am disabled, and vice versa. The client is free to make the assumptions that they need to about my mobility because they cannot see my wheelchair. In a world where my disability is visible and I have no choice but to show it to people, it feels novel to make it practically invisible in my clinical work. The online world is the perfect workplace for me; after all, one of the amazing uses of technology is to lessen the negative impact of disability.

Eleanor says:

> I chose to work online as part of my own professional development, having seen how useful it was as an option for some service users and because I felt it would help me keep pace with the developments in the counselling arena. It was also an expectation of my current workplace, in order to widen accessibility and provide service users with more flexibility and choice. In 2020, it became a necessity to provide counselling sessions remotely due to Covid lockdowns, and it was reassuring to have the confidence that came with already being well acquainted with online/distance working at what was a very challenging time both for clients and their counsellors.

Working in private practice, Rachael found online working the solution to her personal situation:

> The start of my journey into the world of online therapy involved a search for a way that would enable me to practise while at home. My son was recovering from a head injury, and I had been unable to work for some years as I needed to be at home to care for him. I felt stuck and

despondent, as I could not use the professional skills that I had worked hard to develop. Then one day, while I was wistfully searching therapy sites online, I found an advert for a course that offered training in online therapy. This was in the mid-1990s, so before Covid was even known about. I felt very unsure: how would I connect safely with clients from my laptop at home? How could I even consider bringing the techniques I had learnt in psychodynamic psychotherapy practice into an online setting? I hesitated, and this is where I wish I had known what I now know.

Cloie explains her reasons for training to work online:

> I originally chose to train in online therapy at the height of the Covid pandemic so that I could continue to support my clients during what proved to be a very challenging time for most. Since then, I have continued to work primarily online as I have found online therapy offers many benefits, one being that it is accessible for people with mobility challenges who might otherwise struggle to attend sessions – an issue that is relevant to many of the clients I work with.

Transitioning to online counselling

Having shared some varied perspectives on what led these counsellors to work online, I want to explore some of the questions and issues that frequently arise when transitioning to online counselling. As online media offer very different ways to engage in a therapeutic relationship, it is normal for even the most experienced counsellor to have some questions or concerns, ranging from practical and technical to relational. I hope the following will help you gauge whether online counselling is something you would like to venture into, or not.

Q: How do I connect to and engage with my client with a lack of, or limited, body language cues?

A: The key is to use your existing theoretical knowledge, experience and particularly your advanced empathy to consider what may be influencing your client (culture, education, life experiences), and what this may reveal in terms of the explicit, and implicit, feelings and meanings they are bringing to counselling. In audio-only sessions, learn to 'tune in' to your client's verbal way of expressing themself: their accent, dialect, choice of words, phrasing, use of colloquialisms and personal style of speaking. These will all help you to understand their worldview and give clues as to what may be unspoken yet meaningful.

This concern about whether it is possible to create a therapeutic connection and relationship online is echoed by Eleanor:

> I have noticed that for some clients there is a sense or belief that what they're experiencing is not 'real' counselling if done remotely – or that they are not investing so much psychologically when the sessions are not in-person. Some appear to believe that virtual counselling is not real counselling.

She also notes that communicating online can create 'an abruptness to the start and end of a session that is not felt when meeting in-person'.

My response to these is that often a client who begins online therapy thinking it is second best to face-to-face therapy is pleasantly surprised by their ability to connect to the counsellor, develop a meaningful dialogue and benefit from the process. It is certainly true that the beginnings and ends of sessions can feel abrupt, as you do not have the informal element of greeting at the door and walking to and from the counselling room. So, when working online, you need to make time for the greetings and goodbyes and other such 'small talk' at the start of the session, to help the client settle into the space.

Q: How do I express empathy in instant messaging synchronous sessions? Isn't it limiting not to have the non-verbal cues?

A: Be conscious of the words and phrases you are using to convey empathy. Be open, transparent and explicit in demonstrating that you are being tentative and are open to correction and challenge. Literally spell out your rationale and direction of thinking behind your reflections, questions and approach. This will help the client understand the meaning and purpose of your interventions. Explicitly invite feedback and share with the client your experience and responses to them, so they get a sense of you and your reactions to what they are divulging. Ensure that the client feels heard by giving an empathic response to what they are describing before asking further questions or suggesting coping strategies or a different way forward.

Q: I like to use drawing and other art forms to help clients express themselves. How can I use non-verbal creative therapeutic techniques online?

A: It is perfectly possible to work creatively and collaboratively online using a virtual sand tray, paint 3D and screen-sharing images, music, quotes, film clips, exploring emotions through imagery and metaphor, and using the whiteboard feature on the online communication platform you use.

Ellie says:

> As a cognitive behaviour therapist, I know how well online work complements CBT. There are so many online tools that can be used, such as whiteboards for formulations; mood and behaviour monitoring apps, and screen-sharing resources like pictures and diagrams.

Often, when faced with the word 'creative', we immediately think of sand trays, working with stones, pictures, paint and paper, therapy cards, music, poetry, films, dreams, imagery, visualisation and play. But there are a growing number of counsellors who use new technology to work therapeutically – through gaming, for example, whether it's a game created specifically for therapy, such as Proreal[2] or a non-specialist game that the client is already familiar with, like Minecraft.[3] These are 'creative' therapies too. Creating characters or objects to represent real people or aspects of themselves enables the client to explore from a place of safety and a different perspective and opens up new insights and the opportunity to experiment with different ways of being and relating before transferring them to the 'real' world.

Equally, there are more subtle ways to work creatively. Putting the word 'creative' into a thesaurus comes up with 'innovative', 'inventive', 'ingenious', 'original' and 'visionary'. The very act of connecting with clients online fits all these adjectives! By giving serious consideration to your style of relating, use of language and other ways you express yourself online, you are being creative.

Rachael describes how her skills and approach have evolved thanks to the creative opportunities the online world offers:

> I branched out way beyond my psychodynamic training. I will always keep psychodynamic understandings and approaches as a core for my therapy practice, but I have explored ways to work way beyond this. What has excited me the most in online therapy is that I can bring in approaches that may fit different clients and at different times in therapy; it's developed into a really personalised approach for my clients. I trained in mindfulness techniques, complex trauma stabilisation approaches, pain reprocessing techniques, avatar therapy... so many different ways to connect with my clients. Recently, I have explored ways to work with a neurofeedback device called Mendi[4] for clients who have difficulties focusing and have high anxiety, as well as

---

2. www.proreal.world
3. www.minecraft.net
4. www.mendi.io

training in EMDR techniques adapted for online work to work with clients to reprocess trauma.

Q: How do I deal with the inevitable technological glitches? The thought that something technological and outside my control may let me down and I won't be able to fix it makes me tense and nervous.

A: It's important first of all to cover this eventuality in your contract with your clients. Set out clearly the steps you will take to fix any technical glitch if it occurs or find an alternative way to continue the session. What's essential is that you deal with the glitches calmly, with acceptance, and follow the process you have described in your contract, so your client will feel supported and safe with you. Take time to practise how to deal with your stress and anxiety in these moments so that you can remain focused on resolving the problem, whether by reconnecting technically and therapeutically, changing the means of communication (e.g. from video to audio), or by rearranging the session (depending on the situation).

As Cloie puts it:

> Technological issues can impact sessions, and it is very important to develop a contingency plan should technological issues arise and to communicate this plan to the client before issues occur.

Q: How do I respond to interruptions into the client's space, or a lack of understanding about the importance of privacy (what if the client is in a cafe or sitting on a park bench)?

A: This is a common boundary issue for clients and supervisees. People can be remarkably unconcerned about conducting the most intimate conversations in public and in crowded spaces. A client may not understand the importance we give to privacy and confidentiality and to establishing boundaries around the mental space to focus and relate at depth. You need to consider what your ethical framework says about this issue and why it is important, and have the confidence to end the session sensitively and supportively if it is not private. The client may insist that they are okay with the invasion of their space, so you need to be able to explain the reasons for your decision, so they understand that these boundaries are there for their benefit.

Q: How do I minimise misunderstandings in text-based communication?

A: Through openness, transparency and humility. Be explicit in your words and phrasing, and check that you have been clear. For example, you might say,

'I get the sense that you are feeling alone and are struggling to cope. Please correct me if I am wrong.' Be humble in asking, 'Am I making sense?', rather than asking if the client has understood. This, for me, gives a message that I am striving to be clear in my communication, rather than implying that the client is at fault if they don't understand. Routinely explain the rationale and intention behind your reflections, questions and approach. Take time to check how the client is feeling and reacting to your approach and invite their input into the direction of the counselling process.

Q: *Instant messaging takes much longer than talking on video, audio and phone. How do I work effectively in real time with the slower pace?*

A: Take the pressure off yourself in terms of your expectations of the sessions. It is inevitable that you will discuss less using IM than if you were using video or audio in a session of the same length. So, give yourself and your client space to connect and express yourselves. You need also to be aware that the work may go deep very quickly, as the anonymity of IM can lead to online disinhibition (Suler, 2004). You also need to be careful to leave enough time towards the end of the session to ensure the client is in a safe place emotionally, and to summarise, close the session and arrange the next appointment. Think about starting this process with at least 15 minutes to go, and keep focused, as your client may begin to introduce a new topic or may want to respond to the summary or comment about the session. You do not want the ending to feel rushed for either of you.

Q: *What if I make typos, especially during IM sessions where there is less time to correct them? I worry it might affect the therapeutic alliance as I won't be able to check my spelling before I send the message.*

A: In my experience, clients do not expect perfect typing! Consider how often in verbal communication we stumble over the pronunciation of a word, take a couple of attempts to express what we want to say or go round the houses to make our point. These are the equivalent of typos or grammatical errors in text-based communication. It is common for us all to make typos, clients and counsellors alike, and I have never had a client comment on, let alone complain about mine! If I do spot a typo I've made in an IM session, I will make a correction or apologise. For example, if you type, 'It sounds as if you are feeling increasingly isolated and alne. Help me to understand this,' you can follow it up immediately by messaging '*alone'. The * indicates that a correction is being made to a word in the sentence just sent.

Q: Is it okay or even appropriate to use emoticons, emoji and acronyms?

A: First, I'll quickly explain the difference between an emoticon and an emoji. An emoticon is a blend of 'emotion' and 'icon', and is made up of characters from a keyboard, whereas an emoji (a combination of the Japanese 'e' for 'picture' and 'moji' for 'character') is a small image that represents something.

These days, the software you are using, whether you are writing a Word document, email or in IM mode, will automatically turn certain keystrokes into an emoji. In a counselling context, an emoji or emoticon can be used to express empathy, just as you would use a facial expression or gesture when talking to somebody face to face, but make sure the client is happy with this. Ask if they are okay with you using the occasional :-) to show you are smiling at what they are saying, as opposed to typing it out literally: '(I am smiling as I read your words because it is good to hear you sound so pleased with your progress).' Be aware that different clients will have different views about using emoticons and emoji – work with their preferences. Also, you need to be aware that the keystrokes used to create an emoticon will vary from country to country, as some languages use different keyboard characters and lettering. For example, the Russian keyboard does not have a colon, so a smile is conveyed purely with a closing (right) bracket. Perhaps more essentially, the meaning that you intend to convey with an emoji may be very different to the one the client receives. The thumbs-up symbol may be a sign of approval in Western culture, but in Greece and the Middle East it can be interpreted as vulgar and even offensive.

Personally, I limit my use of emoticons and emojis to occasional smiles, which I use to convey warmth (as part of my hello and goodbye), or to show I am positively affected by the client's words. I avoid a sad :-(or confused :-/ face as I believe these may unintentionally convey a negative message and tap into a client's low self-esteem. The client may think, 'I have now made my counsellor feel sad – see, I really am a terrible person,' or 'It's my fault my counsellor is confused, I can never explain properly.' As a rule of thumb, be led by the client, and if you are unsure what meaning they are trying to convey, ask them. The same goes for acronyms. For a long time, I thought LOL meant 'lots of love', and was very confused as that meaning didn't fit what friends were saying when they used it in text messages to me. It all made sense when I was told LOL means 'laugh out loud'. Acronyms come and go in popularity and new ones are being invented all the time, so be cautious and, if in doubt, don't use them.

Q: How do I manage my own time boundaries in asynchronous email sessions and respond to a client who is writing very long emails that I don't have time to answer in the allotted time?

A: This is an issue that counsellors new to working online often struggle with. It is important to give your client a clear word-count limit so that you have time to read, reflect and compose your reply within the time you have allotted to the session. Book the time in your diary, as you would for a synchronous client session. That way you are giving yourself a clear message that this is a 50-minute counselling session, with specific start and end times. Sometimes the client may need a reminder that, regardless of the length of email, you will not continue reading and replying beyond the time you have allocated for the session.

Q: *How do I respond to and manage risk online?*

A: This is another major concern to counsellors, understandably. I can only answer very briefly here. What I want to emphasise first is that risk concerns should not mean you exclude a client from online counselling. Indeed, it may well be that the anonymity and safety that online counselling offers the client is the very reason why they are accessing counselling and disclosing risk. Without the conditions that only online counselling offers, that client may continue to struggle alone, potentially increasing the risk factors due to this imposed isolation.

When I began working online, I made the decision that it is far more ethical to work appropriately with risk issues than deny a client the support that online counselling can offer. However, I am also very mindful that the client needs to be mentally together enough to focus on the therapeutic interventions if they are to benefit from them.

Consider how you assess, monitor and work with risk in in-person practice, and then how you will transfer these approaches and skills to working both synchronously and asynchronously online.

Naturally, it is important to consider the risk assessment tools you use and how you monitor and record risk, and ensure that you have the client's GP details and your contract to refer back to should you need to break client confidentiality. In my experience, this is very rare. I encourage and support my clients to access further appropriate support if necessary. This might include seeking help from their GP or local community mental health team, ensuring they have information about online and 24-hour sources of support (of which there are many now), such as Samaritans,[5] Side by Side,[6] Togetherall,[7] The Calm

---

5. www.samaritans.org
6. https://sidebyside.mind.org.uk
7. https://togetherall.com/en-gb

Zone,[8] and Living Life to the Full,[9] to name a few.

Rachael explains how she felt about risk before training to work online:

> I think my initial anxieties were important and I would not wish them away, as they really helped me to ensure that the therapy I delivered was as safe and effective as I could make it. I took up training courses in online therapy, which gave me an important bedrock of competency in developing my online practice.

Cloie shares how she manages risk ethically and effectively online:

> Perhaps the biggest consideration related to working independently online is ensuring the safety of my clients – specifically those who are particularly vulnerable, such as those who have suffered extensive trauma. When working face-to-face, it is much easier to assess the suitability of the counselling space, for example. Working online requires additional consideration and it becomes necessary for the therapist to educate the client on the importance of accessing sessions from a space that feels safe and within which they are afforded privacy. Similarly, I have found it useful to be in dialogue with other practitioners supporting the client, such as the client's GP, social worker, psychiatrist, support worker etc. to ensure we are all working together to best support the client and promote their safety and wellbeing between sessions.

Q: *What are the legal issues, if any?*

A: What is most important is that your insurance covers you to work online (whether you are counselling, supervising or teaching) in the countries where your clients *are based*. You also need to check that you are legally qualified to practise counselling in those countries, even though you aren't based there yourself. These are two separate points. Your insurer, ACTO and your professional body are all good sources of information and support on legal issues.

Where are the opportunities to work online?

There are several different options for offering online counselling, whether you are in private practice or working for an organisation. If you decide to work independently, there are some key considerations to focus on, including the quality of the technology you use, the platform you use to connect to clients,

---

8. www.thecalmzone.net
9. https://llttf.com

your insurance, and registration with the Information Commissioner's Office (ICO) as part of your compliance with UK General Data Protection Regulation (GDPR) requirements. I have summarised all this in my book, *Online Counselling: An essential guide* (Worley-James, 2022).

Alternatively, you may prefer to sign up to one of the many online therapy platforms now emerging in the independent (commercial) sector.[10] These are set up specifically to connect clients seeking therapy with independent counsellors and provide a secure online space for sessions. This can be an attractive option for counsellors, as the platform will offer ancillary services, such as advertising and an appointments diary, ensure compliance with the UK GDPR with regard to safety of your records and, in many cases, provide a secure online space to write and store your case notes and administer your invoicing and payments. If you sign up, the platform may want to see evidence of your training, supervision arrangements, insurance and Disclosure Barring Service (DBS – criminal records) check. Some may provide supervision or offer opportunities to deliver supervision if you wish to develop your career in this direction. There are several of these platforms based in the UK and, as this is a growing market, more are being developed and launched all the time. Current examples (and their inclusion here does not imply endorsement) are Dr Julian,[11] My Therapist Online[12] and ETherapy.[13]

If you choose to go with a therapy platform, you need to ask about their data storage, security and confidentiality, what qualifications and supervision they require you to have, what insurance you need to put in place, details of how they match clients to you, payments, cancellation policies and so forth.

Another way to practise online is to apply to work with an organisation that offers online counselling, such as Kooth[14] or Sue Ryder Online Bereavement Counselling,[15] or become an affiliate with an EAP provider,[16] which may provide purely telephone or video counselling. These may be either voluntary or private-sector organisations; some will offer clients brief therapy for a fixed number of sessions; others may adopt a single session model, where the client is connected immediately to whichever counsellor

---

10. Note, these platforms are not the same as the client management platforms that are designed to help independent practitioners manage their caseloads and therapy business.
11. www.dr-julian.com
12. www.mytherapistonline.co.uk
13. www.e-therapy.uk
14. www.kooth.com
15. www.sueryder.org/online-bereavement-counselling
16. www.eapa.org.uk/find-an-eap-provider

is available when they make contact with the organisation. The latter is a growing area, with the aim of giving people immediate access to therapy when they feel they need it. EAPs offering telephone counselling often work in this way, as do some online services for young people, where this instant, one-off counselling is often conducted via IM. There are concerns about this way of working as it does not allow for the development of an ongoing therapeutic relationship and process. Also, having instant access to 'your therapist' can detract from the client building their own capacity for emotional resilience. So, when looking into joining one of these organisations or platforms, think carefully about how well this model fits your counselling approach, values and ethics.

Post-Covid, most counselling provider organisations offer a hybrid approach, both online and in-person, and it is worth enquiring about this flexibility, even if this is not mentioned in a job advert.

The opening up of the counselling profession to the possibilities of online therapy means that there are many more potential avenues of work for you. Rather than simply looking for local opportunities, you can apply for an online role across the country or work locally in-person and a day or two for an online company or one based elsewhere.

Top tips

I have two top tips for you. First, do not underestimate the importance and value of high-quality training. The ACTO website is a good place to look for a training provider.[17] The list of common questions explored earlier will have shown you how much there is to consider and learn; it is not as simple as switching on your laptop and logging into an online communications platform!

This was Jennifer's top tip too: 'My gold nugget of wisdom would be that without specific training we cannot possibly be competent or ethical in any online work we do.'

My second top tip is to focus on self-care. I am a passionate believer in the importance of counsellor wellbeing and regular self-care. When working online, we are likely to be working in isolation and spending more time in front of a computer screen. It is easy to forget to take a break – you need to schedule in time to stand up, walk about, take your eyes away from the screen, stretch and breathe. The increased amount of screen time can lead to eye strain, tension headaches, migraines and the physical impact of poor posture and sitting in one chair or position for extended periods of time.

---

17. www.acto.org.uk/training

In terms of the online counselling process itself, the high levels of concentration involved in intently focusing on the limited view of the client, having to attend closely when our only connection is through our hearing, or seeking to uncover feelings and meanings between the written words, is both physically and emotionally draining.

Another important reason for self-care when working online is that, if you are working remotely, it may be more difficult to access peer or line management support to offload after a challenging or emotional session or to explore options and clarify your response when a risk emerges. There are no opportunities for an informal chat in the staff kitchen or a quick check-in with a more experienced colleague or manager, and online meetings tend to focus on the business at hand; there's little space for the small talk you get when you meet in person, which is so important in creating and maintaining bonds between colleagues and a sense of team connectivity.

Ellie's top tip is about client safety and self-care:

> Regular contact with the client's GP is essential, especially when working with eating disorders. This is particularly important if the client feels more comfortable and able to develop trust in the process by engaging through a non-visual media.

Eleanor has a couple of top tips to share. First:

> Be mindful of the disinhibition effect – while having clients engage with counselling on their own turf/choice of environment can come with huge advantages, some clients open-up more easily than when in the room with you. Online disinhibition may seem to be helpful but it can also cause problems. Be prepared to work with it and take it to supervision. Clients who are disinhibited will often need to be paced more actively than you may be used to, and they can be left feeling overwhelmed and/or vulnerable. Online disinhibition can be of great benefit to the therapeutic relationship and process, but it needs to be understood and managed carefully.

Eleanor's other important point is about technology:

> It may seem obvious but get your technology up to spec and ensure your internet connection is strong and reliable. I have found from bitter experience how very uncomfortable and unhelpful it can be, both as counsellor and as client, when there are breaks in connection and the flow of the session is interrupted, especially if it happens several times in a session.

Cloie's top tip is about the value of online supervision and peer support:

> Working independently online can feel significantly isolating at times and does not naturally provide the opportunities to explore one's work with colleagues that working within a school or counselling service might offer. Regular supervision then becomes all the more important, as does creating opportunities to connect with other therapists. Facebook communities and peer supervision groups can be a great way of combating this isolation as they provide ample opportunities to both connect with and learn from other practitioners.

What I wish I'd known when I started

If I'd realised how transformative offering online counselling would be, for me and my clients, I would have done my training earlier! I would say to that younger me, 'Trust the process'. Online working does work, and you will be able to connect to parts of yourself that you don't get to express when working in person. I love words and writing, so working online, non-visually, enables me to focus more on the words, both spoken and written, that pass between me and my clients.

Ellie agrees with me:

> I wish I'd known when training that working online is a totally legitimate and effective setting for good therapy. People have often said to me over the years that online therapy can't work because the therapist and client can't make eye contact. So what?! Sometimes clients just don't want to make eye contact. We meet the client where they are at and working online via email or webcam, with or without the camera switched on, can help clients to feel more ready to access help. I find that the therapeutic rapport tends to be stronger when working online because both therapist and client are very focused on their communication device; fewer visual cues are available and so the therapist and client rely much more on their interaction, which really brings out the essence of the therapy work.

Jennifer says she discovered that online working presents no barriers to effective bodywork – what matters more is therapist competence in using the medium:

> It was surprising to me how well it could be done. I am happy to say I am a bodywork psychotherapist that continues this method in the online world. For me, safety comes from competence and vice versa.

Eleanor notes as a particular benefit the glimpse that online working can offer into a client's personal life:

> I was surprised by how intimate working remotely can be with regard to insight into a client's life that one might otherwise not see. For instance, being able to see background items on display in their personal space, overhearing sounds or other voices nearby, being introduced to a pet cat or dog who casually interrupts the flow of discussion. I have learned over time how these insights can both contribute to the work but also at times interfere.

I'll end this chapter with Rachael's words to her 'hesitant, doubtful younger self', about to embark on online therapy training:

> The anxiety you feel is okay but don't let it stifle you because it can lead you to explore many different rich and exciting ways to connect with your clients that go far beyond the horizons of your initial modality training.

References

Cooper, M., Mearns, D., Stiles, W., Warner, M., & Elliott, R. (2004). Developing self-pluralistic perspectives within the person-centered and experiential approaches: A round table dialogue. *Person-Centered and Experiential Psychotherapies, 3*(4), 179–191.

Reynolds, D.J., Jr., Stiles, W. B., Bailer, A. J., & Hughes, M. R. (2013). Impact of exchanges and client–therapist alliance in online-text psychotherapy. *Cyberpsychology, Behavior, and Social Networking, 16*(5), 370-377.

Simpson, S., Richardson, L., Pietrabissa, G., Castelnuovo, G. & Reid C. (2020). Videotherapy and therapeutic alliance in the age of COVID-19. *Clinical Psychology and Psychotherapy, 28*(2), 409–421.

Suler, J. (2004). *The psychology of cyberspace.* True Center Publishing.

Suler, J. (2015). *Psychology in the digital age.* Cambridge University Press

Worley-James, S. (2022). *Online counselling: An essential guide.* PCCS Books.

Chapter 4

Workplace counselling

Vianna Boring Renaud
with Eugene Farrell and Andrew Kinder,
Nick Wood and Julie Hughes

Introduction – Vianna Boring Renaud

Like many contributors to this book, my career pathway has provided me with a rich array of counselling opportunities. My first university degree was in music, and I worked as an artist manager and university study-abroad specialist. After shadowing my secondary school guidance counsellor, I was inspired to train to be a counsellor. I then got a job as a part-time counsellor at a local university, while also working in a secondary school for girls and as a volunteer youth worker. At the same time, I researched counselling in the workplace and began working for national employee assistance programme (EAP) agencies. It was this line of work that helped shape my workplace counselling career, but all my varied roles have come together to create a unique experience from which I have been able to build further opportunities.

As someone from the USA, I have seen a need for international and culturally diverse counsellors in organisation-based counselling. Perhaps I was self-conscious, coming from a different background and having a strong American accent, but I have found that this has actually been an asset with some of my clients in my work. I have also seen that my wide range of cultural experiences, from studying abroad in a different country to being classified as a migrant in the UK and having to readjust, have all helped me build rapport with my clients.

Working in the EAP and workplace counselling field has brought me and my co-contributors to this chapter great satisfaction because it is a unique environment. You get to understand how organisations operate (well and not so well). You meet people from all backgrounds – from the shop floor to senior management – and cultures. There may be an opportunity to influence positive changes in organisations where problem themes, behaviours or ways of working can be identified and improved – i.e. become a 'change agent'. And there can be opportunities to provide services beyond counselling, like training, facilitation, mentoring, coaching, mediation, trauma support and crisis management.

There are five main areas where counsellors can practise in workplace settings, some with more vacancies and opportunities than others, as follows.

EAP affiliate

An EAP affiliate is usually a self-employed counsellor who is referred clients by an EAP provider. Traditionally, clients were allocated to a counsellor with the most relevant skills or specialist expertise, and by location. Affiliates would either work from an office at home or rent a room in a local business centre. If you were based in, say, central Birmingham, your clients would be likely to work or live in that area. Nowadays, particularly since the Covid pandemic, where you live matters much less as an increasing number of clients have counselling via online/virtual platforms. However, face-to-face counselling is still popular.

EAP provider

Working directly for an EAP provider offers two main clinical opportunities. Most providers offer telephone counselling via a bank of counsellors, and this is the primary work opportunity. Telephone counsellors work in shifts and receive calls 'in the moment' from clients connected with a company that has a contract with the provider. The other opening is for case managers and clinical leads, with responsibility for initial assessments, referring clients to counsellors and managing the 'assignments'. Traditionally, telephone counsellors, case managers and clinical leads have been based at the premises of the provider, although many organisations have shifted these roles to home-working.

Additional non-clinical roles available include account managers and business development managers. The former have responsibility for managing specific corporate accounts and provide the business link between the provider and the organisation buying in the EAP. Business development managers are involved in generating new business for the provider. While these are non-clinical roles, it can be advantageous for account managers in particular to have knowledge of or experience in the clinical work undertaken by the providers, so they can explain the various processes involved to organisations.

Embedded counselling services

Some large organisations still have their own in-house counselling service for their employees, which might be a sole counsellor or a team of counsellors. Often, they are located within the company's human resources or occupational health team. The counsellor(s) will be able to immerse themselves in, and get to know, the culture and policies of the organisation, which can help them better understand work-related issues for clients. Nick Wood writes about working in an embedded service later in this chapter.

Contracted external counsellor

While an embedded counselling service may work best for larger organisations, small-to-medium businesses may contract with a dedicated 'external' counsellor to support their employees' mental wellbeing. They are the organisation's 'go-to' nominated counsellor, and employees will self-refer to them for either face-to-face or online counselling. Being 'external' to the organisation helps the counsellor maintain a professional distance from the organisation, while enabling them to understand its culture and idiosyncrasies. A contracted counsellor will be self-employed and will be paid by the organisation, either on a monthly retainer or by monthly invoice. They may offer the counselling at the organisation's premises or from their own workplace, whether in person, online or by phone.

Private practitioner

Some companies create a list of preferred/recommended local counsellors in private practice, from which employees can choose. This is usually managed by their human resources or occupational health team. This arrangement can be trickier for the counsellor as the work tends to be sessional (rather than, say, a block contract), and they cannot predict how much work (and income) they can expect. The advantage is that the therapeutic and contractual relationship is usually between the client and counsellor and the counsellor is paid directly by the client, avoiding the tensions and complexities of the tripartite contract described later in this chapter.

Perspectives from others

There's no better way to describe the varied roles listed above than to invite those working in these environments to tell their stories. We will start with Andrew Kinder and Eugene Farrell, who outline how EAP providers operate and what they expect of their affiliate counsellors, and an anonymous contributor describes their experience as an affiliate to several EAP providers. Next, Nick Wood describes his work, managing an embedded counselling service with a local authority that draws in affiliate counsellors to work with employees. We end with Julie Hughes, who writes from the perspective of an experienced practitioner and co-director of a small organisation providing workplace counselling to organisations. She looks in more detail at the competences required of counsellors working in any workplace capacity.

Along the way, you'll learn about the challenges and the benefits of this way of working, how to get work as an affiliate, and what will be expected of you when you do.

Working as an affiliate for an EAP provider – Eugene Farrell and Andrew Kinder

EAPs' origins can be traced back to the Industrial Revolution and the welfare initiatives introduced then to support employees, often women, working in factories. Nowadays, the term is used to describe commonplace wellbeing programmes that employers buy in to support their staff. EAPs offer a wide range of people-support services, including counselling, trauma support, consumer advice, legal information, debt advice, health information and wellbeing advice. EAP providers are commercial businesses that create, administer and deliver these wellbeing programmes for client organisations.

There are two ways that counsellors can work for an EAP: as a direct employee of an EAP provider (such as a case manager or telephone counsellor), or as an affiliate counsellor working on a self-employed basis for a provider. Here we focus on the role of the affiliate counsellor, as this is where most of the opportunities lie.

In the past, EAP providers would recruit affiliates in specific geographical locations to provide face-to-face counselling for employees of an organisation based in that location. This has changed with the increase in online counselling but, while online work has become more common in the sector, there's still a demand for face-to-face counselling.

Working with an EAP

According to the EAP UK Standards (EAPA, 2023), all those involved in the delivery of EAP services, and this includes EAP affiliates, must be professionally qualified, competent in EAP practice and familiar with and working consistently within the UK EAPA Code of Ethics (EAPA, 2014). They must also meet the appropriate criteria that reflect their duties.

The standards do not require affiliates to be accredited with BACP or any other professional body, although an EAP may choose to have its own qualification and experience requirements. Most, however, will require a master's degree or other postgraduate diploma in counselling, a minimum of three years' post-qualification experience, and registration with one of the recognised professional bodies, such as BACP, NCPS or UKCP for counsellors and psychotherapists, or HCPC for psychologists (see Appendix for details).

EAPs tend not to dictate exactly how their affiliate should deliver the therapy. Each practitioner will have their own approach to short-term work, and this is likely to be influenced by their style and training. It is important that the challenges and implications of short-term contracts with clients are fully understood. The EAP provider will usually brief the counsellor on a new referral and then seek feedback after they have completed the initial clinical assessment. A client's situation might change from the point of referral to the time they are first seen by a counsellor, particularly if they present in crisis. Short-term therapy is often sufficient in itself, or at least a first step to longer-term support. Often the EAP is used to support clients while they are on an NHS waiting list for therapy or looking for other treatment.

Most EAP providers will offer a choice of face-to-face, telephone and online counselling. Telephone and online work are growing in popularity as they offer flexibility for clients with busy work schedules, travelling commitments, mobility issues and family responsibilities.

EAP services deliver brief models of intervention – typically five to seven sessions of counselling, although a few providers offer more, or even an unlimited number of sessions. Typically, EAPs deliver solution-focused brief therapy, although an integrative approach is popular, as is being able to draw on cognitive behavioural therapy (CBT) techniques. Other therapeutic models such as dialectical behaviour therapy (DBT), eye movement desensitisation and reprocessing (EMDR) and formal CBT may be provided as an additional component of an EAP contract with a client organisation but are not typically included in the standard service delivery.

EAP counselling is delivered within a limited fixed number of sessions, the exact number of which will be confirmed when the provider briefs the affiliate – it can differ between organisations, depending on their contract with the provider. The provider has a contractual and business agreement with the organisation contracting them to deliver the EAP service, and this will set out details of the number of sessions the counsellor can provide. Therefore, it's important to consider client expectations and manage endings. Even though a therapeutic alliance may have developed, and the client may wish to continue with the affiliate once their allocated number of sessions is complete, this is usually not allowed.

However, it is recognised that there will be occasions when a small number of additional sessions beyond the fixed allocation is clinically appropriate and in the client's best interests. In such cases, the counsellor should always follow the processes and protocols set out by the provider and consult their case manager. A clinical case or justification will need to be made by the counsellor, and this may not always be accepted, so client expectations will need to be managed too. It is the exception rather than the norm for extra sessions to be provided. And counsellors should not encourage their client to ask their employer for more sessions. Extra sessions cannot proceed without the provider's authorisation.

Referrals

While the majority of their clients will self-refer, EAPs can accept client referrals from other sources, such as line managers and occupational health departments. The emergence of workplace wellbeing programmes means that increasingly clients are being referred following a wellbeing assessment at work, via a mental health coach, or even signposted by an app.

It may be in the client's interest for the counsellor to provide 'holding' or containing sessions while alternative support is arranged, such as a referral to the client's occupational health team, a GP referral, specialist help or longer-term support.

A 'formal referral' will normally require the EAP provider to feed back to the referrer only basic information such as attendance and the presenting issue; what is discussed between the counsellor and client remains confidential. Formal referrals can only be made with the full knowledge and co-operation of the client, and in these circumstances the response of the client and their attitude towards the counselling process must be considered. This could be positive: 'My employer really cares about me' – or negative: 'I'm only here because I've been told to come, I don't need counselling, there's nothing wrong with me.'

When an EAP briefs an affiliate about a new referral, all reporting requirements should be clarified so that the counsellor can tell the client what might be fed back to whom and why, and when informed consent might be needed. The counsellor should be alert to clients who might feel coerced into counselling, as any counselling relationship should always be voluntary and unconditional.

Tripartite relationship

Clients access counselling via an organisation's EAP, and the organisation pays for the counselling, and yet the organisation may, in some way, be the underlying cause of the presenting issue. Affiliates must remain non-judgemental and detached from views or comments about the client's employing organisation and its actions and policies. The tripartite relationship between the organisation, EAP provider and counsellor means that the affiliate has a responsibility to the individual client *and* to the client's employer.

The EAP provides a confidential service, yet providers have a contractual relationship and duty of care both to those who access their services and to the contracting employer. It is important that the affiliate recognises the nature of this tripartite relationship and its potential impact on the counselling process. For instance, the fact that EAP counselling sessions are funded by the client's employer may lead clients to feel anxious about confidentiality and what might be fed back to the organisation. On a different level, clients may think they are entitled to use all their available sessions, which may or may not be in their clinical interest or necessary.

Complexities

EAP work can involve potential 'conflicts of interest' that can be quite complex. For example, an affiliate may be asked to see someone who is a colleague or close relative of an existing client; a client may want counselling to support them as they resign from their job; a client may be considering taking legal action against their employer, or a third party, such as a client's solicitor or the police, might request to see their case notes. In such cases, affiliates should consult the EAP provider's guidelines and manage the issues in consultation with the EAP case manager or clinical lead, who are usually experienced in these issues.

When a client self-refers to an EAP, they may provide limited information, background and medical history, so a counsellor needs to be able to further assess and work with more challenging issues as they become known during the counselling process, especially regarding risk to self, others and the organisation.

A counsellor also needs to consider whether short-term counselling is going to be suitable and appropriate for a client. It may be more in the interest of the client to be referred to their GP, community mental health team or specialist sources of support. Case managers and clinical leads are there to offer guidance and advice on such considerations. As the counsellor is likely to know more about the availability of local support in their area than the provider, it's a good idea to be aware of a wide range of alternative support and intervention options.

Working with the organisation

While the employee is the counsellor's client, their organisation is effectively also a client 'in the room', as they are funding the sessions. Developing an understanding of the organisation, including the culture, work practices, job demands and pressures, will help the counsellor work with both 'clients'. As counsellors gain an understanding of their organisational client, they may learn about additional internal resources that can support the client, such as specific training or support from occupational health or human resources departments.

The EAP provider will be contractually responsible for the case and has a retained duty of care to the client. The clinical responsibility may be shared to some degree, but the EAP provider maintains an oversight of the case. This sharing of responsibility can be uncomfortable for an affiliate new to EAPs. Therefore, it's important to understand this aspect of the work carefully and consider if it will suit you.

EAP providers place great emphasis on the impartiality and confidentiality of the service. Clients can self-refer to the EAP, usually about any issue, regardless of whether or not it is work-related, and will expect that their use of the service will not be disclosed to their employer, except in extreme circumstances.

Although the service is confidential, EAP providers have a dual responsibility to identify and manage risk, not just to the client contacting them for help but also to their employer. Therefore, clients contacting the EAP will be made aware of the confidentiality boundaries within which the provider operates. This will generally mean that, if the provider believes there could be a serious and immediate threat to the health and safety of the client or those around them, they reserve the right to contact a third party, which could mean the client's GP or even the emergency services.

The provider and counsellor also need to be alert to risk to the client's employer. This might involve risk of harm to other employees but also to the wider public, especially where the use of drugs or alcohol might impair capacity to drive vehicles or operate machinery.

Breaking confidentiality is rare and always a last resort, triggered only after extensive internal consultation with the EAP provider.

Record-keeping and case notes

Affiliates are required to keep concise, accurate and factual written records of EAP sessions and any other client contacts. These must be kept for seven years. This 'client record' belongs to the EAP provider and is the joint responsibility of the EAP provider and the affiliate counsellor.

EAP providers usually want to know the issues that brought the client to counselling, the counsellor's perspectives on the psychological issues faced by the client and a demonstration of movement in the client's recovery and the focus of each session.

Notes should be written according to the ethical and professional guidelines of the counsellor's professional body, as well as the UK EAPA. The client has the right to see their notes and can request these via the provider. Notes also can be subpoenaed by the judicial courts, so should be written with this in mind.

Any records or information about the referral should be kept in a locked container or a secured electronic store that is password-protected. Records should never be sent electronically unless password-protected and/or encrypted. Occasionally, reports may be requested by a third party, such as the client's occupational health team, but they should only be released with the client's informed consent and approval of the EAP provider. Requests for notes or reports should always be discussed with the provider who, most likely, will take responsibility for sending the material to the intended and approved destination.

Requirements of affiliates

As with any counselling context, counsellors should always consider their personal safety when working alone. It is good practice to develop a 'safety plan' to protect against eventualities. This might include a safety alarm or making a nominated person aware of your schedule or whereabouts.

Affiliate work can be lonely and isolating if you don't put strategies in place to counter this. Working alone with clients every day can have many positives but try to ensure you take regular breaks and make time to meet others, whether peers or other colleagues, as you would if you were in a more formal office environment.

Technology and equipment

EAP affiliates need to have a well-functioning computer and reliable internet. And they need to be competent in using them and managing IT issues, as and when they inevitably crop up. They also need an email address and telephone voicemail that's monitored and responded to promptly. Providers are under pressure to allocate cases quickly, usually within three to five days, so if the counsellor does not respond to messages about new referrals, the referral will usually be allocated to someone else. Affiliates who are quick to respond, and meet deadlines for arranging first appointments, providing feedback, case documentation and accurate invoices are more likely to get more referrals.

Case management

Affiliate counsellors must be willing and able to cooperate with all the case management procedures of the provider. EAP providers differ on how closely they case-manage their affiliates (and who conducts the case management), but all providers will have a system in place for monitoring the work of the affiliate counsellor. Regardless of the system that is in operation, affiliates will be expected to fully cooperate with it. The EAPA has published a *Counsellor's Guide to Working with EAPs* (EAPA, 2018), which provides an excellent insight into how best to work with a provider.

Insurance

EAP providers will require affiliates to have appropriate and adequate professional indemnity insurance and provide evidence of this on an annual basis. Some providers require affiliates to get a Disclosure and Barring Service check (DBS).[1]

Premises

Affiliates who work in-person from their own premises will need to ensure their premises are:

- accessible
- comfortable
- quiet
- safe
- clean
- professionally furnished.

If practising from an office at home, the room should not double up as living accommodation, unless all personal effects have been removed. The entrance to the consulting room must also be discreet and any personal effects should be removed from the route through to the consulting room.

EAP providers may request photos or inspect the premises personally. Premises should be free from interruption (phones, pets, children etc.) and clean (no pet hair, cigarette smoke, cooking smells etc.). Toilet facilities should be available and clean, and ideally there should be a waiting area.

Similar considerations should be given to affiliates providing online virtual counselling (see Chapter 3). Counsellors should be mindful of what the client might see in the background via the camera view. Email notifications and other alerts should be disabled during online sessions.

As with working from home in private practice, the affiliate should ensure:

- health and safety risks have been assessed and mitigated
- appropriate fire detection devices are in place
- passageways and exits are well lit, accessible and clear of obstructions
- electrical and gas appliances are regularly serviced and checked and are safe.

---

1. For England and Wales, visit www.gov.uk/dbs-check-applicant-criminal-record. The website signposts applicants to the different formats for Northern Ireland and Scotland.

Pay and client workload

The employer is often keen to know that the support offered by the EAP is having an organisational (and therefore financial) benefit. For instance, has the counselling helped the client take less time off work for sickness, or move on to a different job or role, if that is what they wish? EAP providers use a range of outcome measures to track client progress, and aggregated and anonymous data are usually fed back to the organisation to evidence this. Counsellors will be briefed on the exact outcome measures required when they join the provider's network.

Affiliates are normally paid per session. There is no standard set rate so this can differ between providers. An affiliate with a particular specialism may be able to negotiate a higher rate, but the pay is usually determined by the provider. While rates are likely to be lower than those charged in private practice, the provider will be the source of client referrals. Many EAP affiliates work exclusively with providers and so do not have to cover the costs of marketing, advertising and promotion. Indeed, many affiliates work for several providers. In theory, this can provide even more clients, but it may also reduce availability for each provider. A counsellor can decline a client referral if they aren't available, but this may mean they get fewer referrals from that provider in future. While many affiliates derive a comfortable living from EAP referrals, there's no guarantee of the quantity or flow. This means that many affiliates juggle a portfolio of roles, which might include private practice and EAP work, plus part-time salaried roles.

Finding work as an EAP counsellor

An up-to-date list of EAP providers can be found on the EAPA website.[2] Some providers recruit affiliates via job advertisements and through the main counselling professional bodies.

Most providers will have a standard pro forma application procedure, so it's prudent to check first if this is their way of recruiting. For speculative applications, counsellors should submit an up-to-date CV that evidences appropriate qualifications, skills and experience, together with copies of qualifications, insurance and, if working from home, photos of their premises.

Once the counsellor is accepted onto an affiliate network, the provider will usually provide an orientation session, usually by phone or video conferencing, to explain the procedures and protocols required. As providers work with hundreds of affiliates, their way of working needs to be standardised, so there's often little leeway for deviation.

---

2. www.eapa.org.uk/find-an-eap-provider

Working as an EAP affiliate can provide a very rewarding experience for the counsellor, both financially and therapeutically, as well as a great deal of variety and diversity. Clients of all ages and backgrounds will bring wide-ranging presenting issues from very different organisations. EAP providers' processes and procedures may appear onerous to begin with, but counsellors can find they help them structure and manage their workload. The EAP providers will not only provide the counsellor with expert clinical support and resources but, crucially, will be a valuable source of clients.

What follows is a personal account from an anonymous EAP affiliate, describing their working life – what is good about the work and the challenges.

A perspective from an EAP affiliate counsellor

I love the variety working as an affiliate for several providers. Over a six-session day, I might see a police officer, an accountant, a telecommunications engineer, a nurse, a bus driver and a university professor. While they're all clients at the end of the day, where they work can have a big impact on what they present with.

Providers do have strict protocols and ways of working, and requirements for feedback and administration processes. While this helps offer clarity and guidance for how to work with them, they all seem to be different, depending on the EAP provider, and so this can feel very onerous. I need to earmark at least half a day a week for administration, which is time when I don't earn.

The counselling is always short term, which seems sufficient for most clients, but it's tough on both counsellor and client if they feel longer-term work is clinically appropriate and it's not allowed.

I usually invoice the providers at the end of each month, and while they do all pay up, some can be very slow to do so. I do get regular client referrals, and so a regular income, but hourly rates of pay have barely risen in the 15 years I have been an affiliate and are significantly less than what most private practitioners charge.

I sometimes find the provider is more protective of their client organisation than of the individual clients, so requesting extra sessions when it's clinically appropriate can be a battle. Case managers and EAP clinicians are there to help with referrals and case management, but some of them can be difficult to get hold of and they don't all provide genuine support when required.

Maintaining boundaries is important and a skill to be learnt, but it can be difficult to reconcile the sometimes conflicting demands of an organisation, the EAP provider and the client. I have a good supervisor who understands organisations, and we spend much of our time wrestling with ethical issues that emerge because of these conflicting demands.

But I've been an EAP affiliate for 15 years, so something clearly inspires me to carry on with this work!

Counselling in an embedded service – Nick Wood

Embedded or in-house counselling services commonly provide counselling to just the one employer-organisation that they themselves are part of. This has advantages for the employer as their staff gain exclusive access to the in-house team of counsellors while the employer retains directional control of the business objectives of the service.

Embedded counselling services may be known as staff counselling services in some sectors and are commonly, but not exclusively, found in public sector organisations such as local or regional authorities, NHS trusts and universities, as well as some larger private employers.

Traditionally, an embedded counselling service will be part of, or an extension of, the employer's occupational health provision. Supporting employees back to work and reducing the costs of sickness absence are usually regarded as the main reasons for an employer providing in-house counselling. There is also an increasing understanding among employers that supporting the mental wellbeing of staff is the 'right thing to do' and results in a happier and more productive workforce, which can be a competitive benefit when recruiting and retaining staff.

So, there is an expectation on counsellors working in an embedded service to have an enhanced understanding of the business requirements and workplace culture of the employer, as well as the needs of staff groups within the organisation and any unique or sector-specific challenges they face. Embedded counselling services will be aware of the need to provide information to management about the effectiveness of the counselling they offer, in order to demonstrate the organisation's return on the investment. So, it is routine for counsellors to ask clients to complete clinical measures during the counselling process itself.

Quite often, the embedded counselling service will be based on the employer's premises, ideally in a site allowing discreet access to clients. Traditionally, embedded services offer face-to-face sessions and, overall, make less use of telephone counselling than EAPs. In larger organisations with an embedded service, new clients may be assessed at a central location and then allocated to counsellors working from satellite offices or, like EAP affiliate counsellors, from their own premises.

Mostly, counsellors working for an embedded services will be directly employed by the employer, but there may be opportunities for local counsellors with the necessary experience to provide client sessions on an ad hoc or affiliate basis (see Chapter 2). Like EAPs, most embedded services use a short-term model of counselling and have their own contractual arrangements as to how many sessions are offered and when the limit can be extended, and counsellors should be made of aware of these at induction.

It is always worth newly qualified counsellors contacting local embedded counselling services, where they know of any, to see if they are recruiting and ask if any trainee placements are available. Embedded services are likely to be very receptive to counsellors who have a business background, have worked previously in large organisations, or have experience of that particular sector.

I first came to work in the occupational health team at Gloucestershire County Council in 2010, having seen an advertisement for the role in *Therapy Today*, BACP's membership magazine. I was attracted to the role as I felt it would give me an opportunity both to use my counselling skills and to draw on my previous business experience as a manager in a large commercial organisation.

I had worked for an investment company through the 1980s and 1990s, which was a highly pressurised and competitive environment. It was the time of the 'Big Bang' in the financial sector, when the London Stock Exchange was deregulated, and there were always targets to meet and new product launches. Looking back, I recognise that, at the time I left, I was experiencing burnout. My main memory from that period was how alone I felt in admitting to myself and others that I was suffering from stress. My employer was supportive, but I had to access my own counselling through my GP, which seemed to take forever to arrange, and when I began to feel better, I decided I needed a career change. Retraining as a counsellor was the best decision of my working life.

In 2005, I set up in private practice near the industrial and science parks in the 'northern fringe' around Bristol. I saw several clients, usually male, who were struggling with the kind of workplace stresses I recognised only too well, and I began to develop a model of support into my practice. What concerned me was that, in nearly all cases, the client could have found my help most useful months earlier, before their situation worsened. Isolation, lack of education about mental health issues and lack of access to specialist support were always present in their stories. This sparked my interest in the work of the BACP Workplace division, and I started networking with other counsellors in the field.

What impressed me about the opportunity at Gloucestershire County Council was the council's ambition to provide ease of access to counselling upstream, to assist staff to perform and be the best they could be while maintaining their health and wellbeing.

I am a huge advocate of workplace counselling and, having served for some years on the BACP Workplace executive committee, I was one of the co-authors of its *Workplace Counselling Competence Framework* (BACP, 2021a). This is available free from BACP, and I would encourage any counsellor interested in working in this sector to familiarise themselves with it as a starting point.

One of the major privileges of working in this sector is that many of the clients we see would not have been able to access therapy had it not been provided for them through their workplace. It is one of the reasons I am so enthusiastic about the unique opportunities that embedded services provide.

At Gloucestershire County Council, I and my deputy, the only other counsellor directly employed by the council, manage a team of affiliate counsellors who provide therapeutic interventions for our 3000-plus staff. Our clients cover a vast breadth of roles, including social workers, highways operatives, teachers and social care staff, as well as the local Fire and Rescue Service. The role and what the team does have evolved over the years I have been here. As well as counselling, we provide critical incident support, reflective supervision (similar to coaching) and several health and wellbeing initiatives, such as mental health workshops and coordinating the council's anti-bullying and harassment team.

Benefits and challenges

I would strongly encourage counsellors to investigate opportunities to work as affiliates with an embedded counselling service. It's interesting and varied work – no two days are the same. The organisation provides a constant flow of clients for its affiliate counsellors and may be able to make a room available for them to work on-site, thereby saving some of the office costs of private practice. There is also the added benefit for counsellors that they don't have the worry of chasing clients for payment and that invoices and sessions fees will be paid on time, which helps budgeting and income forecasting.

Counsellors working in the sector say they enjoy feeling part of a team and the fellowship that this brings. Some talk about the added fulfilment they get from working with clients who might not otherwise be able to access counselling and are thankful and appreciative for the opportunity.

Some counsellors do work full time as an affiliate for an embedded service, but it is increasingly common for our affiliates to have portfolio careers and work for us alongside other jobs, roles or private practice. The steady number of referrals can be a reassuring boost to their income stream.

Having said that, the challenges of workplace counselling may not be for everyone. In private practice, the counsellor and client will agree the contract between them, and the relationship is confidential to the dyad. In workplace counselling, the contract is three-party – that is, it also involves the organisation, whether that is the embedded counselling service or the employer organisation itself, as well as the client and counsellor. The organisation will state how many sessions its employees receive, decide the rates of pay and record information about the client's presenting situation (details they may already have collected to ensure the client qualifies for the counselling service).

Experienced workplace counsellors will be used to working with this dynamic, but for some the organisational context may feel restrictive and they may prefer the freedom that private practice provides.

Applying to work with an embedded service

If you are considering applying for a counselling role in an embedded service, the following are some of the things managers and recruiters generally look for.

1. Previous experience of workplace counselling

First and foremost, embedded counselling services are seeking counsellors who can demonstrate that they understand:

a. client issues commonly associated with workplace settings, such as stress, bullying and harassment, interpersonal relationships and trauma
b. models of delivery – short-term or time-sensitive, solution-focused
c. organisational context – ability to work within the organisation's guidelines; awareness of the dynamic of the three-party contract.

A good way for counsellors to start to build experience is by working as an affiliate with the larger EAPs, who are often seeking to add to their 'bank' of counsellors.

Some embedded services will expect applicants to have at least two or three years' post-qualification experience and/or to have completed a required minimum of client hours. It is unusual for agencies to take on newly qualified counsellors with little client experience, but you shouldn't be put off from applying – be sure to spell out how you meet the personal attribute requirements (see further below). Even if you haven't worked directly in a workplace setting, if you can bring a wide range and quantity of post-qualification client hours, you may be able to reassure the prospective employer that you have the necessary depth of experience for the role.

It is less usual for recruiters to be prescriptive about a counsellor's particular modality. This is often seen as less important than experience of short-term working, for example, so core or additional CPD training in short-term and/or solution-focused work will boost your application.

It is important to recognise that most embedded agencies, as in the workplace sector in general, will be governed by financial constraints. The employer is paying for their employee to have counselling and is likely to place some constraints on the cost, such as limiting the number of sessions offered. Short-term, solution-focused work places a particular onus on the counsellor to use their case formulation skills to determine where the focus of the therapy should be in order to be most effective within the limited time available.

For the most part, embedded services will ask that directly employed and affiliate counsellors are both registered and accredited with one of the main professional bodies for counselling or psychotherapy whose register is accredited by the Professional Standards Authority. This is because embedded counselling services need to follow and understand employment law and, if they are a public sector body funded from the public purse, must comply with local or national government procurement regulations. The counselling service will need to evidence its decision-making process for selecting counsellors to work with them and accreditation with a professional body is an effective way of showing that prospective counsellors are likely to have the necessary experience and skill set.

However, some providers will consider those who are registered and working towards accreditation. Any newly qualified counsellor or psychotherapist who is interested in working in the sector will find it useful to gain their accreditation as soon as they are eligible to do so.

2. Personal attributes

The personal attributes an embedded service will look for when recruiting new counsellors will vary from service to service, but some of the common features include:

a. **Organisational skills** – good record-keeping, replying to communications in a timely manner and responding quickly to new referrals from the service.

b. **Presentation skills** – embedded agencies will regard affiliate counsellors as representatives of their service, so it is important that you maintain a professional manner. You could find that your next client is the managing director or the budget holder for the service!

c. **Flexible approach** – there will always be commercial and other pressures on embedded services to provide sessions in accordance with internal service standards or to meet deadlines or peaks in demand as market forces dictate. Nothing puts off a prospective recruiter more than a counsellor at interview saying they are not willing or able to offer flexibility in their approach, model of working or availability.

d. **Additional skills** – recruiters are always interested to hear about other skills applicant counsellors may be able to transfer to the role, whether they are in counselling, such as critical incident work, or from previous work experience, such as facilitating training courses.

e. **Working as part of a team** – experience of working in a team and the ability to contribute to team goals while at the same time being able to work independently with clients is also important.

f. **Interpersonal skills** – perhaps most important of all, the ability to establish the therapeutic relationship quickly with clients is especially important in time-limited counselling, and is arguably the key skill a workplace counsellor needs. The first client of the day may be a managing director, the next a new employee on their first day. In both cases, and often in the first session, the workplace counsellor needs to both establish the therapeutic relationship with that client and begin the process of formulating a case hypothesis to inform how they will work with the client's presenting issue. Recruiters will be keen to see evidence of this skill in any interview or recruitment process. Applicants can evidence this is by reading the role description prior to interview and demonstrating in the interview itself their ability to analyse and feedback their understanding of what the agency is looking for.

Practising as a workplace counsellor – Julie Hughes

I came to counselling following a difficult chapter in my life, when I sought the help of a counsellor. It was a life-changing event that led to my degree, career change and counselling training. Once qualified, I started exploring the many counselling job opportunities out there. I had completed a student placement with Mind Matters Counselling, which was then starting to branch out into the EAP world. Because of my previous career in law, I had acquired many skills that seemed suited to the workplace sector. Had I been offered workplace counselling in my previous role, it might have helped me stay in that career. But I wasn't offered it, and I didn't stay.

Over the past 22 years, I have been developing the workplace counselling component of Mind Matters Counselling. The start of this journey was heavily influenced and guided by their well-thought-through organisational protocols, which provided the solid foundations that shaped and developed my knowledge of workplace counselling.

These organisational protocols made a lasting impact on my practice as a workplace counsellor, and later led me to co-author BACP's *Workplace Counselling Competence Framework* (BACP, 2021a).

The framework provides an excellent insight into the skills required of the workplace counsellor in all five contexts described at the start of this chapter and are increasingly used by employers and EAP providers as a benchmark for competence of their affiliates and direct employees.

The framework covers the following themes:

1. **Core competences for workplace counselling**
   - Knowledge of and ability to work within the legal and ethical requirements of a workplace counselling service
   - Understanding and working in the organisational context
   - Knowledge of the relationships between employment, and health and wellbeing
   - Knowledge of and ability to establish and institute brief interventions

2. **Assessment and signposting**
   - Assessment and signposting
   - Risk assessment and response

3. **Areas of work**
   - Working with common workplace-related issues
   - Offering trauma support

4. **Meta-competences**
   - Meta-competences for providing workplace counselling.

What is a workplace counsellor?

It is common for counsellors who are working as an EAP affiliate or within organisations alongside their private practice not to regard themselves as workplace counsellors.

However, workplace counselling is defined as:

> Counselling provided to an employee by their employer. This counselling may explore work-related issues, personal issues, or a combination of both. The counselling may be paid for by the employer or offered via a salary sacrifice scheme, at a reduced rate. The counselling may be offered via a variety of media, e.g. face-to-face sessions, telephone, online. The counselling could be part of a wider Employee Assistance Programme (EAP), which could also include the provision of legal and financial advice. The aim of workplace counselling is to enhance the wellbeing and

functioning of the client, therefore restoring, or maintaining their fitness to work. (BACP, 2021b, p.7)

This means that any therapist in private practice who accepts referrals from an EAP or an organisation in an employer capacity is a workplace counsellor and so should have the necessary workplace competences.

It is essential to understand the various dynamics of workplace counselling. We need to appreciate how conflicts of interest might arise and the challenges we are likely to face to ensure confidentiality is maintained. The counsellor must be aware of the likelihood of hidden agendas between the employer and the employee, to avoid any ethical or therapeutic collision. Counsellors should ensure that these agendas do not influence their work and stay focused on what can be achieved within a workplace therapeutic contract.

It is not uncommon for workplace counsellors to take on additional roles beyond core counselling, such as involvement in training events, facilitating teams, mentoring and coaching. For example, a workplace counsellor might be asked to train a group of employees (maybe on stress management, resilience, work-life balance and so on), and may also have worked already with some of the participants in one-to-one counselling. Holding dual relationships can be complex and careful consideration needs to be given to how this might impact employees and their ability to access the counselling service later.

There is also the possible repetition of presenting issues when working with several employees from the same department. When a whole department is struggling, this can lead to many individual staff members accessing the service simultaneously about the same issue and/or the same colleagues. This can happen where there's an ongoing bullying and harassment situation, during threats of redundancy, critical incidents or any of a range of potential workplace stress issues (see HSE, 2017).

It may sometimes be necessary to educate an employer or referrers about what counselling is and how it works, the reason for boundaries and how to ensure the service remains safe and ethical. I've had experiences of referrers wanting me to fast-track some employees or offer more sessions than were contractually agreed.

A workplace counsellor should know about the organisation's policies and procedures, including employee rights, sickness policies and complaints and disciplinary processes. This can be helpful when helping a client navigate their way through a policy-impacting issue.

You will face complex challenges in the work, but in my experience this will help you grow as a therapist, to the benefit of all your clients. What drew me to this line of work is the belief that all employees should be able to benefit from workplace counselling, and that passion continues to drive me.

If you want to explore this specialist field of practice, I have two pieces of advice: familiarise yourself with the *Workplace Counselling Competence Framework* (BACP, 2021a), and find an experienced supervisor who understands the workplace environment.

Conclusion – Vianna Boring Renaud

Counselling in the workplace, in any capacity, offers huge variety and diversity because of the very different working environments you may encounter. But those entering this sector for the first time do need to understand how organisations work and the sorts of issues that can emerge. Eugene and Andrew have explained what it's like to be an EAP affiliate and what is expected of them; Nick has provided an excellent insight into working in an embedded service, and Julie has introduced the BACP *Workplace Counselling Competence Framework* as a useful source of guidance.

As the contributors to this chapter have illustrated, there are indeed complexities surrounding potential conflicts of interests and boundary issues. It's really important to find a clinical supervisor who has experience of, or understands, organisations and these conflicts, to reduce the chance of collusion and misunderstanding. But with one in place, I can very much recommend workplace counselling as a rewarding, fascinating and unique context in which to practise.

Good luck!

References

BACP. (2021a). *Workplace counselling competence framework*. BACP. www.bacp.co.uk/media/11051/bacp-workplace-competence-framework-mar21.pdf

BACP. (2021b). *Workplace counselling competence framework: User guide*. BACP. www.bacp.co.uk/media/14455/bacp-workplace-competence-framework-user-guide-feb22.pdf

EAPA UK. (2014). *UK EAPA Code of ethics*. EAPA UK. www.eapa.org.uk/wp-content/uploads/2014/09/UK-EAPA-Code-of-Ethics-2014.pdf

EAPA UK. (2018). *Counsellor's guide to working with EAPs*. EAPA UK.

EAPA UK. (2023). *EAPA UK Standards*. EAPA UK.

HSE. (2017). *Tackling work-related stress using the Management Standards approach*. Health & Safety Executive. www.hse.gov.uk/pubns/wbk01.pdf

Chapter 5

Counsellors who coach

Lucy Myers
with Joanne Wright, Veronica Lysaght, Yvonne Inglis and Carolyn Mumby

My relational, systemic, and solutions-focused way of being with clients is 'about *being present as a human being first; as therapist second*' (Finlay, 2016, p.3; original emphasis). With this in mind, my aim here is to share with you what I think it means to be a dual practitioner of coaching and counselling or psychotherapy. The theoretical information will be brought to life by seasoned practitioners describing their own personal and professional journeys in the coaching-counselling world. My hope is that you'll finish the chapter with some clarity about what practising psychotherapeutically informed coaching can look like. I hope too that this will inspire you to feel, like me, excitement and curiosity about working with clients both at relational depth and with forward momentum, and that you'll know what steps to take next.

What is coaching? The story so far

In 2003, Michael Carroll famously described coaching as 'the new kid on the block' (Carroll, 2003). Twenty years later, the coach-therapy sector is an excitingly evolving space to be part of, with a growing evidence base and a flourishing 'dual-practitioner' community. This growing presence is perhaps reflecting our changing world. Nobody needs reminding of the unprecedented events we have witnessed in recent times: the global Covid-19 pandemic, climate change, Black Lives Matter, Brexit, #metoo, the cost-of-living crisis, the war in Ukraine, the Israel/Gaza conflict and more... So much has happened, causing such noticeable shifts in our collective consciousness, in such a short space of time. With organisations and communities increasingly recognising the need for mental wellbeing support that also builds capacity for progression and positive change, demand for the unique combination of skills that dual-trained coach-counsellor practitioners hold is on the rise.

At the turn of the century, professional bodies including the International Coaching Federation (ICF), the European Mentoring & Coaching Council (EMCC), and later the Association for Coaching (AC), were established to regulate the 'wild west of coaching' (Sherman & Freas, 2004). Since then, significant research into 'whether coaching works' has been undertaken. The consensus is that coaching is an effective methodology for facilitating positive outcomes for clients (Grant & Green, 2018), with at least 80% of people who choose coaching faring better than those in the same circumstances who don't (de Haan et al., 2013).

What are the differences between coaching and therapy?

Rogers writes (2013, p.7):

> Coaching is a partnership of equals whose aim is to achieve speedy, increased and sustainable effectiveness through focused learning in every aspect of the client's life. Coaching raises self-awareness and identifies choices.

As with counselling and psychotherapy, where modalities include person-centred, psychodynamic, existential and CBT, there are many different ways to practise coaching. Alongside the prevalence of sports coaching, there is executive coaching, life coaching, business coaching, NLP coaching, somatic coaching and an array of 'niche' coaching practices, including relationship, parenting, retirement, menopause and divorce coaching.

Debates have raged, with no definitive conclusions drawn, about the perceived differences and boundaries between coaching and psychotherapy. Comparisons include a 'present' (coaching) versus 'past' (psychotherapy) focus; a highly functional (coaching) versus dysfunctional (psychotherapy) client base, and a focus on business performance improvement versus personal healing and recovery (see Maxwell, 2009 and de Haan, 2008 for such detailed discussions). In 2002, Steven Berglas controversially warned of the 'danger' that non-psychologically trained coaches might ignore deep-seated psychological problems they don't understand, leading to negative outcomes for both the client and the organisations they work for. Others are less catastrophist, concluding that, if coaching fails to investigate the 'whole human', the risk are more superficial than dangerous (Maxwell, 2009).

Western (2012) contends that, while modern-day coaching seeks to work with the 'celebrated self', the 'wounded self' will inevitably surface in the coaching room at times, and coaches must be able to work with all parts. Kilburg (2004) supports Berglas' assertion that, in the wrong, 'untrained' hands, certain coaching interventions can do harm, but also highlights the risk that dual-trained practitioners who trained first as counsellors may focus on psychotherapeutic material that feels familiar and comfortable rather than the work most necessary for executives operating in a business context. Others support this, suggesting that a lack of organisational awareness in the 'therapist-turned-coach' population is just as likely to lead to ineffective outcomes for clients and their businesses as a lack of psychological awareness in the coach-turned-therapist (Berman & Bradt, 2006).

The EMCC states: 'Coaching is partnering with clients in a thought-provoking and creative process that inspires them to maximize their personal and professional potential' (EMCC/ICF, 2011, p.3). Clients use coaching to learn about themselves:

> Coaching is facilitating the client's learning process by using professional methods and techniques to help the client to improve what is obstructive and nurture what is effective, in order to reach the client's goals. (EMCC/ICF, 2011, p.3)

So, while the consensus is that coaches *can* work with clients who are experiencing what we might call 'everyday distress', including feelings of anxiety, worry or despair, the purpose of coaching is not to explore at depth or aim to heal deep emotional wounds or trauma. The BACP *Coaching Competence Framework* (BACP, 2022) states that coaching clients should 'have enough psychological resilience to engage proactively with what can sometimes be a challenging process' and concludes:

> Coaching is therefore not generally suitable for clients who are having difficulties with day-to-day motivation and functioning, or who are experiencing, and seeking relief from, persistent and significant distress. (p.17)

I think it's helpful to bring us back to the reason why we do this work – to help people. Clients come to both coaching and therapy because they want, or need, something in their lives to be different. Ultimately, coaching is rooted in a person-centred belief that people can 'self-actualise' (Rogers, 1961), given the right conditions. The focus in both domains is on the client's agenda; both centre around thoughtful conversations, draw on some of the same psychological theories and techniques (more on that in a moment), and regard the client-counsellor relationship as paramount. Coaching research supports findings from the psychotherapy domain (Norcross, 2010) that a strong 'working alliance' is all-important, and report that a coaching relationship typified by factors such as empathy, unconditional positive regard, trust and transparency is necessary to facilitate positive outcomes (Gyllensten & Palmer, 2007). Qualified coaches and therapists alike are also bound by the ethical codes of their respective professional bodies, which require practitioners to work to high standards of ethical and professional practice (see, for example, EMCC, 2021; BACP, 2018).

Integrating coaching and therapy ethically and with impact

How does this integration benefit clients seeking to change? It has been widely acknowledged in the coaching community that a psychological understanding grounded in science underpins the process of human change and that 'psychological mindedness' (Bluckert, 2006) is linked to positive outcomes for clients.

> In the world of therapy, integration is the name given to a way of working in which a practitioner makes use of more than one modality, with the aim of meeting each client's needs more completely than the practitioner believes a single modality can. (BACP, 2022, p.17)

In the context of the coaching competences, 'integration describes a way of working that involves the intentional use of both therapeutic and coaching theories and techniques' (BACP, 2022, p.17). The intentional use of psychotherapeutic theories and techniques has been documented as follows.

Person-centred

Lemisiou (2018) reports that a 'person-centred' psychotherapeutic approach to coaching assists in the development of the levels of emotional and social intelligence competence, resulting in better leadership performance and potential shifts in a client's 'internal frame of reference' that may impact outcomes beyond the completion of the coaching relationship.

Psychodynamic

Critchley (2010) contends that a coach who practises relationally needs an understanding of the nature and implications of a client's unconscious psychological processes in order to facilitate positive outcomes. Kilburg (2004) suggests a coach who can recognise and work with unconscious material in the form of defensive reactions or dysfunctional patterns of thinking is able to explain and change unhelpful or harmful patterns of decision-making and behaviour that clients have been unable to effectively identify or address.

Working in the 'here and now'

Cox and colleagues (2014) describe the efficacy of using 'Gestalt coaching' with clients to achieve significant positive developmental change. The co-created 'here-and-now' relationship is the central vehicle for transformation and development in coaching, with coaches who draw on Gestalt therapeutic influences being able to acknowledge the influence of past experience while remaining focused on how they manifest in the present.

Working with emotion

The ability of an integrated dual-practitioner to effectively contain and explore the emotions of clients within a coaching relationship is seen by both clients and coaches to heavily influence positive results (Bachkirova & Cox, 2007). De Haan (2019) suggests that experienced coaches with the appropriate psychotherapeutic training are most able to draw on their intuitive understanding of psychodynamic unconscious processes in 'critical moments' within coaching, and to possess the ability and courage to put these powerful observations forward to the client in a way that will allow them to be received and insight and change to be created.

Why do therapists and coaches want to integrate their practices?

In his 1895 *Studies on Hysteria*, Sigmund Freud famously stated: 'Much will be gained if we succeed in transforming your neurotic misery into ordinary unhappiness' (Breuer & Freud, 1895). Oh the optimism! Of course, things have moved on considerably since then, and while all psychologically trained practitioners believe that alleviating misery is important, the coaches among us wish to help our clients go much further than this – not just to survive but to really thrive. While every dual-practitioner journey and approach may differ, it seems many of us find the dynamic tension between an excavation of the past and proactive movement towards the future simultaneously energising, joyful and fulfilling – for us and for our clients.

Within the coach-therapist community, one of the current topics of discussion is what we call ourselves and how we describe our integrated practices. Some of the different ways my peer group with similar training across coaching and therapy describe what they do include psychological coaching, therapeutic coaching, and personal consultancy (we'll call this Group 1). Others who are dual-trained continue to describe their practices as distinctly separate, and may use the terms executive coaching or life coaching, and/or counselling or psychotherapy, depending on their training and their understanding of what a client needs from the work (Group 2). Many highly experienced dual practitioners focus solely on delivering coaching, usually with senior executives, and openly share with clients that their psychotherapeutic experience informs their way of being and approach to working with coaching clients (Group 3).

Another commonly asked question is how we ethically and professionally contract to work with clients. Again, it varies from practitioner to practitioner, but practitioners in Groups 1 and 3 will usually explain their approach as drawing on their coaching and therapy skills and backgrounds throughout the relationship, and usually have a single paper contract for clients to sign. Practitioners in Group 2 may have two separate contracts and, depending on the client's initial presenting issues, will discuss and agree with them the approach they feel is the best fit. How this works in practice will be helpfully illustrated by my co-contributors in the next part of this chapter.

Practitioner journeys
Joanne Wright
Joanne is director of Wright Insight Ltd, and a coach, counsellor, mediator and organisational development specialist. She is also an executive member of BACP Coaching and an associate at Insightful Exchange and the Therapeutic Coaching Consultancy.

How do I describe what I do?
I've been a coach since 2009 and qualified as a counsellor a few years later. It's taken me a very long time to find something that feels like a good fit. But I can now say with much conviction that I work mostly as a therapeutic coach.

My previous work experience has helped define the space I now work within. I run Wright Insight, a company that supports individuals and organisations through tough times at work. I bring my entire 25-year career of working with complex work situations into the room. Clients tend to choose me because of my organisational development background, not because of my coaching or counselling qualifications. They often say, 'I selected you as I thought you would understand the situation I am in at work.' They focus on factors that resonate with them, not my modality of practice. Many practitioners feel that coaching and counselling should be kept separate but, as my supervisor would say, you can't leave bits of yourself outside the room.

For me, it's impossible to remove my counsellor head when I'm coaching or my coaching head when I'm counselling. I work in a person-centred way and adapt how I practise to meet the needs of the person sitting in front of me. I explain what I do when I contract with my clients and will often unpack what I am doing with them when I feel that would be of benefit to the client, but they all get all my 25 years' experience when they see me – there are no longer several versions of me they can hire.

I spent many years trying to separate my coaching, counselling and organisational development work into different camps. I was constantly reinventing my business model and I felt really confused about what I was doing and where my business was going. Organisations came to me because they knew I was a counsellor and wanted help with their more 'challenging' staff issues, but trying to keep the disciplines separate was a complete minefield. After one quite tricky situation, I felt I had no choice but to take a leap of faith and merge all my offerings under a 'therapeutic coaching' banner. However, at the time there was no model for this and I wondered if I was doing something unethical. It was just at this moment that I landed a role on the BACP Coaching executive committee. It was great to be with like-minded practitioners and feel I wasn't doing anything wrong in merging my offerings. I now support the BACP Coaching network meetings and speak regularly to people who practise in a similar way or want to learn more about the approach. It has been a huge relief – I feel clearer about how I define my work and clients have a better idea of what to expect from me. My contracting is far simpler now, which is ideal for someone whose passion doesn't lie in paperwork. I feel I have found my home, my safe space, or – as the marketing people would say – my niche or USP.

How did I get here?

I think it probably started when I undertook Myers Briggs training in 2003. I absolutely loved it and I credit this with making me take a really hard look at who I was and where my heart lay in terms of my work. Funnily enough, my Myers Briggs profile said I'd be a great counsellor. At the time I was working for a company whose values did not align with mine. I searched for a job that matched my Myers Briggs profile and found myself in the NHS. This is where my coaching journey began, as I was lucky enough to gain a fully funded place on a coaching course accredited with Strathclyde University, with the aim that I would coach aspiring leaders in the organisation. The qualification took me almost a year of part-time classroom study and many practice hours and I eventually qualified. I say 'eventually', as I wasn't the best student and had to re-sit one section.

Looking back, I think my very person-centred way of practising was already fighting against the more structured coaching model we were assessed against. So, my advice is never give up if you are doing something you are thoroughly enjoying, even when things don't go the way you expect. However, although I had many coaching success stories during my first few years of practice, I always felt there was something missing in the sessions – but I had no idea what that was. I now feel they were probably a bit robotic and lacked relational depth. The GROW coaching model, developed by Sir John Whitmore (Whitmore, 1992/2017), with its delineated four steps, certainly doesn't fit with my own style of practice now. My clients do get to where they need to go but in a way that works for them, which may not follow a structured model and stick to four sequential steps.

After a couple of years of coaching practice, I decided to quit my job and embark on a full-time counselling degree with Essex University. Student life didn't work well for me: going from the boardroom to the classroom was a huge adjustment. Also, the discovery at the age of 47 that I was dyslexic brought unfamiliar obstacles in an academic setting but it has proved to be a real superpower in the counselling room. Dyslexia isn't about being poor at spelling and reading; it's often described as a different way of thinking, having great problem-solving skills and loads of empathy. The most surprising thing for me on the course was that I had seen many of the theories covered in leadership training years before (in a somewhat diluted version), so maybe my coach-counsellor journey started much earlier than I thought.

What do I wish I'd known at the start of my journey?

I feel it's important to evolve into what you feel is going to work for you. No two coaches or counsellors are the same. It's important to have an open, inquisitive mind, accept the challenges along the way, take on all the placements and volunteer experiences you can, work in different sectors, find out what it all means to you and, most of all, enjoy every minute (even the tough bits, as that's where you learn the most).

I wish those starting out on their counselling journey the best of luck. To those seeking to merge the two disciplines, my message is: be brave, be ethical and, most of all, be kind to yourself and embrace the journey.

Veronica Lysaght

Veronica is former BACP Lead Advisor, Coaching, and previous Strategic Regional Director for Europe, Middle East and Africa for the International Coaching Federation.

How do I describe what I do?

On its website, in the section on coaching, BACP tells us:

> Coaching is about change and action. The core purpose of coaching is to increase self-awareness, to make choices explicit, and to close the gap between potential and how things are currently. While counselling is reparative in nature, coaching has a developmental focus. We look at how the 'there and then' may be impacting on the 'here and now', but it is not primarily focused on understanding the past or overcoming traumatic events. (BACP, 2023a)

In practice, I cannot tell you now when I am counselling and when I am coaching. At the heart of it is contracting with the client. I find there is constant re-contracting 'in the session'. My guiding principle is to make the subconscious conscious. I remember a client who came for career coaching and, when I asked about a block they were experiencing, they said, 'I think this is because of the sexual abuse I suffered as a child.' At that point, I felt my client would be much better served by seeing a counsellor who specialised in working with sexual abuse survivors. So, we then discussed how she could get the support she needed and I advised her that if, down the track, she wanted to return to me for career coaching, that would be fine.

I love the evolving flow of coaching. First, the client always decides the content; I bring knowledge and experience about the process of coaching. Second, I have faith (in the universe/god/time/spiritual energy – call it what you will) that whatever emerges will be the perfect thing to emerge in our time and space together. Third, my role is to hold the space for that emergence – to make it safe to say the unsayable, to admit to the darkness, grief and despair and know that the person will still be okay.

For me, coaching is also about purpose and meaning, and about going forward – it's what we do with clients and how we live as coaches. After a tragic family bereavement when I couldn't see the world through the same eyes again, I challenged my husband to do what he'd been talking about for years – buy a yacht and sail back to Aotearoa/New Zealand. He said, 'Yes, as long as we have a purpose to the trip,' and I added, 'Let's take an interesting route home.' And from this, the idea of the Novara One Planet project was born.[1] As this book goes to print, Nigel and I are leading an adventure to work with coastal communities to adapt to climate change. We plan to initially to engage with communities in high-latitude coastal locations along our route – the Scottish Highlands, Shetlands, Faroe Islands, Iceland, Greenland Labrador Coast and Newfoundland. How does all this relate to coaching? Not only will we and our crew need coaching, but we will also be offering ongoing coaching and

---

1. http://novara.world

mentoring to people in those communities who want to find ways of adapting to the impact of climate change in their part of the world.

How did I get here?

When I started my journey in the 'helping' professions, I was bouncing away from a career as a journalist and press secretary to a government minister. I remember asking myself, 'How do I make a positive change in the world?' It seemed to me that the role I then occupied didn't really make much of a difference.

So, I resigned from the job and had a brief stint working for the Office of the Race Relations Conciliator (in New Zealand), before giving birth to my daughter. Soon after this, my career-change plans really started to take shape. I co-authored a book, *The Sun Will Shine Again: Stories of survival and optimism in the face of mental illness* (Fahy & Lysaght, 1999), and I enrolled in a master's counselling course.

My counselling degree was eclectic, which meant we had a taste of many counselling methodologies. The one I enjoyed most was psychodrama – for several reasons. First, psychodrama offers the protagonist the opportunity to step into someone else's shoes, to see the issue/world from a different perspective, and to shed light on an area that has been in darkness. There is a freedom and creativity in it that goes far beyond words.

Second, the idea that our emotions are lodged in our bodies and we have to move our bodies to release them makes perfect sense to me – as well as being my personal experience. I've always found that moving my body, even with a 'walk and talk', releases something that sitting a chair can't access.

By the time I finished my master's, my daughter was a toddler and I had picked up a gig doing career counselling for a company that supported organisations with outplacement, team building, retirement workshops and individual career development work. I loved the job. I also worked part-time for the counselling service at my local university. Again, I enjoyed that work, but I always felt my style of counselling was a bit inadequate because I was less interested in going into a client's past and more enthused by how they were going to cope with today and what they could do differently tomorrow.

Landing the role as Lead Advisor, Coaching, with BACP helped reinforce for me the essence of coaching. In my latter role with ICF, I discovered that many of the theoretical models I'd learnt about in my counselling degree had been adapted for coaching. One time, when attending an ICF conference, I decided to go to a demonstration on constellations. I had heard about constellations but didn't know much about them. As the event got underway, I was amazed to find I was experiencing a psychodrama workshop – the theories and principles of psychodrama had been adapted for coaching. It was a light-bulb moment!

I could suddenly see how I could apply my counselling theories to a coaching context. If I could do that with psychodrama, what about the drama triangle, transactional analysis between line managers and direct reports, Gestalt principles of being in the moment – all of these have a relevance (but often under different names) in the coaching world. It was like my favourite Rumi quote, where he compares a person to a guest house with many rooms, and advises us to welcome whatever comes our way (Rumi, 2004). I interpret this as not only welcoming what each day brings as it unfolds, with all the beauty, sadness, joys and pains, but also welcoming all of yourself – all your experience, wisdom and knowledge that has come from all of your life.

What do I wish I'd known at the start of my journey?

The answer is simple and yet not easy: be yourself. Twenty-three years ago, my ego, my wishes for others, got in the way of being truly myself when with a client. I swallowed the guidelines of professional bodies about boundaries, being a conduit/mirror and so forth, and consciously thought I was not bringing myself into the room. On reflection, I think this is at the heart of why coaching suited me better than counselling. Within safe, ethical boundaries and guidelines, I like the freedom that coaching gives me to bring my whole self into the experience. In coaching, I am more me. I share, when appropriate, my experience. I offer suggestions on a range of practices that may (or may not) assist someone to embed a new behaviour. I celebrate with my clients. Sometimes, I feel their sadness or frustration. Mostly, I 'hold' the space that we're in together.

Recently, I was asked to be a coaching supervisor and I wondered if I needed to follow a specific supervision model, but so far I haven't found one that works for me. Which brings me back to where I started: walk into this practice of being a therapist who coaches knowing you will develop your own way. You may align with one professional body, or many, or none – only you will know what is best for you. Follow ethical guidelines and your consciously stated values. Be open about who you are and bring all of who you are into your practice. This way of living, where we take time to reflect on who we are and how we live, is an ongoing joy.

Yvonne Inglis

Yvonne is an executive coach, accredited to senior practitioner level with EMCC, and a psychotherapist and supervisor accredited with BACP. She is also a member of the BACP Coaching Executive committee.

How do I describe what I do?

My approach to coaching and therapy is very much about bringing all of me into every session, regardless of whether it is coaching or counselling. I have a very varied bag of tools and skills gained over the years and will use whatever I feel is useful for each client. I suppose you could call it bespoke, but I do not separate out my coaching/therapy skills – it is an integrated approach.

However, it really does depend on the source of the initial contact. So, if it's an approach for counselling, I will mainly use counselling skills and will bring in coaching tools if/where I feel they are appropriate. It may be a natural progression and may not necessarily be labelled as a switch from counselling to coaching. In the same way, I wouldn't tell the client 'This is a person-centred approach in this bit but now I am going to introduce a bit of cognitive behavioural therapy or transactional analysis.'

If I were approached for coaching, I would use a different contract and involve individual coaching sessions or follow a programme. The benefit of being a coach who is also an accredited therapist means that I can work at depth and with the whole of the person. For me, it's more holistic. Many coaches who do not have any mental health training shut the client down when they start discussing mental health or emotional detail and refer them for therapy because they don't feel equipped to do this work; worse are those who think it can't be that difficult and deal with it unskilfully. Both responses can cause real emotional harm to the client.

I feel that particularly since the Covid pandemic. People's mental health and wellbeing are very much recognised in modern working culture, but many organisations are falling short in providing what their workforce needs. They need more than Wellbeing Wednesdays or Talking Tuesdays. This is why therapeutic coaching, which follows a holistic approach, is valuable for all organisations, as it can increase engagement, support retention and increase productivity.

The biggest challenge for a coach in the current economic climate is to demonstrate our value to organisations. Right now, organisations face considerable recruitment difficulties; they need to incentivise and retain staff. Staff turnover and the hiring and training of new staff costs approximately 40% of pre-tax income for the average company, whereas retraining existing employees incurs only training expenses. So why not use coaching to develop and grow your existing workforce?

How did I get here?

My therapist journey began while I was working full-time in a financial services organisation and my husband was diagnosed with stomach cancer. I was 44 when he passed away and, while raising two teenage children and working through my grief, I completed a postgraduate diploma in counselling and psychotherapy. There was an opportunity at work to train as an in-house coach and I quickly realised that I was using the same skills in coaching as I was as a person-centred therapist but there was more of an emphasis on focused goals and outcomes. I would say that this has also become more of a feature in short-term therapy in recent years.

I made the decision to leave corporate life after 30 years when both my parents died within six months of each other. A trusted adviser counselled me to continue to use my business experience, hence the transition to train as an executive coach. I obtained my Institute of Leadership and Management (ILM) Level 7 in executive coaching and mentoring and through this have had the privilege to work globally with senior leaders in several sectors.

I would say my journey was never specifically planned this way but, by being open to opportunity, I have found the journey to be enlightening and enriching and am always excited to see what is round the next corner.

What do I wish I'd known at the start of my journey?

Whether you are a coach looking to become more skilled in mental health or a counsellor looking to add coaching to your skill set, I would advocate talking to colleagues who have taken that step, to find out more. Perhaps experience a bit of coaching or counselling yourself to see how you feel about it as a client. There are, of course, numerous models of counselling and coaching, and coaching itself has its own disciplines, such as life coaching, executive coaching, business coaching and so forth. So, you need to decide what you want to do and what would align itself best with your values and skills, then sign up for training and get yourself a recognised qualification.

I have seen a definite shift in demand from pure coaching to a dual approach, and this will be a challenge for the coaching industry if it does not take steps to integrate more mental health qualifications/resources/awareness into its training. Coaches need to be able to hold that space for their clients without panicking. Not everyone needs therapy; some people just need to be heard. So, it's important that you know your boundaries and feel safe to practise at the border between these two arenas, and always to work ethically and with the appropriate level of supervision.

I feel that people who are not dual practitioners can become very fearful of stepping outside their comfort zones and like to have what they should do and when they should do it mapped out for them. I wish people would become more relaxed around the use of multi-layers of skill and expertise and have more confidence that they know how to use their skills well, at whatever their level of practice.

The other challenge is around pricing – counsellors and coaches command fees at very different ends of the scale, with some meeting in the middle. Is there a case for making coaching more affordable and accessible without coaches feeling their work is disvalued? Should counsellors be expecting to be paid more for what they do? Or is this simply about what the client expects to have to pay and is willing and able to afford?

I am sure the debate for these issues will continue for some time to come but I do see some of the lines breaking up and skills merging.

As I continue my journey, I see endless new possibilities ahead for me. Having completed my advanced diploma in supervision, I am considering moving into an arena with relatively little provision – that of supervising qualified dual practitioners. I am a passionate believer in the value of supervision, not just to ensure ethical practice but also to provide a supportive, non-judgemental space for practitioners to bring themselves and their entire practice. At the moment, many dual practitioners have a coaching supervisor and a therapy supervisor, so combining these roles is where I see my role evolving.

Lucy Myers

Lucy is Founder and CEO of Therapeutic Coaching Consultancy and took up the role of Chair of BACP Coaching in 2021.

How did I get here?

It probably makes sense to briefly begin with where I came from, because diversity, equity and inclusion are important to me now as a result. I was good at English, so I studied a BSc in communications and media studies at Loughborough University. A fortuitous phone call from Sky to my university in my final year landed me my first TV job.

Having a hug with Harold Bishop from *Neighbours* and convincing David Attenborough to do an interview; producing a surprise marriage proposal live on TV and getting cut in half by a magician for a promo; flying to LA and New York for conferences and taking the flak for an ex-footballer who ruined an expensive sofa by deliberately smashing eggs on it… All these formed part of my first career, and you wouldn't necessarily think they'd help me in my current one. And yet…

While I've never disclosed any of this history to clients, I believe everything we experience in life contributes to how fully we are able to show up in the coaching or therapy room. If people are encouraged to 'bring their whole selves to work', doesn't it make sense that we (within the framework of ethical practice) model the same for our clients? I've experienced wobbling self-esteem as a result of disillusion with my career, and feeling financially and emotionally trapped as a result – so yes, having lived experience of successfully transitioning to a new vocation inevitably helps me work with certain professional dilemmas in the coaching room. But of equal, if not greater, importance are the challenges I've overcome (or not) and the mistakes I've made along the way, because they've given me a deep understanding of my own human fallibility and the inevitable imperfections and messiness of life. I think it's my hard-won self-compassion and self-acceptance that enables me to hold compassion for everyone and everything that is brought into the coaching room.

Fast-forward nearly two decades and I'd come to realise that, while working in the media gave me an incredible experience, it no longer felt 'like me'. Fate then played its hand in the following five ways:

1. My employer paid for me to see an executive coach – the experience fascinated me.
2. A colleague began training in psychotherapy and I watched her fall in love with it.
3. I realised the bits of my jobs I'd most enjoyed were helping my own team members grow and being inspired by strong leaders to 'be better' myself.
4. I'd watched people close to me struggle and I'd faced my own demons. I felt an intense need to know why some of us thrive in life, some of us barely survive, and some swing like a pendulum between the two.
5. I was offered the opportunity to take redundancy, and with it the opportunity to take a huge leap of faith.

Enthused by the experience of being coached, and learning from my psychotherapy colleague, at the age of 40 I began studying both coaching and psychotherapy, concurrently, on two separate courses.

I formalised my experience of management training and coaching experience with an ILM Level 7 executive coaching and mentoring certificate, choosing this because it was an industry-respected and accredited qualification. Alongside this, I completed a MA in integrative counselling and psychotherapy with the University of Roehampton, and went on to develop my own integrative practice, drawing on humanistic, psychodynamic and CBT modalities. Is it advisable to study both at the same time? My master's course leader said no, because 'it would be too confusing for you'. Reflective of my personality (impatient) and practicality (I'd already been accepted on the courses and paid deposits for both), I pressed ahead anyway.

Rather than confusing, I actually found the work highly complementary. For example, coaching is rooted in the Rogerian belief that people can evolve or 'self-actualise', given the right conditions and assisted by curious, non-judgemental, humble inquiry. What better way to help a coaching client understand a tricky relationship with their boss than with an awareness of psychodynamic theories of attachment theory or object-relations, or by challenging unhelpful thought patterns with CBT techniques? It works the other way too. Solution-focused brief therapy feels strongly aligned with a coaching ideology. This way of doing things might not be right for everybody but, as I reflect back now, I think I had begun from day one to integrate my understanding of how we can help to overcome distress while also finding ways to move proactively towards something new.

How do I describe what I do?

Today, I am an executive coach and psychotherapist delivering an integrated 'therapeutic coaching' approach in private practice. My consultancy combines the solutions-focussed energy and structure of therapeutic coaching with the healing empowerment and psychological insight of psychotherapy, working with organisations to deliver one-to-one coaching, team coaching, leadership development training and workshops, and coaching supervision and CPD events for in-house coaching networks.

I now advertise my service transparently as an integrated approach.[2] But how did I decide whether to use coaching or therapy skills with new referrals before? For me, the work begins even before a client contacts me. I have always been transparent in my marketing materials that I'm dual-trained with a business background, and many people tell me they've sought me out for precisely these reasons. Some aren't sure whether they need coaching or therapy because they're experiencing issues at home and at work and are confused about which came first and which is more problematic. Others are attracted to my solutions-focused approach, telling me they have tried counselling before but found that, while they felt an initial relief from being listened to, after a few sessions they were left with a frustrating feeling of '... and now what?' With these clients, I'll have a chat with them and come up with an initial plan of how we'll begin our work together, and then, with creative collaboration at the core of my approach, we review as we go.

I've discovered that even clients who come with the most intense and devastatingly distress often emerge from a period of therapy with greater clarity about what they want from life and an energy that they now wish to harness. At this point we might discuss moving into more of a coaching relationship, and if the client wishes, re-contract with clearly defined goals and success measures.

---

2. www.therapeuticcoachingconsultancy.co.uk

When I'm contracted to work with coaching clients in senior positions within a business, they have usually selected me from a bank of coaches (including those without therapy training) because they are naturally psychologically minded and, being competitive, extremely curious about increasing their self-awareness of blind spots as well as capitalising on their strengths. So, while we begin with the necessary organisationally agreed objectives and key performance indicators, these are usually swiftly followed by a deeper and more therapeutic excavation of emotional responses to relationship issues and workplace challenges.

How does my previous career support the work? To borrow a phrase from Mearns and Cooper (2017, p.163), my 'existential touchstones' in coaching include an understanding of working under pressure within competitive environments, challenging bosses and targets, excitement and success (and frustration and failure), restructures and organisational change processes, and the complexities of working relationships in terms of building, influencing and maintaining them, and of conflict resolution within them.

My private practice provides a fully integrated 'therapeutic coaching' approach for all clients, combining the emotional depth of psychotherapy with the strategic structure and energy of executive coaching. I'm most inspired by the practices of coaches whose corporate fees enable them to provide low-cost or free coaching for disadvantaged individuals and community groups, which aligns with my personal values and purpose. Continuing to work with a few purely psychotherapy clients in addition to therapeutic coaching clients is not only highly rewarding but also feels vital to my continued professional development. To explain this further, my recent psychotherapy client roster includes lawyers, teachers, artists, students, authors, accountants and health care professionals. Collectively, they struggle with anxiety, OCD, depression, suicidal ideation, ADHD, autism, gender dysphoria and transitions, bereavement, addiction, and personality disorders. In contrast to the myth that therapeutic clients are 'dysfunctional', almost all are highly 'functioning' members of society, holding down jobs, raising families and completing qualifications.

We know mental health difficulties are increasingly commonplace in the general global population, so why wouldn't they be present in business executives managing high levels of responsibility and stress while often feeling isolated by their seniority in the office hierarchy? When the symptoms of any of the conditions above present themselves in coaching clients (the prevalence of sociopathic and personality disorder traits in senior leaders is well known), I am able to notice and identify them, privately formulate their potential origin, and then, without the client ever needing to know (unless ethically appropriate and relevant), work as effectively as possible in the interests of serving the personal and professional goals of my client.

What do you need to know before you start on this journey?

If any of the following statements ring true for you, then adding coaching to your therapeutic skillset could be something to explore further:

- You feel insight alone doesn't necessarily lead to change.
- You believe people have the potential to achieve behavioural change. faster than standard therapeutic processes allow for.
- You want to support clients' need towards the end of therapy for something more future-focused.
- You feel your business background or strategic mindedness may help your clients.
- You feel the energy and goal-focused forward momentum of a coaching relationship will suit your personality.

But there are some issues you need to be aware of. While the world is changing and demand for coaching is growing, the therapy-coaching world is still predominantly white and middle class. Although the counselling profession is largely female, the upper echelons and thought leaders of the coaching world are still mostly male. To fully represent the client base, we need more diversity in coaching, across gender, race, class, religion, sexuality and disability. I am proud of my own working-class roots and my confidence continues to grow to be truly who I am, with all I meet.

We need to professionalise this evolving area as effectively as possible. We are working to avoid a 'new Wild West' of therapeutically informed coaches, and I'm hopeful that the next few years will see progress in formalising training, registration and accreditation for coach-therapists, in alignment with the structures and frameworks established by the professional bodies for counsellors. Collaboration between professional bodies from both the therapy and coaching worlds will be necessary.

And if any of this whets your coaching appetite, my advice would be to reach out, connect and get your questions answered. My experience of the coaching-therapy community is that it's inclusive, supportive, authentic, friendly, warm and passionate. So get in touch with a group or join a network and start to feel your way into what might be right for you next. After all, to use a classic coaching question, what's the worst that could happen? And what's the best?

Carolyn Mumby

Carolyn is as a coach, supervisor, facilitator, consultant and author. Here she focuses on the supervision needs of the dual-trained coach-therapist.

How did I get here?

Entering the river that flows between the banks of counselling and coaching is exciting and challenging, and supervision is an essential part of the navigation:

> Supervision provides practitioners with regular and ongoing opportunities to reflect in depth about all aspects of their practice, in order to work as effectively, safely and ethically as possible. (BACP, 2018, p.22)

Whether the dual-trained practitioner maintains separate counselling and coaching practices or works in an integrated way, they are drawing on two different established professions, so to ensure safety and promote innovation, they will need a supervisor with some experience of the benefits and challenges of dual practice. Modality, context and speciality and/or client group will also need to be considered.

At the time of writing, BACP is one of the few professional bodies supporting dual practitioners. Yet, finding the right supervisor can be tricky as there is currently no way to search for them on the BACP register or directory. Joining networks and events through BACP Coaching can link you with recommendations from other colleagues.

Questions to consider as a dual-trained practitioner in supervision might include the following: If you offer separate practices, how will you delineate and explain them? How would you move from one to the other practice, if requested by the client? If you have different pricing scales for each, how will this be managed? If offering an integrated practice, what is the entry point – are you offering counselling as the foundation and then moving into coaching? Are you starting from the position of coaching and working therapeutically as needed, or just to some extent? Are you positioning the work as entirely integrated? Within the 'continuum' between counselling and coaching, where is your territory? This will depend on your theoretical approach and may also be determined by the level of distress that you will work with, how much 'holding' and regular contact you want to offer, and how experienced you are in the different types of coaching (life, specialist, business, executive, leadership and so forth). What is the framework or approach that supports your integrated practice?

Themes that have arisen in my supervision practice include how to understand and describe a new identity as a dual-trained practitioner. Practitioners often want to explore how to move into new markets for their work and introduce new pricing structures. The process of contracting is a big part of this reflective inquiry. A common mistake for practitioners new to coaching is to slip into feeling responsible for the delivery of the client's goals. This can be explored by returning to the mutual assessment process before the work starts. What is the contract between you? What is the shared understanding of the process? What are the expectations of what the practitioner and client will differently bring to the work? How will you know when the work has been successful (which may include, but also go beyond the specific outcomes desired at the outset)?

One of the questions I'm most frequently asked by therapists seeking to develop their knowledge and skills in coaching is which training they should choose. There's a plethora of training options available, ranging widely in duration, depth, level, accreditation, focus and cost, but (currently at least) limited options for those already qualified in counselling or psychotherapy. My advice would be to consider the client base and context that interests you most, and look for a course that maps as closely as possible with the competences required to practise coaching ethically and impactfully with your future ideal clients. BACP's coaching training curriculum (BACP, 2023b) offers training providers a framework for delivering core coaching training and integrating therapy and coaching training, and may assist you with this.

You can access further information via the websites of the main professional bodies for coaches and counsellors: BACP[3] and the British Psychological Society[4] (BPS) (both of which have coaching divisions), the International Coaching Federation (ICF),[5] the European Mentoring and Coaching Council (EMCC),[6] the Association for Coaching (AC),[7] and the Academy of Executive Coaching (AoEC)[8] (see also Appendix for more details).

Conclusion – Lucy Myers

I hope you have enjoyed this theoretically and experientially informed perspective on how counselling and coaching might be woven together to form new ways of working with clients. While we're still only beginning to explore the nature of effective dual practice, the evidence base for the benefits of psychotherapeutically informed coaching is growing, and much positive collaboration between the psychology and coaching sectors is already under way. If we are to put clients at the heart of what we do, we need more research that will deepen our knowledge, skills and abilities as practitioners and enhance our understanding of how we can both alleviate distress and help clients flourish.

---

3. www.bacp.co.uk
4. www.bps.org.uk
5. https://coachingfederation.org
6. www.emccglobal.org
7. www.associationforcoaching.com
8. www.aoec.com

I hope that together we have achieved two things in this chapter: first, that we've given you a flavour of the enjoyment and satisfaction that we experience in our work and as a community of practitioners; second, that you've been able to glimpse the opportunity and freedom the dual-practice role offers to create, design and grow into a practice that feels right for you and for your clients.

To build on Carolyn Mumby's metaphor, the river of dual practice is dynamic and ever evolving, with different depths and speeds of movement; it's impacted by what feeds into it from either bank and it flows into future ways of being.

Thank you for joining me for this chapter, and I hope you enjoy your future journey, whatever comes next for you.

References

Bachkirova, T., & Cox, E. (2007). Coaching with emotion in organisations: Investigation of personal theories. *Leadership & Organization Development Journal, 28*(7), 600–612.

BACP. (2018). *Ethical framework for the counselling professions*. BACP. www.bacp.co.uk/media/3103/bacp-ethical-framework-for-the-counselling-professions-2018.pdf

BACP. (2022). *Coaching competence framework: User guide*. BACP. www.bacp.co.uk/media/17020/bacp-coaching-competences-user-guide-2022.pdf

BACP. (2023a). *What is coaching?* BACP. www.bacp.co.uk/about-therapy/types-of-therapy/coaching

BACP. (2023b). *Coaching competences: Raising training and practice standards in coaching*. BACP. www.bacp.co.uk/events-and-resources/ethics-and-standards/competences-and-curricula/coaching/

Berglas, S. (2002). The very real dangers of executive coaching. *Harvard Business Review, 80*(6), 86–92, 153.

Berman, W.H. & Bradt, G. (2006). Executive coaching and consulting: 'Different strokes for different folks'. *Professional Psychology: Research and Practice, 37*(3), 244–253.

Bluckert, P. (2006). *Psychological dimensions of executive coaching*. McGraw Hill.

Breuer, J. & Freud, S. (1895/1955). Studies on hysteria. In J. Strachey (Ed.), *The standard edition of the complete psychological works of Sigmund Freud, vol. 2*. Hogarth Press.

Carroll, M. (2003). The new kid on the block. *Counselling & Psychotherapy Journal, 14*(10), 28–31.

Cox, E., Bachkirova, T. & Clutterbuck, D. (2014). Theoretical traditions and coaching genres. *Advances in Developing Human Resources, 16*(2), 139–160.

Critchley, B. (2010). Relational coaching: Taking the coaching high road. *Journal of Management Development, 29*(10), 851–863.

de Haan, E. (2008). I doubt therefore I coach: Critical moments in coaching practice. *Consulting Psychology Journal: Practice and Research, 60*(1), 91–105.

de Haan, E. (2019). A systematic review of qualitative studies in workplace and executive coaching: The emergence of a body of research. *Consulting Psychology Journal: Practice and Research, 71*(4), 227–248.

de Haan, E., Duckworth, A., Birch, D. & Jones, C. (2013). Executive coaching outcome research: The contribution of common factors such as relationship, personality match, and self-efficacy. *Consulting Psychology Journal, 65*(1), 40–57.

EMCC. (2021). *Global code of ethics*. EMCC. https://emccuk.org/Public/Public/Accreditation/Global_Code_of_Ethics.aspx

EMCC/ICF. (2011). *The professional charter for coaching and mentoring*. EMCC/ICF. https://emccuk.org/Common/Uploaded%20files/Professional-Charter-EMCC.pdf

Fahy, M. & Lysaght, V. (1999). *The sun will shine again: Stories of survival and optimism in the face of mental illness*. The Schizophrenia Fellowship.

Finlay, L. (2016). *Relational integrative psychotherapy: Engaging process and theory in practice*. Wiley-Blackwell.

Grant, A.M. & Green, R.M. (2018). Developing clarity on the coaching-counselling conundrum: Implications for counsellors and psychotherapists. *Counselling and Psychotherapy Research, 18*(4), 347–355.

Gyllensten, K. & Palmer, S. (2007). The coaching relationship: An interpretative phenomenological analysis. *International Coaching Psychology Review, 2*(2), 167–177.

Kilburg, R.R. (2004). When shadows fall. *Consulting Psychology Journal, 56*(4), 246–268.

Lemisiou, M.A. (2018). The effectiveness of person-centered coaching intervention in raising emotional and social intelligence competencies in the workplace. *International Coaching Psychology Review, 13*(2), 6–26.

Maxwell, A. (2009). How do business coaches experience the boundary between coaching and therapy/counselling? *Coaching: An International Journal of Theory, Research and Practice, 2*(2), 149–162.

Mearns, D., & Cooper, M. (2017). *Working at relational depth in counselling and psychotherapy* (2nd ed.). Sage.

Norcross, J.C. (2010). The therapeutic relationship. In B.L. Duncan, S.D. Miller, B.E. Wampold & M.A. Hubble (Eds.), *The heart and soul of change: Delivering what works in therapy* (pp. 113–141). American Psychological Association.

Rogers, C. R. (1961). *On becoming a person: A therapist's view of psychotherapy*. Constable.

Rogers, J. (2013). *Coaching skills: A handbook* (3rd ed.). McGraw Hill.

Rumi. (2004). *Selected poems*. Penguin.

Sherman, S. & Freas, A. (2004). The Wild West of executive coaching. *Harvard Business Review, 82(11)*, 82–90, 148.

Western, S. (2012). *Coaching and mentoring*. Sage.

Whitmore, J. (1992/2017). *Coaching for performance: The principles and practice of coaching and leadership* (5th ed.). Nicholas Brealey Publishing.

Chapter 6

Counselling in higher and further education settings

Géraldine Dufour
with Desmond Channer, Mark Fudge, Jane Harris, Dominic McLoughlin, Allie Scott, Stella Sookun and Stefan Wilson

Introduction – Géraldine Dufour

I am thrilled to have been asked to edit this chapter on counselling in universities and colleges. Becoming a university counsellor was my dream job when I started training – a feeling I know is shared by many of the contributors to this chapter.

However, like being in love, our work has its ups and downs, and our passion does not blind us to the challenges of our roles. I hope that this chapter, with its diverse contributors sharing their honest experiences and insights, will give you a real sense of what it's like to work in a university or college counselling service. I hope too that you will discover much to inform and inspire you amid the wealth of knowledge that we have accumulated from our personal involvement and from working in the field alongside talented colleagues with whom we reflect on our work and its rewards and challenges.

I discovered counselling as a career by chance after benefitting from it when I was an Erasmus exchange student more than 30 years ago. Not only did I gain emotionally and mentally – I realised that this might be a job for me! It brought together different strands of my life and interests: I believed in social justice, wanted to help people, and felt that I had found my niche at university.

I went on to work in social care, trained and then found work as a counsellor with young people, victims of sexual violence and in a community alcohol team. I never had a career plan in mind, but I kept wondering what it would be like to work for a university counselling service. When I furthered my counselling training, I chose a university counselling service as my placement. This valuable experience helped me to secure a position as a counsellor at Birmingham City University. I very much enjoyed working there and went on to work as a supervisor, then as the manager of the service. I was appointed on national boards for university and college counselling before moving to the University of Cambridge as the Head of Counselling, overseeing the provision of psychological support for the collegiate university and leading a multi-disciplinary team of more than 40 counsellors, CBT therapists, mindfulness teachers, the university sexual harassment and assault advisor and mental health advisors. I now work outside the university sector, but I continue to support the work of counselling, mental health and wellbeing services as a consultant, trainer and supervisor.

I am sharing my journey because it illustrates the route that many of us take in the sector, starting out as unpaid trainees and moving on to work in both paid and volunteer positions. I managed my first shift to a paid role by working full-time alongside my counselling studies, but this may not be an option that is available to all. As a profession, since we want to increase the diversity of our teams, we need to consider whether to offer paid internships (and even training places) to counsellors from less represented groups, such as working-class people and those from racially minoritised communities. This is crucial at a time when students and staff are asking rightly that their counselling services are more representative of the population they serve.

Before looking at our counselling roles, it might be helpful to think about why universities and colleges offer counselling to students. It stems from a pastoral support tradition (Bell, 1996), but it also serves another purpose – enabling students and staff to engage better with their work. For institutions, there is a clear economic incentive in attracting new students, retaining them and enabling them to succeed in their studies. While there is undeniably an economic imperative for student retention, I would argue that it is also a moral responsibility. Once they admit students, universities have an ethical obligation to support them so they can complete their course. This is particularly important for students from population groups and backgrounds that are under-represented at university (known in the sector as 'widening participation students'). For students who face additional barriers to accessing education and career opportunities, universities can act as an agent of social mobility. The importance of social justice in our work is crucial to many of us and it certainly resonates with me at a personal level: I was the first in my family to go to university and I experienced first-hand the transformational impact on my life, enabling me to enter and progress in a professional career.

As you will see in this chapter, we have all developed an awareness of the impact of the university and college sector on our work as counsellors. Those of us who lead a counselling team have learned to align the objectives of our services to the strategies of our universities, but the context is present in many other aspects of our work – from the way we assess (Dufour, 2016), to the times at which we take our holidays (mostly out of term), and many other facets, which we will share with you here.

In the following pages, we will tell you about the range of work opportunities in our sector and how to get work, and share insights about the recruitment process, particular areas of concerns and presenting issues, the peculiarities and idiosyncrasies of the sector (in sixth form and further education colleges as well as universities), client access issues and attitudes towards counselling, general working conditions, the joys and woes of our work and why we love practising in the sector.

Finding work in the sector – Géraldine Dufour, Allie Scott and Desmond Channer

Much has been written about student mental health (Hughes & Spanner, 2019; Auerbach et al., 2018) and, with more than half of each generation entering further and higher education, student mental health has a huge impact on the health of the nation. The rise in demand for support services (Barden & Caleb, 2019) has also increased the number of positions available to those holding counselling qualifications. These encompass a range of different roles, such as counsellors, mental health advisers or coordinators, wellbeing advisers and mental health mentors. Some services have moved away from offering purely counselling to more generalised wellbeing support, which may be at a lesser level of expertise (see Percy in Lightfoot, 2018); other institutions have increased the range of support available to students, adding wellbeing and mental health support to existing counselling provision.

Opportunities to work as a counsellor in higher education institutions are generally advertised on university websites, on the academic website jobs.ac.uk and by counselling bodies and directories, such as the weekly vacancies email sent to subscribers by BACP. Requirements for qualifications and essential and desirable criteria vary between institutions. However, if you keep checking the advertisements, you will quickly get a sense of what different institutions expect.

Applying for a job in a university counselling service – Jane Harris

I am writing here to share my professional experience over many years as head of service, recruiting and inducting colleagues in a university wellbeing, mental health and counselling service.

A strong job application will be well researched, tailored to the role, and demonstrate how you meet all the candidate requirements. Take time to read the university strategies as well as sector guidance. It's worth learning about the university and the service you are hoping to join. The university webpages will outline the student support structure and provide information for students on what to expect. This research will both help you to understand the role and establish that this is a setting you would like to work in, considering the diverse range of responsibilities and duties.

Universities value the services and departments that support students through the difficulties that can undermine their engagement with and success in their degrees. When recruiting university counsellors, we look for evidence that candidates understand the role within its institutional setting. In some respects, you have two clients – the individual student and the wider university.

Large organisations increasingly use online application forms, though some still ask for a covering letter and CV. Regardless of format, the assessment and shortlisting system will be a formulaic process, with each response scored on the extent to which it answers the relevant point on the role description/candidate brief. Your answers should be precise, long enough to illustrate your points, but not too long – good quality applications typically convey all the necessary information in one or two short paragraphs per question.

For each question, you will need to clearly demonstrate the specific skills, knowledge and experience you bring, providing clear examples of what you have done or achieved and the impact or outcome. Ensure that you explain technical terms and acronyms and do not repeat responses from earlier answers, even if there are overlaps in the subject matter. Make sure to check your written submission for basic spelling, grammar and punctuation errors. The role will require you to write clinical notes, letters and sometimes reports, so evidence of good writing style and accuracy is important and will be assessed through your application.

As with therapy, there is both an art and a science to a strong application, and a need to balance personal and professional discourses. Prepare for possible interview questions and spend time thinking about how you will communicate your theoretical model and demonstrate how this translates into your way of working.

As therapists we are all potentially 'wounded healers' but, unlike on our training courses, be cautious about self-disclosure in the application and interview process. Disclosure of personal struggles and difficulties should be contextual and serve only to illustrate a broader point. It may be relevant to cite specific experiences if they relate to what you are seeking to demonstrate, particularly to illustrate insight and maturity.

Think about your appearance and what to wear at the interview. Counselling is a professional role in a university; how will you convey this at your interview? Interviews are difficult processes, and you may feel challenged: think about leaving a good impression, and try to respond positively to constructive feedback, as there might be other opportunities or jobs that come up with the same university, so this is also a chance to lay some groundwork.

Competences and supervision – Géraldine Dufour

Student counselling services were established more than 50 years ago in universities (Bell, 1996), and counsellors' work has changed considerably since, to adapt to the needs of students and developments in the sector. Most counselling services are now part of wider student support services, and you may be working alongside other welfare, disability, mental health and wellbeing advisers and colleagues offering help with finances and career development. Knowledge about what other support is on offer is key, as you will need to be able to collaborate with other services, particularly in your initial client assessments (Dufour, 2016).

Due to these specificities, counselling in universities and colleges is now seen as a specialist arena, with a set of guidelines for good clinical practice in the further and higher education sector developed by BACP with the sector (BACP, 2017),[1] as well as its own resources and journals. Through the years, these guidelines have been invaluable in establishing some fundamental practice standards across the sector. They address many issues that are of concern to supervisors, such as the number of client contact hours for a counsellor working full time. The guidelines also urge counselling services to set up working agreements with supervisors that clarify issues around clinical responsibilities: it is generally agreed that the heads of services hold clinical responsibility for the counselling service clients, rather than the counsellors themselves.

The skills required for this work have been further mapped by BACP in a set of competences (BACP, 2016). These are well worth reading, as they will help you decide if this is the sector for you and if you need any further specialist training post-qualification. The competences include, for example, the ability to work with young people and the need to adapt to the vagaries of the student life cycle.

It would seem important that a supervisor has an understanding of the way a counsellor is expected to work, but a supervisor with this expertise can be hard to find – they will need to understand and ideally have experience of working in the university or college context, as well as extensive experience in brief therapy (see below), and be able to guide the counsellor as they adapt

---

1. There is also a more detailed description of the competences at www.bacp.co.uk/media/2042/bacp-competences-working-in-further-higher-education.pdf

their modality to working in an institutional context. Supervisors need to understand the impact of the whole context on the work, and the tensions created when different agendas are competing. This tension can create a specific ethical concern when the needs of the client (the student), the counsellor and the institution collide, and supervision is where this will need to be unravelled.

For counsellors to do good work, the reflective space created by supervision is invaluable. I would argue that the reflective and restorative spaces offered by supervision are sorely needed by university and college counsellors. Like many other practitioners, they have to cope with increasingly larger and more complex caseloads.

Common presenting issues – Mark Fudge

University student populations are generally diverse and this can impact on the severity and nature of problems students present with. In considering a career in student counselling, you should therefore expect to work with a diverse and ever-changing clientele.

The problems brought by students attending counselling services could be presented statistically as a data spreadsheet, but to appreciate this more, it's relevant to consider the broader context – the culture of higher education and its funding, societal pressures to achieve and conform, and developmental issues linked to identity/life experience. We also must consider the uniformity and quality of the data defining the presenting problems and the measures used to describe distress levels and subsequent changes (improvement or deterioration) during counselling. To achieve an accurate picture, then, data would need to go beyond self-reporting surveys of students to statistically valid measures and uniform data collection.

Returning to the common presenting issues, as flagged up earlier, the breadth of choice of data collection systems means there is no reliable single source (see Barkham et al., 2019 for a discussion of this). By contrast, in the US, some 750 higher education counselling services contribute standardised data to the Center for Collegiate Mental Health, giving a reliable insight into effectiveness, severity of presentation and types of appointments accessed by students, along with service workloads.[2] It's a model of data collection and analysis to which the UK should aspire.

Very often, when meeting people for the first time and being asked what I do, my reply, that I am a university counsellor, gets the response: 'That's just homesickness and people worried about exams, isn't it?' Those of us working in the sector know that the breadth and complexity of problems faced by students

---

2. See https://ccmh.psu.edu/annual-reports"https://ccmh.psu.edu/annual-reports

mirrors the complexity of distress within the general population. Students cross the breadth of age groups, but younger students (who are still the majority) will have fewer life experiences and shorter narrative biographies, and the emotional pain of experiencing something for the first time can be acute, and for some difficult to navigate.

In the UK, we do have some data sets relating to students generated by standard measures such as CORE-OM, CORE-10, CCAPs, PHQ-9 and GAD, which uniformly measure presentation alongside severity. Data collated by the Student Counselling Outcomes Research and Evaluation (SCORE) project[3] from four participating university counselling services found that academic distress, followed by social anxiety, generalised anxiety and depression were the most prevalent causes for concern for students (Broglia et al., 2023).

Universities can be wonderful places to study and work. Each is subtly different, depending on size, location, degree programmes and reputation. Likewise, academic enquiry and learning can be rewarding, creative and challenging. But universities are in competition with each other for students, meaning students are also exposed to increasingly skilled and complex marketing. The 'hard sell' raises expectations, hopes and pressures on younger students setting out on their career pathways. It's fanciful and a polarised distortion to think that all students achieve, and that the promised careers happen for all those who graduate. A shadow side of any learning experience is that of failure, rejection, struggle and frustration. Our universities teach, research and create, but they also judge, fail and reject students – and, indeed, academic staff. Those of us who have been working in the sector for a long time have observed a culture shift from primarily academic to a corporate business model, where the payment of fees can increase levels of pressure on students and changes the staff/student relationship to a provider/consumer dynamic. One view of a counselling service in an educational setting is that its role is to support the corporate model of education by facilitating academic attainment and engagement. Likewise, students may have particular expectations of how therapy can help them. This isn't new. Back in 1962, Audrey Newsome, a careers advisor, founded a counselling service at Keele University because she realised that emotional problems were a block to students gaining employment following graduation (Newsome et al., 1973).

Facilitating transformations – Dominic McLoughlin

At the beginning of a counselling contract, when meeting a student for the first time, I tend to introduce the idea that any presenting problem they bring can

---

3. https://score-consortium.sites.sheffield.ac.uk

be seen as dynamically related to their learning environment. When things are going well on the course, we are likely to feel well in ourselves; when the course is a problem, personal difficulties can increase as a result. The studies the student has chosen can be used to meet their personal development as well as their educational needs. This sense of purpose enters the counselling room too, where the brief intervention frame requires the counsellor to be active and focused while also providing space for reflection and the ability to tolerate 'not knowing' (Bion, 1970). Academic enquiry can take many forms, from essay writing to model making, from lab work to pattern cutting. In the therapeutic realm, active learning in personal development involves as many different iterations or idioms as there are students to create them. For counsellor and client, this search for understanding and truth can be seen as operating in parallel to learning in any discipline or subject area, from the arts and humanities to law, from social sciences to business and technology.

This is not to say that in every case the student will want to talk about their university experience. Many will bring problems that are conceived as family or relationship difficulties that have nothing to do with course demands. However, it is crucial to keep the context in mind, as it can have more impact than you or your client might think. Beyond its relationship to the client's mental and emotional state, the learning environment can be used as a therapeutic tool. The counsellor can help the student use the educational impulse as an object of attachment, leading to emotional security and the possibility of transformation in the internal world.

An awareness of this potential for growth is implied in the contract between institution and student, with each party believing that success on the course will mean increased opportunities in the future. Furthermore, symbolically, university can represent a period of transition from youth to maturity, or from dependence to independence (Coren, 1997). But if the student is not able to sit alone and think creatively, operate in a group or gain insights from people who know more than them, they are going to struggle in an academic environment. At a more basic level, the student has to be well enough mentally to function day-to-day, maintain a degree of self-care and enjoy a social life and network that supports their endeavours.

The academic subject they have chosen might turn out to conflict with their sense of self. Equally, the subject area can be a place of self-discovery and personal affirmation. Being alive to these dynamics enables the counsellor to bring the activity of learning into alignment with the student's desire to make personal changes to improve their wellbeing. The work that is done on campus takes place in individual sessions, but also in workshops and outreach activities, bringing to the wider university community the benefits of an emotional and psychological perspective on what it is to flourish and reach one's potential.

Beyond stereotypes, it is important to consider how different academic specialisms might entail particular challenges. Not all computer scientists are binary thinkers and not all fine artists are disorganised. What we can say is that architecture students have to be able to share their work and receive feedback in a group; bio-medical science students have to be able to deal daily with disease and ill health; music and drama students have to be able to perform. These demands can be the seeds of growth and development, alongside which the student may also be grappling with personal, social and cultural history, sexual or gender identity, physical disability, neurodiversity and other learning differences and health challenges, as well as the need for adequate material comfort in an unequal society. The pressure of being assessed can bring further powerful feelings around competition and self-esteem, and these too will find their way into counselling material.

Counselling in further and higher education is shaped by the student's pursuit of knowledge of the self and the world. This may not give rise to the presenting problem, but their learning environment is always meaningful, however far in the background. The student is not at university primarily for developmental or therapeutic reasons and yet their academic work can be a means and a process that leads to beneficial change. A student counsellor is in the privileged position of facilitating and witnessing such transformations.

Sector specifics – Géraldine Dufour, Allie Scott and Desmond Channer

Working in universities and colleges, we need to be mindful of the context in which we are practising and its impact on the students and staff we counsel. Boundaries need to be malleable. We must adapt our model to practise more flexibly to accommodate the changes necessitated by fluctuating teaching timetables, deadlines, exams and placements (where relevant to the course). We need to be aware of the demands placed on a student – for instance, helping them to contain rather than work through their distress if they are approaching the examination term, so that they are able to continue to study. We also commonly work with difficulties related to specific aspects of learning, such as procrastination, group work or the relationship with a PhD supervisor. We support students with additional learning support needs, such as those diagnosed with ADHD or ASD, and write letters of support for mitigating circumstances – all tasks specific to the student context.

High levels of suicidality among the younger student groups mean there is likely to be a complex dynamic within the institution and the counselling dyad (Reeves & Mintz, 2001). In addition, in the case of student deaths, a counselling team might be supporting the whole community or giving advice to staff concerned about a very distressed student. For counsellors working with younger students, a good understanding of safeguarding and duty of care (DfE, 2022) is crucial.

That said, there can be a more relaxed and informal vibe in the college sector, by comparison with universities, which can be a good thing, but it can also impact on the way a counsellor works. There is often an expectation or assumption that you are able to share information about your clients, and you are likely to need to hold boundaries and continually re-establish them with your teaching and administration colleagues.

Across the whole sector, counsellors will need to have a dynamic and flexible approach and be able to adapt to an ever-changing environment – to respond in the moment, move appointments around and accommodate students in distress as well as understand the wider education system.

There is also the pressure to continuously evidence outcomes and present them in a way that others can understand. Clinical outcome measures help us with our work and ensure we are identifying risk but may mean little to senior academics and administrators. However, to demonstrate the value we bring and secure extra funding, we need to find a way to show how our works impacts on academic outcomes, attainment and recruitment, which can be a challenge for the head of service. Sector research has demonstrated that embedded counselling provision can help students continue their study, improve their academic achievement and overall student experience, enhance their employability, improve their self-confidence and boost their hopes for the future (Wallace, 2012).

In the college sector, you may find that you are the sole student counsellor on site and must be a jack of all trades, managing all the bookings and administration and attending numerous meetings with external and internal agencies, such as intra-departmental meetings, multi-disciplinary team meetings with local mental health services and CAMHS, staff training, report writing and promoting the service you provide (at freshers' fairs etc.).

Short-term working – Stella Sookun

Working in the student counselling sector, you will find that there is considerable pressure to turn over your caseload (due to the growing waiting lists), which means you can only offer clients a limited number of sessions. Models such as one-at-a-time and single-session counselling are increasingly popular in the sector and have a good evidence base, and can help to keep waiting lists down (Dryden, 2020; Worley-James, 2020).

Short-term counselling can mean different things depending on the service, from an average of four sessions (Broglia et al., 2023) to between six and eight sessions maximum for a student in distress. This can be a shock for counsellors new to this sector and only trained to work in an open-ended way. In my view, short-term work does require a level of clinical flexibility that can feel challenging at times. You will often be facilitating sessions with a client group who developmentally, by and large, are in a very specific period of flux, anxiety and transition. An ability to 'start with the end in mind' will help counsellors to be clear about the limits to the therapeutic support they can (and can't) offer, within the constraints of the client contact. You will need to develop the skill of taking concise assessments and your capacity to think with a student about their starting goals while maintaining a professional resilience towards the numerous 'beginning and endings' you will experience throughout the academic term, given the volume of students you will have to see and the short-term nature of support.

The higher education environment can be a real gear-changer for some counsellors. Short-term client contracts and fixed academic term times reflect the stressful and ambiguous experiences of some students within institutions where independent learning and academic achievement are the main features. Considering the variety of presentations, it can be really useful for counsellors to be clear about the strengths of their clinical model and how it can be adapted to fit this specific environment. Supervision can be an invaluable space for self-regulation where you can regain confidence in the merits of your own ethical and professional boundaries in the role – particularly given that academic institutions are likely to be dominated by the priorities and fragilities of business decisions and academic visions.

University counselling services can be heavily oversubscribed, like any other therapeutic services. For some students, this is the first time they will have ever spoken to anyone about their early life or current challenges, let alone to a trained counsellor. Student counselling services are seeing clients with an ever-widening range of mental health conditions, complex trauma and neurodiverse presentations. This is compounded by the current context of austerity and chronic underfunding of youth and adult mental health services, and deficits in robust and early therapeutic interventions in schools. Within an almost exclusively short-term counselling model, the stresses on counselling service managers and counsellors can at times be challenging and require a high degree of flexibility.

Last, as much as I always hope to be able to support someone in distress, I think it is useful to consider that sometimes short-term counselling is not the most useful or complete clinical response for a student in difficulty. In these circumstances, counsellors may need to feel confident enough to articulate why this is to other professionals involved with the individual (such as GP, university mental health advisory teams and academic tutors). Importantly, it also raises the profile of counselling and demonstrates why therapeutically informed thinking is so important in this setting.

> **Why I love my job – Stella Sookun, Allie Scott and Desmond Channer**
>
> - Working within a limited number of sessions is a skilful way of working and can raise useful learning edges and growth areas for counsellors. Employment can also offer much financial stability, rewarding work, and a good experience of multidisciplinary ways of working within a larger mental health framework. (Stella)
> - No day is the same, and as I have always felt passionate about learning and mental health, it allows me to combine the two. I also get to meet the most amazing people and to see some of the most beautiful places in Scotland. (Allie)
> - It's rewarding! There is something really special about changing the trajectory of a young person who comes seeking assistance and leaves with a plan. Students in the 16–20 age group are often confused about what they want to do, particularly if they have mental health issues. To see a student take a more rewarding path as a result of your work with them is a wonderful feeling and a gift. It's very different to working in the NHS or in secondary schools. I have found the work with the 16–20 cohort to be challenging at times, but also engaging. You may also have more freedom to jazz up the clinical space in a way that may not be possible in other sectors. Students here have enjoyed contributing towards the décor we have in our counselling service, and we've created a really nice space where they can decompress. (Desmond)

Affordability, access and client attitudes – Géraldine Dufour and Jane Harris

Counselling in universities and colleges is free at the point of delivery, which makes it very accessible to students and staff alike. One of the ever-present tensions of working in the sector is that, at times of pressure, staff and students may find it hard to prioritise their counselling sessions over academic or other demands. This is an issue that a service needs to address though clear policies and contracting, while responding to individual students' circumstances with compassion.

Also, the casualisation of academic contracts means many teaching staff are excluded from accessing university counselling services.

A significant, more recent change in how counselling is accessed is the use of digital self-help platforms and online courses, and the growing popularity of online student support packages that universities and colleges can contract to support their students. These include counsellors working remotely within a wider wellbeing package of support. Some of these collaborations are an attempt to manage growing waiting lists, but universities and colleges are also seeking to adapt to the needs of digital natives, who may find this method of getting support more acceptable than traditional models of weekly in-person counselling sessions. Also, they are more flexible for students who wish to maintain their support during periods away from campus during their studies. It's important here to bear in mind that overseas students travelling home for vacations and those on overseas placements as part of their course are subject to the laws and regulations of the country where they reside during their absence. You may not be registered, insured and qualified to practise there, so check this if you are counselling a student while they are outside the UK (Dufour, 2021).

There is a particular pleasure and opportunity in working therapeutically with someone at a point in their life when their educational, professional and personal development goals converge. We know that clients approaching counselling are seeking to resolve, understand or change something of their lives, experiences and futures. An additional dimension is that a student at university is already pursuing change in the educational-professional domain of life, lending a fertile synergy to the therapeutic task. Intrinsic to this is the hope that lies within the ambition to pursue a higher degree, and therapy can be a powerful tool to identify and mobilise these more or less latent dimensions of the client's internal world.

Generally, there is quite a positive attitude towards counselling in universities and colleges, and little stigma attached to seeing a counsellor. When students do complain, it is often that they would like more frequent access to counselling and more sessions (Shackle, 2019). However, given the broad demographics of the student population, there are likely to be some members of university communities, such as international students, who might not have the same understanding of counselling, or come with very different expectations seeking advice and guidance, rather than self-exploration.

Why I can't imagine working anywhere else – Stefan Wilson

In terms of institutional settings, it is hard to beat working in a university. Major pluses of working in this sector include:

- a diverse client group (particularly in the newer universities) along many dimensions – race, ethnicity, gender identity, socio-economic background, disability, age and so forth
- being able to work with people at a very interesting stage of life that affords many opportunities as well as challenges
- a relaxed yet professional environment
- a well-resourced sector, where counselling is embedded in a wider student support department and has excellent links to mental health, wellbeing, disability, and health services
- a good remuneration and pension package
- less bureaucracy and fewer constraints than the public sector
- a vibrant atmosphere of learning, creativity, and potential.

Some of the challenges in terms of working conditions include a high throughput of clients and short-term interventions (typically six sessions). At my university, we have adopted one-at-a-time counselling, where each session is standalone and the student books in again as and when required (more and more universities are adopting this approach). This means that I generally do not see clients weekly – usually there's at least three weeks between appointments, and sometimes it can be several months. This means it is very important to keep detailed notes in order to help keep track of client material because I have many more clients on my books. For example, I currently have more than 200 clients allocated to me. This still represents a normal weekly caseload of 20–25 client sessions, but it also means I have to keep more people in mind at the same time.

An unfortunate aspect of universities, in my opinion, is that they have become increasingly corporate over the past few years, caused by the eradication of the grants system in favour of student loans, and by the introduction of tuition fees, league tables and a market-driven ideology.

Relatedly, while universities typically make bold public statements about the importance of student welfare and safeguarding, in some institutions it can sometimes feel like the main concern is managing reputational risk rather than actually acting in the best interests of the students. This can be quite demoralising at times. Having said that, these issues rarely make it into the counselling room.

In terms of support, I have found that we are strongly encouraged to engage in self-care and that the university management are truly on board with this. There are regular opportunities for CPD, high-quality learning resources are widely available and there is a general sense of being valued and treated well.

Overall, I would say the higher education sector is a really great place to work. I honestly can't imagine working anywhere else!

A day in my counselling life – Stefan Wilson

My typical working day is, of course, mainly spent seeing clients. At the university where I work, the expectation is for five client hours per day, leaving ample time for writing up notes, dealing with emails, lunch and breaks and so on. Those client hours include team meetings, departmental meetings, updates from the Vice Chancellor and suchlike. We also have a fortnightly meeting just for the counsellors, where we discuss client work and wider university happenings that may impact on our team, or just talk more generally about broader issues within counselling and psychotherapy, which we find of great value as a source of mutual support.

Another regular commitment is a 'duty' day, where my role is also to respond to students presenting with more immediate concerns (our client hours are reduced on duty days to allow for this). For example, the university has an online tool for reporting safeguarding issues, and we will deal directly with those that are relevant to our service. This might involve calling a student where a concern has been raised to make sure they are okay and to assess any risk, encourage them to register with our service, or perhaps to see their GP, or refer them to an external service if necessary. This can be challenging work, and perhaps more a wellbeing role, but it can also be varied and interesting, with some chances to really support students in a time of acute need.

There are quite a few other things to do and get involved in. For example: giving induction talks for new students about our service; giving presentations to university staff about mental health issues; taking part in or running workshops, and taking part in university open days to promote the service. There are also opportunities to contribute to the university's commitment to improving equality, diversity and inclusion within the workplace. University settings tend to be open-minded as well as interested in research, so if you have an idea about a novel way to help students that might be useful, you may well get a chance to put that idea into practice and pilot it with students. University counselling departments commonly offer placements to trainees and volunteers seeking to gain their clinical hours towards qualification or accreditation or learn about our specialist area of practice, and this can offer mentoring opportunities.

More generally, outside of work, you might find time to be part of the university community and attend one of the many events in the university: talks by guest speakers, lunchtime or evening concerts put on by music students, plays, art exhibitions – and all of these are generally free of charge.

I hope I have given some indication of how a day might go in a university counselling service. The main work, as I said, is seeing clients – but there are plenty of opportunities to do something a little different every now and then, which keeps the working day varied and interesting.

Conclusion – Géraldine Dufour

We hope that you have found reading this chapter helpful. As we write, we are aware that things are constantly evolving, bringing new challenges and opportunities. In a sector that welcomes new undergraduates every year, we are continually having to embrace new ways of working and keep up with wider changes in society. To give just one example, when I trained as a counsellor, brief work was a 16-session model (Malan, 1995), very different to the single session therapy or one-at-a-time counselling now offered by many services

We hope that some of our readers will be inspired and enthused to work in university and college counselling services and, in your turn, you will encourage future generations of counsellors to do the same.

Recommended reading

Barden, N. & Caleb, R. (2019). *Student mental health and wellbeing in higher education: A practical guide*. Sage.

Mair, D. (2016). *Short-term counselling in higher education: Context, Theory and practice*. Routledge.

References

Auerbach, R.P., Bruffaerts, R., Alonso, J., Benjet, C., Cuijpers, P. & Murray, E. (2018). WHO World Mental Health Surveys International College Student Project: Prevalence and distribution of mental disorders. *Journal of Abnormal Psychology*, 127(7), 623.

BACP. (2016). *Competences required to deliver effective counselling in further and higher education*. BACP. www.bacp.co.uk/media/2043/bacp-competences-working-in-further-higher-education-counsellors-guide.pdf

BACP. (2017). *University and college counselling services. Sector resource 003*. BACP. www.bacp.co.uk/media/2237/bacp-university-college-counselling-services-sector-resource-003.pdf

Barden, N. & Caleb, R. (2019). *Student mental health and wellbeing in higher education: A practical guide*. Sage Publications.

Barkham, M., Broglia, E., Dufour, G., Fudge, M., Knowles, L., Percy, A., Turner, A., Williams, C. & SCORE Consortium. (2019). Towards an evidence base for student wellbeing and mental health: Definitions, developmental transitions and data sets. *Counselling and Psychotherapy Research*, 19(4), 351–357

Bell, E. (1996). *Counselling in further and higher education*. Open University Press.

Bion, W.R. (1970). *Attention and interpretation*. Karnac.

Broglia, E., Ryan, G. Williams, C. Fudge, M. Knowles, L., Turner, A., Dufour, G., Percy, A., Barkham, M., on behalf of the SCORE Consortium. (2023). Profiling student mental health and counselling effectiveness: Lessons from four UK services using complete data and different outcome measures. *British Journal of Guidance & Counselling*, 51(2), 204–222. https://doi.org/10.1080/03069885.2020.1860191

Coren, A. (1997). *A psychodynamic approach to education*. Sheldon Press.

Department for Education. (2022). *Keeping children safe in education 2022 - Statutory guidance for schools and colleges*. www.gov.uk/government/publications/keeping-children-safe-in-education--2

Dryden, W. (2020). *The single-session counselling primer: Principles and practice*. PCCS Books.

Dufour, G. (2016). Assessment. In D. Mair (Ed.), *Short-term counselling in higher education: Context, theory and practice*. Routledge.

Dufour, G. (2021). University counselling across borders. *University & College Counselling Journal*, 9(2), 20–24.

Hughes, G. & Spanner, L. (2019). *The university mental health charter*. Student Minds.

Lightfoot, L. (2018, July 17). Universities outsource mental health services despite soaring demand. *The Guardian*. www.theguardian.com/education/2018/jul/17/universities-outsource-mental-health-services-despite-soaring-demand

Malan, D. (1995). *Individual psychotherapy and the science of psychodynamics*. Routledge.

Newsome, A., Thorne, B. & Wyld, K. (1973). *Student counselling in practice*. University of London Press.

Reeves, A. & Mintz, R. (2001). Counsellors' experiences of working with suicidal clients: An exploratory study. *Counselling and Psychotherapy Research*, *1*(3), 172–176.

Shackle, S. (2019, September 27). 'The way universities are run is making us ill': inside the student mental health crisis. *The Guardian.* www.theguardian.com/society/2019/sep/27/anxiety-mental-breakdowns-depression-uk-students

Wallace, P. (2012, November). The impact of counselling on academic outcomes: the student perspective. *University & College Counselling*, 6–11.

Worley-James, S. (2020). The evolution of the Cardiff Model. *University & College Counselling*, *8*(4), 14–18.

Chapter 7

Counselling in the third sector

Jeremy Bacon
with Sabrina Bailey

In this exploration of the rich range of opportunities offered to counsellors by the third sector (also known as the voluntary, community and social enterprise (VCSE) sector, or any one of those single identifiers), I have drawn on my 25-year career spanning four organisations and services of different sizes, structures and functions.

My first role in the sector after completing a diploma in social work presented me with opportunities, challenges and learning that have stayed with me and that shaped my subsequent career. I had one of only three paid roles in a small, recently founded organisation in Northampton. My role was to develop and deliver a new, independent mental health advocacy service. The service was led by a management committee at whose core were users and survivors of psychiatric services who had come together in common cause to support others to have a voice in a system that was rooted in a medical model that they had found to be disempowering and ineffective in promoting recovery. Committee members shared a passion for the mission of the service, which was to support and redress systemic power imbalances for people in statutory mental health services. The impact of working with individual clients and seeing the value that they placed on the support provided by the service gave me a sense of vocation – it was unlike any work I'd done before. The defining features of this organisation were its explicit independence from statutory services, a wider advocacy role in promoting and canvassing change, and its proud status as user-led and person-centred in its planning and practice. I recognise many of these features in my contacts since with third-sector organisations. Each has been unique, but their roots are in common.

I currently (2024) work in the policy team at BACP, advocating and campaigning for increased access to and provision of talking therapies. Third-sector counselling services are a rich source of evidence of the impact of talking therapies in improving the lives of individuals and their communities and promoting better mental health and greater emotional literacy more widely. Many are small charities rooted in local communities, created to respond to a particular need. One such is R-evolution for Good, based in Moray in Scotland, which has combined its offer of counselling, coaching and practical assistance to support families to build resilience and navigate their way out of child poverty. Others include counselling services delivered by national charities as part of a wide range of support and advocacy work, such as Barnardo's UK-wide counselling service for people who arrived under the UK government's Homes for Ukraine scheme.

Whatever the size, delivery model or specific client focus of third-sector counselling services, all have in common the ability to reach and respond to people in ways that make psychological therapies accessible and acceptable and remove barriers, such as stigma and the absence of cultural awareness in many mainstream services, that can stop people accessing the help they need.

Background

The third sector is complex, made up of a large and diverse range of organisations with the common defining characteristic of being neither public bodies nor private enterprises and operating on a strict not-for-profit basis. Any profit or surplus income is ploughed back into service delivery. It includes registered charities and community-led associations, self-help groups and community groups, social enterprises such as community interest companies (CICs), mutuals and co-operatives. In surveys conducted by BACP, one-third of its 67,000+ individual members report that they work either part-time or entirely in the third sector, for dedicated counselling organisations or in organisations whose counselling service is part of a range of support and advocacy activities (BACP, 2023). Many counsellors report working in the sector in a portfolio career, alongside private practice or roles in the NHS, teaching, schools or universities and colleges.

The third sector in the UK can trace its roots back many hundreds of years to medieval times and the establishment of religious orders and monasteries that provided aid to the poor and sick. During the 16th and 17th centuries, the emergence of the tradition of philanthropy led to the creation of charitable organisations focused on helping specific groups, such as children and older and disabled people. In the 19th and 20th centuries, charities expanded their scope to address broader social issues, such as poverty, education, social inequalities and health. In more recent decades, the sector has expanded to play a significant role in identifying and addressing social issues and improving the lives of individuals and communities, with varying connections into government departments and policymaking. Through all of this change, development and growth, the sector has been defined by its flexibility and ability to adapt rapidly in order to respond to the changing needs of the communities it serves, with new charities and organisations coming into being in response to new and growing needs as they emerge throughout society.

The 1980s brought a seismic shift in the role of the third sector when the Conservative government introduced legislation that opened the doors to the voluntary sector to deliver what were previously public services. The voluntary sector was seen to be able to provide cost-effective and flexible services, and this diversification also supported the government's neoliberal agenda to reduce the role of statutory services in providing health and social care. Over subsequent decades, the delivery of government contracts by the third sector has increased significantly, particularly in areas such as health, social care and housing. This trend has continued to the present day.

In 2022 an estimated 165,758 voluntary organisations were operating in the UK, most of them either micro or small. They employed almost one million people (950,000), accounting for about 3% of the UK's workforce (NCVO, 2022). England has the highest proportion of charities per head of population in the four UK nations, while Northern Ireland has the lowest. The sector also contributes significantly to the UK economy, with a total value estimated at more than £20 billion in 2019 (NCVO, 2019). This includes the direct value of the goods and services provided by charities, as well as their indirect impact on the economy through increased employment and spending.

Today, third-sector counselling services are resourced from a variety of funding streams, each of which has a bearing on the service models and impact measures used and the ways in which services record and report outcomes. For many third-sector organisations delivering talking therapies in England, the introduction of IAPT (the Improving Access to Psychological Therapies programme, now known as NHS Talking Therapies) from 2008 created opportunities to play a key role in its success (see Chapter 1). Input from the third sector has significantly contributed to the data showing that high-intensity counselling is achieving recovery rates from depression on a par with those of high-intensity CBT (Pybis et al., 2017).

Independence from government is an important part of the history and culture of the sector, with many leading charities involved in campaigning and advocacy as well as service delivery. With the growth in commissioning and greater involvement in delivering public services under contract to statutory bodies, the independence of third-sector organisations has arguably become less clear cut. Some third-sector counselling organisations have taken a principled decision not to bid for NHS contracts. MindOut, a counselling service specialising in work with clients from the LGBTQI+ community in Brighton, operates with an understanding that client trust is paramount when engaging with people who have good reason not to trust or have experienced harm from engagement with mainstream mental health services. MindOut relies on grants, donations and client fees, with counselling delivered by volunteer qualified counsellors and students on placement completing their client hours towards qualification. The service receives referrals but no funding from the NHS, prioritising its independent ethos and values rather than damage its reputational standing in the communities it seeks to reach.

Reflecting on the challenges and dilemmas faced by third-sector counselling services considering seeking funding through delivering services for the NHS, Duncan Craig, chief executive and founder of Manchester-based charity Survivors Manchester, notes that the experience has 'been fraught with anxiety, frustration and conflict, but has also been an opportunity for enormous resolution and growth' (Craig, 2017). For that service, the increased complexity and costs of implementing the standards of data collection and reporting required by its NHS contract presented a considerable burden for a small third-sector organisation but doing so reaped rewards: the service has grown and can now reach many more clients.

Many other third-sector organisations successfully blend NHS contracts for the delivery of talking therapies with other services funded from grants, charitable fundraising and client payments. Working flexibly, these services are able to offer their clients a choice of model and duration of therapy, match clients to the part of the service that best meets their needs and provide opportunities for therapists at different stages of their careers to work within their skills, competence and experience. With their lower overheads, third-sector services are also able to pioneer specialist services for marginalised client groups, opening up the reach of counselling into new arenas that mainstream services cannot serve cost-effectively.

Support for older people

One example of the ability of the third sector to drill down into and reach out to populations that mainstream statutory provision can overlook is its support for older people. Despite age being a protected characteristic under the

Equality Act (2010), ageist attitudes and views remain common. Advertising promoting anti-ageing products and negative portrayals of older people across all media reinforce the idea that old age is a time of decline and depression, and that older people are out of touch with and somehow 'other' than the rest of the adult population. The Royal Society for Public Health reports that one quarter of young adults (18–34 years) believe that it is normal to be unhappy and depressed in old age (RSPH, 2018).

Data from the IAPT programme have consistently shown that, despite better-than-average completion and recovery rates for those who receive therapy, referral and uptake rates among older people fall well below the target of 12% for all referrals (NHS Digital, 2022).

Research and data analysis indicate that, despite the significant prevalence of depression in this age group, people aged 65 and older are less likely to recognise symptoms of common mental health problems, and those that do are less likely to seek help from family, friends or a healthcare professional. Barriers to older people accessing therapy can be attitudinal, structural and practical, and include lack of knowledge, familiarity with and understanding of what therapy is, the stigma and shame that can be attached to the concepts and language of mental health, and a reluctance among family and others to suggest or recommend therapy. Community-based third-sector organisations such as local Age UK services play an important role in providing much-needed support, and many local organisations include psychological therapies in their wider suite of services.

As part of the UK-wide Big Lottery-funded Ageing Better Programme, Sheffield Mind was funded to deliver a three-year project to focus on improving access to talking therapy services for older people experiencing or at risk of loneliness. 'Doing therapy differently' included offering clients appointments in their own homes. In its report on the project, Sheffield Mind reflected on the learning gained:

> Therapists were very aware that, for this client group, it was the first time that many of them were confronting certain issues and emotions. The depth and quality of therapeutic relationship will be a factor in allowing the client to come to terms with their loneliness and with life as it is. By showing warmth, compassion and honesty, the therapist is modelling a healthy relationship. The outcome from the final data may indicate that the person is in the same position as before but with greater inner peace and potential to change. Therapy with this client group was not aimed at 'fixing problems' but rather at increasing the levels of comfort a person feels with themself and encouraging them to want to have healthy connections and build positive relationships with others. In many cases

people were not simply isolated from other people but they had become isolated from themselves, from nature, from hobbies and interests. Loneliness was so much more than the absence of company. Therapy led to new levels of self-awareness for many of the clients, which in turn led to the admission that they were indeed lonely and had become socially isolated. (Brocklehurst & Cliff, 2021)

The messages from the Sheffield project about the value of therapy increasing comfort for older adults is reflected in Helen Kewell's book *Living Well and Dying Well: Tales of counselling older people*, in which she draws on case studies of counselling eight older people ranging in ages from 75 to 95 (Kewell, 2019). In her analysis of the case studies, what emerges is the value for older people of having the opportunity to tell their life stories, find meaning in their lives and reconcile fears of mortality. Kewell urges therapists working with older clients to believe that growth is possible at any stage of life and argues vehemently that older age or perceived frailty should not be a barrier to therapeutic work.

Yet older people are still rarely seen in the therapy room. An analysis of data from a small sample of third-sector counselling services across the UK found that, in services open to adults of all ages, only 4.1% were aged 65 and older, despite making up 19% of the UK population (O'Donnell et al., 2021). As the UK population ages, demand for later-life psychological support will increase and the third sector is well placed to recognise and respond to this growing need. Within the psychological research community, there is a growing focus on the value of therapy for people affected by dementia (Bell et al., 2022) and a recognition of the importance of increasing access to therapy in care homes.

Racially minoritised communities

Third-sector counselling services, because they are often pioneered by individuals from a particular community for that community, can use their status as trusted sources of support to make therapy more accessible and acceptable to marginalised groups known to under-use mainstream psychological services. There is longstanding evidence that racialised communities are least likely to seek help for their mental health and have poorer outcomes from services. Cultural stigma associated with help-seeking, mistrust of the statutory mental health services, the sense that clinicians in mainstream services have a poor understanding of different cultural needs, and the expectation and experience of racism within these services contribute to deterring people from racialised communities from accessing the help and support they need (see, for example, Bignall et al., 2022).

Pattigift Therapy, located in Birmingham, specialises in working with clients of African ancestry – adults, couples and families. Pattigift is contracted by the Birmingham NHS commissioners to deliver NHS Talking Therapies services to its client group, ensuring they have the same choice as any other adult in England to access free counselling. Often clients completing the NHS therapy move on to continue to attend Pattigift's group therapy sessions and peer-support groups. To supplement its NHS contract, which is its primary source of income, Pattigift seeks funding from grant-making and charitable bodies to run its other services. It also raises some monies from charging people who self-refer to the service, on a sliding scale.

Pattigift's approach is psychodynamic and integrative, and founded on an African-centred understanding of human psychology. Consciously, the service ethos reaches back to the African heritage of clients as the point of connection, rather than 'Blackness' as a common identity. Pattigift founder and clinical director Rameri Moukam argues:

> Being Black in a majority-white community includes having a racialised identity and being 'othered' by the white majority. At Pattigift, a client is encouraged to step away from and challenge the definitions and identities that others give them and bring their true self into therapy. In their therapist, a client will have someone who has significant shared experience and connection. (BACP, 2022 p.8)

Pattigift's service delivery models are constantly adapted to ensure that it is meeting the needs of service users. In addition to using routine, established outcome measures (GAD-7, PHQ-9), as required by its NHS commissioners, Pattigift draws on learning from the American Black psychological movement to assess clients' progress and outcomes: for example, if Black people are engaging and completing therapy, that is seen as a positive outcome, not just evidence of improvement.

It does not conceptualise its clients' difficulties as mental ill health, and instead turns the focus towards wellness and prevention of poor mental health. To that end, Pattigift has been able to build strong links with other community organisations, churches and community networks and become a trusted resource for people from Black communities.

As noted earlier, the stigma attached to mental ill health generally, and reluctance to talk about personal issues that are painful or troubling, can impact on older people of all backgrounds, and can have particular resonance in some communities. In her exploration of attitudes towards talking therapies among older African Caribbean women, Helen George (2015) found both a deep-rooted cultural belief that you 'don't talk your business to people', as well as a fear and distrust of health services and the consequences of being labelled 'mentally ill'.

Serving communities

Pattigift's links into Birmingham's communities of African heritage is just one example of how third-sector organisations often have strong ties to the communities they serve. This gives them insights into and understanding of the specific needs of those communities and thus the ability to address health inequalities. Another is the hospice movement, which has grown substantially in the UK over the past 50 years in response to the palliative care needs of an ageing population. Hospices are charitable bodies offering a unique level of care that is not available directly from the NHS. The work is often closely linked to oncology healthcare. Many hospices have in-house counselling services that work with people who are living with a terminal illness or receiving end-of-life care, and with their grieving and bereaved families (see Chapter 8 for John Wilson's discussion of working in this sector). Hospices mostly have strong links with their local communities and benefit from charitable funding raised within those communities.

The physical locations and settings of third-sector counselling services are also important in increasing access to therapy as a valued community resource. Aisling Centre, located in County Fermanagh, Northern Ireland, serves a largely rural community from its base in the town of Enniskillen. The counselling service emerged in response to the economic and social conditions of the time, which included the ongoing political conflict and violence (commonly referred to as 'The Troubles') and the trauma felt in the community following the Remembrance Day bombing in 1987. In the early days of Aisling Centre, the founders brought in specialist services from organisations outside the area, such as support for survivors of sexual abuse. Over time, the service developed to establish its own in-house offer of therapy and support, and today it is funded through GP contracts, grants and donations, and offers student placements as part of its delivery model. The centre is now widely considered to be part of the fabric of the local community. Alongside its counselling service for adults, the centre has a community hub, with support groups, classes and a coffee shop that are open to all and provide a first step for many to access its services.

One of the enduring strengths recognised in the UK voluntary sector is its flexibility and responsiveness to changing needs and circumstances. Many third-sector counselling services have emerged in response to specific problems in a distinct community that will not be effectively dealt with by services designed to meet wider population need.

Lenadoon Community Counselling Service was established in 1998 as a direct response to rising suicide rates among young people locally. Situated at an interface between two predominantly Catholic/Nationalist/Republican and Protestant/Unionist/Loyalist housing estates in Belfast, in an area that is still deeply impacted by the traumatic legacy of political conflict and violence in Northern Ireland, people from within the Lenadoon community came together to set up a service to support bereaved families, with the aim of tackling the underlying mental health problems contributing to the suicides. Set up as an ad hoc response to support those affected by suicide, the service received support and advice to become established as a counselling service. Initially it was part of a pilot suicide prevention project to increase take-up of counselling through GP referrals from across west Belfast. Over time, it has become part of the fabric of its local community and is able to respond rapidly to events that impact the community, as well as lead on suicide prevention work. The development of a crisis intervention service has been a key extension to the service provision within the community. The closeness of the organisation to the community it serves also plays out in its provision of student placements, encouraging people from the community to train as therapists, with many staff having first encountered Lenadoon Community Counselling as students.

Because they are often based within the communities they serve, third-sector services are better able to build relationships, understand needs and adapt the ways they work accordingly, and flexibly. Moray-based counselling and coaching service R-evolution for Good has its roots in the Moray School Bank, which was founded to provide practical support to families living in poverty. Through conversations with families about their practical and material needs, it became apparent that there was a deeper unmet need and, despite following each of the three steps to reduce child poverty recommended by the Scottish government – increasing earnings from paid employment, reducing household costs, and accessing eligible benefits (Scottish Government, 2018) – families still felt trapped. Beyond the practical help of providing families with school uniforms, footwear and stationery, an additional need for guidance and support to make lasting changes emerged. With business planning support from a community development initiative, in 2018–2019 services were extended to include the choice of coaching and counselling, and R-evolution for Good came into being. To date, the service has found that most families initially opt for coaching support and move on to counselling if further needs are identified by a family member during the coaching sessions to address underlying trauma that may sit alongside their experiences of poverty.

Development manager Debi Weir describes how the service is able to flex to meet changing needs so that the client retains agency over how and whether the counselling progresses:

> We put the processes in place that support and enable them to do that work, but the family decide where and when the work happens and the pace at which they work. People's situations change and impact upon the way they work. For instance, someone who may have recently started a new job will need to adapt to the increased demands on their time and changes in income. Once things have settled down and they have adapted to their changed circumstances, they may choose to end our work together, and that will be their decision when the time feels right. (BACP, 2021)

Advocates for change

In addition to providing counselling services, third-sector organisations in the UK play an important role in advocating for change through public campaigns, policy briefings, lobbying, networking and coalition building, and engaging with policymakers. By advocating for change and highlighting the needs of communities and individuals, charities help to ensure that the perspectives and experiences of those they serve are taken into account in policy and legislative debates. This can be seen at local and national levels. For example, under the banner 'Fund the Hubs', some 50 third-sector organisations have come together, supported by some of the larger mental health charities, in a campaign calling on the government to establish community-based one-stop hubs to widen choice for children and young people aged up to 25, including access to free counselling in community settings.

Large national third-sector organisations such as Barnardo's and the Refugee Council take active policy roles in campaigning for change, drawing on the direct experience and themes that come from contact with those they support, including clients in therapy. The Refugee Council works directly with politicians across the UK parliaments through the All-Party Parliamentary Group on Refugees. It holds regular meetings in parliament and provides parliamentarians with the latest research and developments in UK and global asylum and refugee policy. This work includes campaigning and lobbying for increased provision of mental health support and therapy.

Student placements

For many counsellors, the third sector offers an invaluable and eye-opening opportunity while they are training, through its offer of placements to students seeking to build up their practice hours prior to qualification. The student gets work experience and support from experienced colleagues in a real-life, rewarding setting, and in return many third-sector counselling services are able to offer free or low-cost counselling because they do not have to pay the students who are delivering it. In addition, host organisations will often offer professional mentoring and personal development opportunities and activities, CPD resources and in-house training. For some students, the placement experience leads to lasting connections with the host organisation and paid employment once they qualify.

'Trust your instincts and be true to your values and ethos'

Bedfordshire Open Door is an award-winning charity offering free and confidential counselling to young people aged 13–25 resident in the borough of Bedford and North Central Bedfordshire. Founded in 1995 in response to a gap in support for young people, the service has grown and developed over time, gaining accreditation from BACP in 2011. Sabrina Bailey completed her student placement with Open Door and found it a career-defining experience that shaped her counselling practice. This is her experience.

I didn't set out to be a therapist and it wasn't an ambition that I'd held from earlier years. I was working as a self-employed freelance physical trainer – work I really loved. Many of my clients had goals relating to weight loss, and as I worked with them, it became more and more apparent to me that, alongside the need for physical exercise programmes, many people were facing emotional and psychological barriers. Successfully working with them to achieve their goals inevitably involved acknowledgement of these, so I started to become interested in psychological wellbeing. At the same time, I was finding that my chosen profession was becoming increasingly competitive, and that the viability of my own business was at risk from other providers charging lower fees. The work was also unpredictable and seasonal, with an influx of clients in the New Year that dropped off over time. I took on a role with a large gym, hoping that it would be a more supportive and secure environment, but it proved to be just as cut-throat and competitive, and this sat uneasily with me. It was my partner who first sowed the seed for my change in career. 'You're very good at giving advice,' he said, 'Why don't you consider becoming a counsellor?'

My first step was to contact the local college and enrol to complete the 10-week introduction to counselling course. This was my first eye-opener! Everything that I'd thought counselling would be about was proved wrong – it was nothing to do with giving advice and instead I was surprised to find myself beginning a journey of self-exploration that enabled me to better understand myself, my motivations and relationships, and even to be a better mum. Looking back now, I can see how the personal development and healing that came from that initial training made me want to go further with my learning and development as a person and as a therapist.

Over the next three years, I continued working through the training, until I was ready to undertake the Level 4 course at the same college. My college tutor was one of the most empathic people I'd ever met, and by the time I was ready to embark on my first placement, I'd developed a focus and knew that I had to find somewhere I would feel safe, where I could be true to my values and honest in my work, in a supportive collective, rather than a competitive working environment.

We were given a list of counselling services covering a wide geographical area around the college. Initially, I contacted a counselling service that specialised in work with survivors of rape and sexual abuse. I was accepted and completed the service's 10-week induction training. However, when I was asked to immediately start my placement working with three clients, I felt that this would be too much for me and that it would take me beyond my skills and competence. Although my course-mates were progressing with their placements, for me it was more important to 'get it right' than to 'get it done', so my unease at the size of the caseload, coupled with the practical demands of a long journey to work and its impact on my self-care, persuaded me not to continue with this placement.

At my tutor's suggestion, I made email contact with Bedfordshire Open Door, having looked at the organisation's website and been struck by the values and purpose of the service. Although it's a service for children and young people, it continues to see clients up to the age of 25, which was important for me, in order to get enough client hours with adults. The reply from the service lead was positive, warm and encouraging, and we set up a first meeting. I instantly knew, on visiting the service and meeting Donna, the clinical manager, who would also be my supervisor, that this was the right place for me. When we spoke, I was able to be honest in my responses to her questions. Asked about how I felt about working with my first client, my honest response was, 'I've spent so much time learning about Carl Rogers, that I kinda want to be him. But I'm not him. I'm Sabrina, and I don't know if that's going to be enough.'

I'll never forget Donna's reply. She told me that the work was going to be about the relationships and that, by bringing myself into the therapy room, I would allow the client to do the same, and that is what would make the therapy work. She gave me permission to be Sabrina. This set the tone for the whole placement and for my subsequent relationship with the service. Allowing me to be myself also included practical assistance with travel costs and working with me to fit my counselling sessions around my family commitments. I felt understood and valued, and this was the culture of the organisation, with no hierarchy or division, just a real sense of shared purpose, openness and support.

I started with two clients, who had been assessed as having moderate needs related to anxiety stemming from pressures at home and school, and I saw each of them once a week for 12 weeks. I'd done some practice contracting sessions with Donna, where she'd encouraged me to do the contracting in my own way, naturally, not following a formal text-book process, and this allowed me to set the scene for the work that followed.

The supportive culture of the organisation came into its own when I started working with another client. Initially assessed as presenting with moderate levels of anxiety, as the work progressed the client began to bring problems that were more complex and related to a history of abuse. My initial response was that I needed to step back and let the client work with a more experienced therapist, but supervision with Donna gave me confidence that the therapeutic relationship was strong and that it was this dynamic that had allowed the client to disclose their hidden hurt and so provided the basis for ongoing therapy. To support my continued work with this client, the service paid for me to have personal therapy in addition to my in-house supervision.

As my placement progressed, my confidence grew and I felt able to increase my caseload to five clients – a prospect I would have found daunting at the outset. The support of the service was constant and vital to this growth.

As the only Black, female therapist working in the service at the time, I was able to bring issues related to race and identity into my supervision conversations and this was important in allowing me to truly be myself. On one occasion, a colleague witnessed a racially framed microaggression directed towards me from the parents of a client, and she stepped in immediately to address it sensitively but forcefully. They had my back.

Another key element of my placement was access to regular one-day CPD opportunities, giving me access to training from experts. The events were often delivered on Saturdays and Donna was always there to welcome and introduce the learners to the presenters. Topics for CPD were rich and varied and included training on anger, working with autistic clients, trauma and sexual violence. In 2019, before the Covid-19 pandemic was even on the horizon, I took up the offer of 80 hours of training to work remotely by telephone and online. When the pandemic lockdown restrictions came into force, I was able to immediately switch to remote working, still receiving support and supervision from the service. After every training session, I was given formal feedback and encouraged to suggest new topics for CPD sessions.

On completion of my placement in 2020, I decided that I wanted to continue to work for Bedfordshire Open Door. It's a service that reflects my own values and all that I am as a person, so it was an easy decision to take. Initially I took on unpaid client hours to develop my skills and competence. Over time, this developed into paid sessional work as my caseload grew, and I was able to fit this in around my personal life and other commitments.

Five years after my first contact with Open Door, I'm now moving on to a new full-time role in another service, delivering long-term therapy to victims of sexual violence. I'm going into this work with the empathy, skills and abilities that I believe can help empower clients to be themselves, all of which have been gifted to me by the opportunities, support and growth I experienced after sending that first tentative email to Open Door. Looking back on my experience, I'd advise counselling students to trust their instincts and be true to themselves and their own values and ethos in choosing a third-sector organisation for their placement or to work in. I'm not Carl Rogers, I'm Sabrina – my placement and all that it provided, has set me on this course.

The vexed question of volunteering

There are dilemmas associated with volunteering in the third sector. They are complex and relate not only to funding but also to the requirement for high-quality student placements, post-qualification experience for counsellors and availability of services and choice of therapies for marginalised and under-served clients. Counselling services in the third sector have been criticised for their use of unpaid students and volunteer qualified therapists to allow them to keep their services affordable and accessible. And volunteering is by no means exceptional in the profession. In a workforce mapping survey, BACP found that 60% of respondents in the third sector worked some unpaid hours every week, compared with 30% in private practice, and a quarter of members working in the third sector reported no earnings (24%) – a higher proportion than among those working in private practice or the public sector (BACP, 2023).

It is a complex situation created in part by how services are funded, partly by the need for trainees to gain practical experience and accreditation, and partly by the personal choice of some therapists to volunteer with services with which they have a particular connection or interest in supporting.

As a professional body representing 67,000+ members across the four nations of the UK, BACP campaigns for increased paid employment opportunities for qualified therapists and more government investment in counselling services to meet growing demand for psychological support. The reality for many third-sector services, and perhaps particularly for those whose ethos and mission precludes them from taking on publicly financed contracts, is that they cannot afford to pay all their therapists if they are to ensure what they offer is affordable for the communities they strive to reach. However, many therapists consider that unpaid work devalues what counsellors offer and their skills and training, and undermines their professional status. These are issues that counsellors considering working in the third sector will need to consider.

For those wishing to work in the voluntary sector, this may present a dilemma if they need to earn a living from counselling. Indeed, counselling may not be considered an affordable career for those without a second income stream, which inevitably impacts on the demographic profile of the counselling professions. The training itself can be hugely expensive, which also restricts access to those with alternative incomes. But, while organisations and professional bodies grapple with these ethical and moral issues and campaign for increased state funding for therapy, it remains the case that, without these volunteers, many clients would not have access to vital support and many third-sector services would not be able to continue to operate.

Toby Sweet, CEO of Sunderland Counselling Service, explains the importance of volunteering for him, personally, and the opportunities and benefits that it presents for counsellors:

> In my sector, there is a long tradition of people giving their time and labour for free, which benefits not only the service or the client, but also the volunteer. In the course of my career, I have done a lot of voluntary work, alongside paid roles. For me, there was something powerful in

the knowledge that I was making a deliberate choice to give my time to help someone – and that brought its own rewards. In many parts of the voluntary sector, such as the hospice movement, that tradition of community involvement has been a powerful and mobilising force. (Sweet, 2022, p.29)

There should be no contradiction in vigorously making the case for increased state investment that ensures all qualified therapists get a fair rate of pay that recognises the value of what they do while acknowledging the critical need for volunteers to support the survival of the third sector. Without it, clients would be denied the life-changing therapy that more affluent people can afford.

Conclusion

The third sector in the UK plays a vital role in our social and economic landscape, providing essential services and support to individuals and communities in need and advocating for change on behalf of these communities. Through its flexible and responsive approach, high-quality services and commitment to social justice, the sector strives to make a positive and lasting impact on the lives of people across the four UK nations. These values are also central to counselling as a profession, with its overall aim to facilitate all individuals to live their lives to their full potential. The sector provides a vast range of opportunities for counsellors to deliver life-changing therapy to clients and communities, often at low cost or free, and in accessible and acceptable settings within the communities themselves. It also offers the chance to counsellors to specialise in work with particular groups, thereby providing a vast array of opportunities for learning, development and innovation and the chance to bring their values to bear on their professional practice.

Acknowledgements

I am grateful to therapists and managers from the third-sector counselling services who have shared their insights and experiences in this chapter. I am particularly grateful to Sabrina Bailey for her generosity and trust in contributing her personal story.

References

BACP. (2021). R-evolution for good. *Coaching Today, 39*(July), 22–23.

BACP. (2022). *Race for the soul of the profession: Tackling racial inequalities in the counselling profession.* BACP. www.bacp.co.uk/media/15293/bacp-presidents-paper-race-for-the-soul-may22.pdf

BACP. (2023). *2021–2022 workplace mapping survey.* BACP. www.bacp.co.uk/about-us/about-bacp/2021-2022-workplace-mapping-survey

Bell, G., El Baou, C., Saunders, R., Buckman, J.E.J., Charlesworth, G., Richards, M., Brown, B., Nurock, S., Michael, S., Ware, P., Aguirre, E., Rio, M., Cooper, C., Pilling, S., John, A. & Stott, J. (2022). Effectiveness of primary care psychological therapy services for the treatment of depression and anxiety in people living with dementia: Evidence from national healthcare records in England. *EClinicalMedicine, 52*, 101692. doi: 10.1016/j.eclinm.2022.101692

Bignall, T., Jeraj, S., Helsby, E. & Butt, J. (20-22). *Racial disparities in mental health: Literature and evidence review.* Race Equality Foundation.

Brocklehurst, R. & Cliff, G. (2021). *Why we need to do therapy differently: A therapist's guide to working with older people.* Sheffield Mind. https://agefriendlysheffield.org.uk/wp-content/uploads/2021/09/Why-we-need-to-do-therapy-differently-report-1-1.pdf

Craig, D. (2017). Eyes on the prize: Achieving IAPT compliance within third sector mental health provision. *Healthcare Counselling and Psychotherapy Journal, 17*(1), 18–21.

George, H. (2015). 'You don't talk your business to people'. *Therapy Today, 26*(9), 12–16.

Kewell, H. (2019). *Living well and dying well: Tales of counselling older people.* PCCS Books.

NCVO. (2019). *UK Civil Society almanac 2019. Data. Trends. Insights.* NCVO. https://ncvo-app-wagtail-mediaa721a567-uwkfinin077j.s3.amazonaws.com/documents/ncvo_uk_civil_society_almanac_2019_final.pdf

NCVO. (2022). *UK Civil Society almanac 2022:. Data. Trends. Insights.* NCVO. https://www.ncvo.org.uk/news-and-insights/news-index/uk-civil-society-almanac-2022/#/

NHS Digital. (2022). *Psychological therapies: Annual report on the use of IAPT services, 2021–2022.* NHS Digital. https://digital.nhs.uk/data-and-information/publications/statistical/psychological-therapies-annual-reports-on-the-use-of-iapt-services/annual-report-2021-22

O'Donnell, J., Pybis, J. & Bacon, J. (2021). Counselling in the third sector: To what extent are older adults accessing these services and how complete are the data third sector services collect measuring client psychological distress? *Counselling & Psychotherapy Research, 21*(2), 382–392.

Pybis, J., Saxon, D., Hill, A. & Barkham, M. (2017). The comparative effectiveness and efficiency of cognitive behaviour therapy and generic counselling in the treatment of depression: Evidence from the 2nd UK National Audit of psychological therapies. *BMC Psychiatry, 17*, 215. https://doi.org/10.1186/s12888-017-1370-7

RSPH. (2018). *That age old question.* Royal Society for Public Health. www.rsph.org.uk/static/uploaded/a01e3aa7-9356-40bc-99c81b14dd904a41.pdf

Scottish Government. (2018). *Every child, every chance: The Tackling Child Poverty delivery plan 2018–22.* Scottish Government.

Sweet, T. (2022). Third person. *Healthcare Counselling & Psychotherapy Journal, 22*(1), 29.

Chapter 8

Counselling in hospice settings

John Wilson
with Paul Parsons

I need to say from the outset that working in a hospice is not for everyone. It's a cliché to say that it takes a special kind of person, but in my experience, I think it probably does. I've worked with amazing doctors, nurses, social workers and many different ancillary workers, as well as volunteers. A hospice is a community, an extended family, where it's easy to make friends for life. Yet the idea of working with death, dying and bereavement worries many therapists. Even the idea of walking into a hospice can make some people anxious.

It's a common misconception that hospices are where you go to die. Only a small part of a hospice work is about peaceful death. Mostly it's about helping people to live a full, pain-controlled life for the time they have left. We're all dying, but some people have more idea when that will be than others. Hospices are places where people with life-limiting conditions come to receive palliative medication, sometimes as day patients, sometimes with a stay on the inpatient unit until their optimum medical care is established, after which they can return home. The day centres are lively places where patients meet friends, engage in activities and are entertained. Many hospice patients also have access to complementary therapies, as well as physiotherapy and occupational therapy, as part of their treatment. If you feel that this work is for you, hospices are a rewarding and fulfilling place to work.

CPD opportunities

It isn't just the day centre that is a bustling hive of activity. Most hospices have an education centre that offers training for health professionals. This means they also have well-stocked specialist libraries. If you work in a hospice, you never have to look far for continuing professional development (CPD) opportunities, and if your hospice doesn't offer the training you seek, another within reach certainly will. The hospice education centre will probably also host self-help groups for people with life-limiting conditions and their carers. Many hospices have support groups for carers, which offer both respite from the caring role and a chance to share thoughts and feelings without being judged. These support groups tend to be run by nurses, social workers or counsellors/psychotherapists. Very often, teams are multi-disciplinary, and this can raise ethical dilemmas around confidentiality for counsellors and psychotherapists. But I will discuss this further later in the chapter.

A tradition of professionals and volunteers

Counsellors who work in hospices will generally be part of the hospice bereavement support service. For various reasons, mostly historical, this service is not always managed by a counsellor. Many such teams are led by qualified and experienced social workers, who have considerable expertise and experience in using counselling skills to support bereaved people but may also problem-solve and offer practical support consistent with a social work model, rather than a person-centred therapeutic one. Some teams will include counsellors and social workers and may be coordinated by a manager from either profession. For these reasons, your job title may be 'bereavement supporter', although my name badge from my hospice days did describe me as a counsellor.

As well as having paid staff, it is a long tradition, dating back to the earliest service at St Christopher's Hospice, for hospice bereavement services to use teams of volunteers. Colin Murray Parkes, a pioneer of bereavement studies, demonstrated that well-trained volunteers are effective in offering bereavement support using a person-centred counselling skills model (Parkes, 1981, 2002). Four decades later, such teams often include counsellors and psychotherapists whose day job is in private practice and who wish to give something back to their community. In these teams you are also likely to find people from many other occupations who wish to offer their time freely to bereaved people. My hospice role included managing and mentoring a large team of volunteers and teaching counselling skills and bereavement counselling theory and practice. It was this aspect of my work that was the genesis of my first book (Wilson, 2013). Many volunteers become so interested in the work that they go on to train in counselling or psychotherapy. Some may remain as unpaid volunteers, while others may seek paid employment opportunities.

I was a volunteer for a few months before I got a paid post in the same hospice. Volunteers generally receive travel expenses, free in-house CPD and free group supervision. Ideally this supervision should be from outside the hospice and independent of management. I greatly valued group supervision because of the opportunity to learn both from my peers and from an experienced supervisor. My volunteer group supervisor became my one-to-one supervisor for 20 years, until she retired.

Student placement opportunities

Many bereavement support services offer counselling student placements. These placements are highly sought after and highly selective. Tough selection processes are an ethical imperative. More than once, my line managers and I interviewed a cohort of students looking for placements and didn't accept any of them. Bereaved people are, for a short time, very vulnerable, and students must be committed to working with grief, rather than just looking for any placement to meet their course requirements. The client must always come first, before the needs of the placement student.

Those successful in gaining a placement will have done their homework in acquiring a basic knowledge of the models of grief, will have explored the hospice and bereavement service website in order to be able to answer some searching interview questions, and will have convinced the interviewers that they genuinely want to work with grief. If a service is big enough to take students on placement, the chances are that it will be an excellent experience, with opportunities for furthering your knowledge and experience through mentoring and in-house CPD. You may receive free supervision as part of your placement, but this isn't guaranteed.

Securing a professional post

To successfully apply for a permanent job as a bereavement counsellor in a hospice, you are likely to need experience in this field, either from a student placement or from volunteering. The strongest candidates are not always the volunteers in that service, but internal applicants are advantaged in knowing how the service works and what is expected of them.

Experience and expertise are essential components in hospice bereavement work. Since the client/therapist relationship is central, so too are your personal qualities. The vicarious emotional load can be great, so self-care and the ability to switch off from work when you leave at the end of the shift are vital. All this comes from experience. You will not necessarily have to be accredited, but there may be an expectation that you are working towards accreditation. This is an area of work where older counsellors are welcomed. I was over 50 when I got my first paid hospice role. If you consider the demographic profile of bereaved people, you will see that most prefer to work with somebody near to their age or older (Furnham & Swami, 2008). This doesn't preclude younger counsellors from the role, but mature counsellors may be at an advantage.

Back in 2001, when I first began working as a paid hospice counsellor, I found it a huge culture shock. Having volunteered to see a maximum of two clients each week, suddenly I had a diary with up to five clients every working day – men and women bereaved of loving relationships, often in tragic and traumatic ways. I was aware that my predecessor was only in the job for a short time, and for a few weeks I wondered if I was up to it myself. It was only after discussing my concerns honestly with my line manager that, with their reassurance and good supervision, I overcame my fears. If you can do the job, this is some of the most rewarding work you will find anywhere in counselling. I stayed in that post until 2017. I fell completely in love with the work and valued the privilege of being trusted by so many people at the lowest ebb of their life.

The broad spectrum of work

Hospice counselling can take many avenues. While some hospices work only with the bereaved families of former hospice patients, others may work in the wider community. The service I worked for was community based. Hospice-related bereavements were only a third of our workload. Beyond those, we saw clients bereaved from any cause, and that included miscarriages and neonatal deaths. Counselling after traumatic and violent deaths presented more complex challenges, since it is recognised that sudden, unexpected and violent deaths generally lead to more complicated grief (Burke & Neimeyer, 2013) than peaceful, 'good' deaths, which in fact are the norm in hospice inpatient units. When counselling for any bereavement, I strongly believe that the work should not be time limited. In some circumstances – typically, the loss of a child or a partner – normal grief can continue over two years or more (Bonanno, 2010). However, as a counsellor/researcher, I have found that most clients require six sessions or less (Wilson et al., 2016). Some do require longer work, and they push the mean number of sessions up to ten. I have long maintained that bereavement work should never be a fixed number of sessions, precisely because most people need little or no help, but a few can benefit from more significant input.

Who benefits from counselling

By its very nature, a hospice is a place where recently bereaved and very distressed relatives will be passing through its doors, and it might be tempting to routinely offer bereavement support to all those who have lost loved ones. The weight of evidence suggests that it is far better to wait for people to self-refer than routinely to offer support for all (Schut et al., 2001). The same study concluded that there were no benefits in offering support in the first six months of loss. Indeed, there are indications that early support for no reason other than a person has been bereaved may do harm (Fortner & Neimeyer, 1999). Many services have taken this research on board, and although they may meet potential clients to reassure, normalise and offer guidance on getting through the early weeks and months of bereavement, they do not offer formalised support during the initial period of grief.

I mentioned earlier that, as a qualified counsellor in a hospice bereavement service, you will very possibly be working alongside social workers and volunteers who may or may not be counsellors. However, for historical reasons predicated on bereavement research dating back to the genesis of bereavement support (Parkes, 1981), these services tend to use a person-centred counselling skills model. This model embraces the Rogerian core conditions and skills. One of the first training manuals used in hospices (Faulkner & Wallbank, 1998) took such an approach.

Hospice services tend to embrace such a breadth of knowledge and expertise that bereaved clients, once assessed, can be allocated to the member of staff or volunteer who is best equipped to meet their needs. A triage system (NICE, 2004) is often the basis of allocation. Component 1 describes normal grief that does not require formal support, although information and guidance may help. Component 2 offers space and support to explore thoughts and feelings, and this can be provided by trained volunteers. Component 3 interventions are the task of counsellors or counselling psychologists, who will work within their professional competency and will know if they need to refer on to other mental health professionals.

The assessment of the needs of bereaved people is vital. George Bonanno (2010) found in his observations of trajectories of grief that roughly half of people bereaved of someone close are resilient, and Schut and colleagues (2001) confirmed that this group is not helped by counselling. Nevertheless, in the early weeks following the loss, even the most resilient person may be frightened and confused. My experience is that the first session should provide a therapeutic space for the client to tell their story and discuss their thoughts and feelings. It is often helpful to explain the process of grief, to allay any fear and confusion. When this is done sensitively, around half of the clients I meet in hospices need no further sessions, so long as the initial assessment session is conducted therapeutically (Wilson et al., 2016).

The counsellor working with clients who are assessed to need specialist bereavement support requires not only the personal qualities essential to relating to bereaved people, but also knowledge and understanding of the grieving process. In all my experience of interviewing counsellors and students for courses, placements and jobs, I have met many who have little knowledge of what is needed. If you are considering applying for a job in bereavement counselling, familiarise yourself with the principal models of grief before completing your application form and preparing for your interview. Why is it so important? Bereaved people are often at a very low and vulnerable time in their life. They are confused and puzzled by their grief reaction. Experience has taught me that what the client in front of me wants is someone who understands their experience and can reassure them with informed explanations. Psychoeducation has an important role in this work.

Applying theoretical models

A number of models and theories of grief have been developed since the 1990s. Before then, counsellors tended to use 'stage' models of grief (Bowlby & Parkes, 1970; Kubler-Ross, 1969). These models typically describe an initial period of numbness, denial or dissociation from reality. This is followed by protest at the reality and searching behaviour to locate the lost loved one. When that inevitably fails, the bereaved person typically goes through a phase of despair and depression, followed by, in the case of normal grief, a period of reorganisation and recovery as they adapt to life without the deceased. But this is seldom a linear process; clients move to and fro between these phases.

However, stage models have become largely of historical interest and are no longer considered best counselling practice in bereavement services. As Parkes (2009) subsequently recollected, one of the problems in the early years of hospice counselling was that counsellors tended to use the stages as a prescription for bereavement counselling, which was never the intention: they were intended to describe the dying person's process of coming to terms with a life-limiting diagnosis. Parkes also more recently (2013) revealed his belief that the Kubler-Ross stages were based on his own work with John Bowlby (1970), rather than an original idea. Since that time, Margaret Stroebe and colleagues (Stroebe et al., 2017) have also critiqued the limitations of stage models of grief. They have proposed the dual process model (Stroebe & Schut, 1999), where the bereaved person oscillates between engulfment in their sense of loss and a resilient getting on with life and its practicalities.

Another idea that has become largely outdated is the concept of 'grief work'. The idea goes back as far as Sigmund Freud (1917/1957), when he posited that people prone to melancholia (or depression, as we would now call it) needed grief work in order to let go. This belief perpetuated unchallenged until Wortman and Silver (1989, 2001) and Stroebe and Stroebe (1991) addressed the issue. Not every grieving person is helped by being encouraged towards a cathartic display of emotion. As I mentioned above, almost half of the bereaved we meet are naturally resilient (Bonanno et al., 2008, 2002; Bonanno, 2010). Even if an individual is not resilient, there can sometimes be a case for not encouraging a client to try to make sense of the loss (Stroebe & Schut, 2002). Grief is a very individual process, and some people work through the worst of their grief by distraction activities, including keeping busy. The good counsellor listens carefully to the client and works with what works for that person. The counsellor may be an expert in the theories and models of grief, but the client is an expert in their own experiences and emotions.

From the 1990s and into the 21st century, hospice counselling practice changed. You will find that all bereavement services now use the theories and models that are briefly described below (for a more detailed account, see Wilson, 2013). If you are considering applying for a hospice post, familiarise yourself with these models. You will almost certainly be asked about them if you are interviewed.

1. Finding and making meaning

Meaning-making theory is predicated on the idea that homo sapiens is an animal that survives and thrives by making sense of their world. Being unable to make sense of a situation, such as a bereavement, throws the individual into a state of cognitive dissonance, resulting in negative affect. The process of making sense and constructing new meaning results in restorative healing. Most bereaved people need to make sense of the death, to know exactly what happened in as much detail as they can get. That alone may not be enough, because grief can rob us of our meaning and purpose for living, especially if it deprives us of a role – we are no longer a parent, a partner or a sibling of a living person. Part of coming to terms with loss involves finding new meaning and purpose to carry on. We also express meaning to ourselves through our internal voices. For example, it is very common in the early phases of grief to tell ourselves that we cannot, must not, be happy. To smile or laugh leaves us feeling guilty. In time, and often with counselling, the bereaved person comes to realise that it's okay to enjoy ourselves, and that our loved one would not want us to stay unhappy, and from this our life takes on new meaning and direction. Much of the work on meaning-making theory is attributed to Robert Neimeyer and colleagues (Neimeyer et al., 2010).

2. A changed assumptive world

Colin Murray Parkes' research preceded Neimeyer's work by several decades. He too noted that one aspect of bereavement is the loss of the world as you knew it before your loved one died. With their death, particularly if they were a significant part of your life, comes a disruption in your daily narrative. The personal world you took for granted, assumed would always be a constant, has suddenly gone. Parkes called this 'assumptive world theory' and labelled it a theory of psychosocial change (Parkes, 1971). Dramatic and traumatic sudden changes to our assumptive world are major stressors. This includes bereavement, redundancy, relationship breakdown and radical surgery. As Mary-Frances O'Connor (2022) has observed, grieving is very much about learning to adapt to changes brought about by bereavement.

In noting the disruptive effects of bereavement and the need to adapt to a new, post-loss life, Thomas Attig coined the phrase 'relearning the world' (Attig, 1996, 2001). In bereavement counselling, we bring the client's need to make sense of the death together with helping them recognise and name what has changed, and then support them as they adapt to this new life.

When Colin Murray Parkes revisited his 1971 assumptive world theory (Parkes, 2009), he was able to reconcile it with the link he and Bowlby had established when they saw grief as an analogue of disrupted attachment between the child and their main caregiver. I said earlier that the stage models have little practical use in counselling now. This is not because the theory is irrelevant; indeed, the neurology of grief is at last revealing the veracity of Bowlby and Parkes' model – in particular the protest and then despair phases of grief (Freed & Mann, 2007). In bringing together his two theories – the need to stay close to the loss while at other times seeking to restore a new life – Parkes saw Stroebe and Schut's dual process model (1999) as the appropriate fit.

3. The dual process model

Stroebe and Schut (1999) developed the dual process model from recognising that grief typically involves periods of immersion in the loss punctuated by spells of distraction and avoidance. This model posits that healthy grief is characterised by an oscillation between loss-orientation (grief) and restoration-orientation (avoidance, distraction). The role of the counsellor is to encourage healthy oscillation between the two extremes, governed by the client's needs, without one side or the other becoming dominant in the client's everyday life. Bereaved people will of course react very differently: some clients do better if they stay on the restoration orientation side until they feel ready to face the reality of their loss. Other can only think about the reality of what has happened – they dwell on loss orientation and need support to acquire skills of distraction.

4. Continuing bonds

Until the closing years of the 20th century, bereavement counselling theory and practice was very much fixed on the idea that we had to encourage our clients to let go of the deceased and move on with their lives. I and those I worked with found this was not the case. Our clients had no intention of letting go, so it came as a relief to discover the work of Dennis Klass and colleagues (Klass, 2006; Klass et al., 1996), who developed a theory of continuing bonds. They recognised that, following the death of someone close to us, we do not let go of the loss and move on with our lives. Rather, we form a new symbolic bond of closeness with them that is comforting, and we take them with us into our future, despite their physical absence. This again is a very individual response. In some cultures, particularly in the East, this is highly ritualised in the form of 'ancestor worship' – veneration of our forebears – to the extent of keeping a shrine to them in one's home. In the industrialised West, we use counselling; we support each client to find their own unique way to construct a continuing bond with the person they have lost. This takes time and is unlikely to develop fully during the time that the client is receiving counselling.

5. Grief and growth

Lois Tonkin's circles model (Tonkin, 2007) is very popular with counsellors and widely shared in counselling groups on social media. Tonkin describes how she was working with a bereaved mother with the expectation that in time the woman's grief for her child would diminish. She then realised that it was not that the mother's grief for the lost child diminished; rather, the woman grew around her grief, so it remained, but as a smaller part of who she became (see also Wilson, 2020). Many bereaved people have told me they find this helpful in explaining how they can return to living a full and even happy life, despite a terrible loss.

Valuing clients' resilience

We know that half of all bereaved people present with a level of resilience, meaning they are able to cope without a counselling model of intervention. My own research (Wilson, 2017) indicates there are key criteria that indicate that a client is coping well. These criteria are also used to decide when a client is ready to leave bereavement counselling. The first is that the client must be able to talk in detail about the death without becoming overwhelmingly upset. The second is that they can make some sense of the death. Third, they should be able, as in the dual process model, to move comfortably between sadness and getting on with life. The fourth criterion is that the client is at least beginning to form a continuing bond that will bring the person who has died with them into the future. And last, the client needs to have begun to find new meaning and purpose in life and be adapting to a new, post-loss world. As an extension of my 2017 research, with colleagues I developed these five criteria into a more detailed eight-phase sequence, supported by a case study of one hospice client's grief journey following the loss of her husband to cancer (Wilson et al., 2021).

The vexed question of grief as a disorder

At interview for a bereavement counselling post, you could be asked about your views on complicated grief. Over the half-century of hospice-based counselling in the UK, there has developed a cultural consensus in which grief is viewed primarily as a natural, healthy process, rather than medicalising it by seeing it as a disorder. This view is not universal, and for many practitioners and researchers, the jury is still out. Prolonged grief was classified as a disorder in the main diagnostic manual of psychiatric disorders, the *DSM-5* (APA, 2013). In the US, inclusion in this manual is necessary if you are to get any care covered by your health insurance. The *DSM-5* listing also established a time limit of six months, beyond which, if you continue to grieve, you will be considered to have complicated (or prolonged) grief disorder and be in need of psychiatric intervention.

It is a vexed question and one that continues to be a topic for debate. There are some useful texts that you might wish to explore. Margaret Stroebe and colleagues (2013) brought together experts from both sides of the fence in an edited a book where contributors discuss the arguments for and against the concept of prolonged grief as a disorder. From my own clinical experience with hundreds of clients, I can only identify six who met the criteria (Prigerson et al., 1995) and showed a trajectory of continuing symptoms (Bonanno et al., 2008) over two years. Some of my clients did demonstrate grief prolonged over two years, but their trajectory showed a steady decline of symptoms (Wilson et al., 2021), which I considered normal in their individual circumstances. There is, however, emerging evidence from neurological research using functional MRI scans that the brain activity of individuals diagnosed with complicated grief does indeed differ from that of people who are considered to be grieving healthily (O'Connor, 2022).

No two days the same

The tasks of a hospice counsellor can be many and varied. As you would expect, most of your work will be one-to-one with clients. If you are joining a team, your clients may have been initially assessed by a more experienced colleague, which will have included a risk assessment. Of course, there is an element of continuing, less formal assessment in each session, which will include regular appraisals, through discussion with your clients, of how they feel their grief is changing over the course of the support you offer them. Some, but not all, services collect data, using clinical measures, especially if they are expected to demonstrate service efficacy to funders and stakeholders. A non-intrusive measure I have routinely used is the Assimilation of Grief Experiences Scale (AGES) (Wilson et al., 2021), which compares how the client talks about their grief against a detailed set of descriptors of the sequence typically observed in grieving people. But, as previously discussed, clients will vary hugely in their trajectories: some may only need a couple of sessions, most will need no more than 10, and a small minority will need longer-term work.

Most of your counselling is likely to be at your hospice, in dedicated counselling rooms. You may also work in the community, perhaps from a room in a local GP practice. In my experience, this works well, as the staff understand and respect the importance of confidentiality, although you may have to judiciously rearrange the chairs away from the desk and examination couch, to lessen the 'medical consultation' ambiance. Your hospice may offer home visits, although even where this does happen, the visits are generally restricted to clients with mobility problems, transport difficulties and geographical isolation. Inevitably, the majority of these clients will be elderly and frail, and typically bereaved of a partner. Often the grief is compounded by loneliness. Sometimes these visits are to an elderly person in a residential home or sheltered accommodation. In such cases, the client may have recently moved from a lifelong home into care, and this may be another change involving loss and a secondary factor in their grief.

Although we must never make assumptions, you may also encounter some age-related cognitive impairment, which can make it difficult to establish a therapeutic relationship. Boundaries that are relatively easy to establish in your hospice-based sessions may be harder in a community setting. You are likely to find carers and relatives in the client's home, who may not understand the need for privacy; cats and dogs may push closed doors open, and the television may be switched on. In some instances, there may be a risk to your own safety. I have felt vulnerable visiting a client in a poorly lit housing estate with a high crime rate, and perhaps even more so on a home visit to an isolated farm on a dark evening, where I encountered moving agricultural vehicles, a guard dog on a long chain, a flock of belligerent geese, and an excitable and protective terrier.

Another issue with working outside the hospice settings is whether the client has actually consented to counselling. They may have been cajoled by concerned relatives or their GP, who may have effectively made the referral for them. They may not fully understand the nature of counselling either, and you may need to explain this to them and your expectations of their engagement in the initial session.

It's important that a hospice has clear risk management policies and procedures for home visits if they are expected of counsellors.

Working with groups

In addition to your one-to-one sessions, you may be asked to facilitate support groups. If you are joining an established team that offers these groups, one way to learn this skill is to join a group initially as an observer. This way you can gain helpful guidance from seeing how the group facilitator operates and the processes of the group members. Because bereaved people are often so vulnerable, I believe it is good practice for such groups always to have at least one facilitator, and preferably two, as well as an observer who can watch out for anyone who may become distressed, allowing the facilitator to continue to engage with the others. Facilitating groups is a specialist skill if the group is to be anything more than simply a setting for clients to exchange experiences and mutually empathise. Some of the larger hospices offer training in facilitating group work, and there is an excellent book on this by Dodie Graves (2012), drawing from her many years of experience.

There may also be groups for relatives and carers of hospice patients, which tend to be the domain of the social work team or palliative care nurses. However, counsellors may be called on to offer their skills. Thanks to ever-improving treatments for conditions that in earlier days were more swiftly fatal, many hospice patients live for a long time, sometimes years, with a life-limiting illness. Hospices support families as well as patients. Carers are often exhausted, frightened and frustrated, even angry, in their role. Those caring for a spouse will tell you how difficult it is to negotiate the change in relationship from partner to carer. Anyone close to a person with a life-limiting illness will be living with uncertainty. Anticipatory grief is something to be faced, whether you are working with a patient or with someone who loves them. This work seeks to find a balance between hope for a future and realistic recognition of an almost certain outcome (Clukey, 2007). Colleagues who have specialised in this work tell me it is a privilege to be part of this relationship, and a deeply moving intimate experience.

Listening to dying patients

Equally moving and an immense privilege is to be invited to the bedside of a patient in the last days of their life. When a dying patient has what counsellors call 'unfinished business', they will often offload to anyone who is with them, whether that is a nurse, healthcare assistant, doctor, chaplain or a volunteer coming round with a tea trolley. Sometimes they may ask for the counsellor. I recall a patient I visited several times in her final days. She could only manage five-minute sessions and I didn't feel I had done anything to help her, but after she died, a nurse sent me a message to tell me I had made a difference. That's one of the many examples of the rewards of hospice counselling.

I invited a colleague from another hospice to write briefly here about her 14 years of practice as a specialist palliative care social worker in hospice, community and hospital settings.

A time to talk

For some people, grieving can start long before someone has died. This is known as 'anticipatory grief' or 'pre-bereavement'.

Having the opportunity to talk to a good listener before death can be a huge benefit to these patients and their families. It is normal and natural for patients and carers to notice feelings of loss, such as overwhelming sadness, anger, fear, confusion, forgetfulness and isolation. These emotions can mirror those that people may experience in bereavement. It can help them to talk and acknowledge that, although the person has not died, they are grieving all the losses that occur as an illness progresses. People who are dying often seek to protect loved ones around them from their deep feelings, and so having an opportunity to open up can offer some relief.

Talking about dying can give people the opportunity to consider important conversations with the people they love. They may want to say, 'I'm sorry', 'I love you', 'I forgive you', 'Thank you' or simply 'Goodbye'.

Supporting open communication can help everyone to better understand each other and make the time remaining to the dying person more comfortable and meaningful. It may be that a client requests a visit from an estranged relative in order to say these things.

Opportunities for honest discussions about advance care planning, wills, powers of attorney, finances, funeral planning, memory work and letter writing can be hugely beneficial for family members and ensure that the dying person's wishes are reflected in their care, even if they lose the ability to express these themselves.

The founder of the modern hospice movement, Cicely Saunders (Saunders, 1984, p.472), wrote, 'How people die remains in the memory of those who live on.' In my experience of talking with people before a death, it can help with acceptance of the imminent loss and, for some family members, help to relieve them of guilt they may feel afterwards.

Negotiating boundaries

Working closely with other hospice departments means negotiating boundaries with other professional codes of practice and ethics. It means, for example, protecting client confidentiality. In an organisation where hospice care notes are electronic and centralised, there needs to be a system in place to ring-fence and protect counselling notes from being viewed by colleagues. There may also be occasions when a nurse, social worker or chaplain supporting a family asks about the counselling you are doing with a family member. You may have to remind them that you cannot discuss it unless you have the client's expressed consent. Negotiating the confidentiality boundary in the hospice setting is often a matter of educating colleagues. Within your own department, it is helpful to agree team confidentiality. Then, when contracting with your client, you will explicitly explain who has access to their notes and about your supervision arrangements, and that it may be helpful for you to be able to discuss the client, with their permission, with your immediate colleagues, who are signed up to a counselling code of ethics. In large teams, a bereavement support service may include volunteers who are not qualified counsellors or psychotherapists, so it is important that anyone using counselling skills in the service understands counselling ethics and practice. All members of the team, paid and volunteering, should be contracted to follow the ethical framework of a recognised membership organisation.

A secondary, but no less important, reason for team confidentiality is that it can be helpful to be able to debrief with a colleague after a particularly difficult session with a client, and perhaps receive validation and a hug. Many years ago, working in isolation in a GP practice, I met and assessed three clients in one afternoon, each with a story of sudden and violent death and each traumatised by the unexpected bereavement of their loved one. The afternoon left an effect, but I was unable to debrief with colleagues until the following day. As I mentioned previously, good supervision is an imperative in this setting. This should be independent of management, at least for the paid staff, and if possible for volunteers too, who ideally will have group supervision, and it should be provided by independent practitioners.

On-the-job CPD

The multidisciplinary nature of a hospice team offers invaluable opportunities to extend your knowledge about death and dying, life-limiting conditions, palliative care, end of life and the process of death. Some of this I picked up in conversations, or when seeking answers to a client's questions, but some was from in-house training delivered by colleagues. I learned about how to relate to people with dementia, what 'Do not resuscitate' means in practice, what a care pathway involves, and the physiological process of dying, including (from sitting in on a consultant's lecture to medical students) how to tell conclusively that life has ended. I have talked to mortuary attendants, visited crematoriums, and seen funeral directors at work. My experience is that clients greatly appreciate having a counsellor they trust who can answer questions about their loved one's hospice death, such as helping them understand their loved one's final hours on the care pathway. Clients sometimes ask about behind-the-scenes funeral procedures. I can, for example, categorically confirm that it is your relative's ashes, and only theirs, in the urn you are given after a cremation.

Fielding potential complaints

There are times when a client's questions can be one step from a complaint about their relative's hospice care. At the end-of-life stage, when a loved one is admitted to the inpatient unit (IPU), doctors have made a judgement, based on a medical assessment, that death is not far away. Once in the warmth and security of a hospice bed, the patient may stop 'being strong' and relax into acceptance of their death. To relatives, it may look as if the patient has rapidly 'gone downhill'. Clients often mention this in counselling, asking what happened to bring about this apparent rapid deterioration. It helps if, with the client's permission, a nurse or doctor can be invited into the counselling room to explain. Sometimes, once this is done, no further counselling is needed.

Raising and maintaining standards

Bereavement service provision across the UK hospice network varies greatly, since such services are limited by the size of the hospice and what it can offer within its budget. For this reason, Cruse Bereavement Support and the Bereavement Services Association came together to produce the *Bereavement Care Service Standards* (Chaplin et al., 2014). This 11-page document sets out what is needed for a bereavement service to be safe and effective. Its authors recognise that not all services will have the capacity to reach a gold standard. For this reason, it sets out three levels of service provision under seven headings. These are:

1. Planning to address community needs.
2. Awareness of and access to local services that optimise client choice.
3. Assessment of client needs.
4. Support and supervision of staff and volunteers.
5. Education and training of staff and volunteers.

6. Allocation of available resources.
7. Monitoring/ evaluation of the service.

By auditing a service against these standards and levels, a management team can identify gaps, optimise effectiveness and plan service development. These standards are also useful criteria for stakeholders to appreciate their service, and for those commissioning a service. Auditing a service against these standards provides evidence of what can be commissioned.

ABSCo – your professional body

Although the larger hospices seek to recruit counsellors as part of a team, some of the smaller hospices employ just one bereavement counsellor, who may manage the service or be managed by a professional from another discipline. If you are responsible for coordinating bereavement work, you are eligible to join ABSCo, the Association of Bereavement Service Coordinators. ABSCo was once part of Hospice UK but is now an independent organisation, although membership is still limited to hospice bereavement services. Although I did not manage the service in my hospice employment, I did coordinate the volunteer work, in that I was responsible for training and mentoring. That entitled me to join as a full member. Other hospice bereavement supporters can join as associate members.

ABSCo offers training events and an annual conference, and subsidises regional training events. Regional meetings throughout the year bring together coordinators over a wide area. At both a national and regional level, ABSCo is a friendly organisation that supports its members and can be an emotional lifeline to lone therapists in a small hospice. It is another place to make lifelong friends.

Before I conclude this chapter, I'd like to introduce Paul Parsons, who shares his experience of working as Adult Bereavement Co-ordinator for St Christopher's Hospice in south London.

Working at St Christopher's Hospice – Paul Parsons

I find working in a hospice environment such an uplifting experience. My own life struggles are immediately dissolved by the sense of hope, joy and laughter in equal measure that is palpable as soon as I walk through the door of St Christopher's Hospice in south London.

As John has indicated, it takes a special kind of person to work here, and the staff at the hospice are indeed very special human beings. As St Christopher's covers five London boroughs, its patients, staff and volunteers are extremely diverse. I am very proud that, over the years, our volunteer base has grown in size, and within that increase, so has the diversity of the individuals within it. We are here for the community and driven by the community itself.

Training people to become a bereavement support volunteer is certainly not just about achieving qualification placement hours or popping in to see if anyone needs some help because they might be 'sad'. This is a serious commitment for the volunteer and the hospice.

'Volunteers are not free, you know' is a phrase I often say to people. There are applications to sift through, interviews to arrange, on-boarding and vetting to be done, training to conduct and continuing professional development workshops to plan and provide. Then we get to the actual clinical work, with clients to allocate, supervision to support the volunteer and dilemmas to answer, including safeguarding and risk. 'It's not boring here' is also a well-used phrase of mine!

It requires a team, and certainly valuing staff and volunteers in equal measure is very important, so that everyone feels part of something special. Undoubtedly, working in the palliative care arena is a very special environment to be involved in.

Most of the paid staff in the adult bereavement team at St Christopher's were volunteers before they were employed in a salaried role. I am a good example of that, having volunteered for the hospice for more than three years previously. Volunteers have their own life experiences, previous (or current) job skills and interests to bring to the work, which is why we welcome our volunteers to apply for any of the roles we advertise here.

Many of our bereavement volunteers stay with us long after the two-year commitment we initially ask for. Why? Some cite professional accreditation needs, work-life balance, good quality supervision – and then there's the subsidised lunch! However, all talk about the power of the work, making a difference, and the rewards and privilege of supporting people in their hour (or therapeutic 50 minutes) of need.

There are other opportunities for the bereavement volunteer beyond seeing the two or three regular clients assigned to them. A volunteer can co-facilitate bereavement groups with a member of staff, help at memorial events, and perhaps expand on their own skills and interests by facilitating a training workshop. Volunteers can also take other posts in the organisation, such as helping in administration, meet-and-greet roles, or working in the Candle bereavement service that supports children and families in their grief. The opportunities are endless.

Grief theory talks about reconnecting with meaning and purpose in life after a traumatic life experience such as a death. We feel that our volunteers gain meaning and purpose in their lives and community from working at the hospice.

Assessing the client's need is an important aspect of our work. Most bereaved people do not need formal counselling. Understanding grief, normalising their experiences and offering support through psychoeducation, information and advice are paramount to helping a bereaved person back on their 'normal' trajectory or pathway through the grief journey. It can be a very painful journey indeed, but the hospice is there for the bereaved person throughout.

We have early intervention assessors who contact the bereaved next of kin by telephone, soon after a death. We write to the family a few months later and then again within the first year. We offer opportunities for reconnecting with the hospice during quarterly memorial events, fun runs or other charity events. It is important that people feel able to make contact at any time; there is no time limit to grief and St Christopher's door is always open to anyone asking for our help. It is also important that bereaved people have support that is easily accessible. Formal therapy does not suit everyone. Social prescribing has been part of primary care provision for a good few years now, and St Christopher's offers a range of these opportunities, including a drop-in service called Bereavement Help Points, healthy walks and creative art and music spaces where people can express and share grief therapeutically as an alternative way to pure talking therapy. These offer more opportunities for volunteers to make a difference.

It is important to note that death is inevitable and all of us will experience the pain of grief, although some more than others. Hospices play a hugely important role in demystifying death, dying, loss and grief by engaging with and informing the community, and our valued volunteer workforce plays a vital part in that.

Working therapeutically with bereaved people offers opportunities to explore emotions, practical issues, identity changes, philosophical reflections and health concerns, as well as cultural differences. It is a great opportunity to learn about loss in its wider context and a great stepping stone towards paid counselling work.

Concluding comments

I hope we have managed to convey the many and varied aspects of hospice counselling. The work is rewarding because almost all clients report being more than satisfied with the outcome of their therapy. Their gratitude is heartwarming. I can say from my own clinical experience and from the outcome measures we have used, almost all clients show a measurable improvement. Moreover, clients have sometimes sought me out many years after their counselling to let me know that the changes were lasting, and that what they learnt in their sessions had equipped them to deal with subsequent losses. If you have what it takes to work with death, dying and grief, this is an arena I can recommend as a career.

References

APA. (2013). *Diagnostic and statistical manual of mental disorders* (5th ed.). (DSM-5). American Psychiatric Association.

Attig, T. (1996). *How we grieve: Relearning the world.* Oxford University Press.

Attig, T. (2001). Relearning the world: Making and finding meanings. In , R.A. Neimeyer (Ed.), *Meaning reconstruction and the experience of loss* (pp.33–53). American Psychological Association.

Bonanno, G.A. (2010). *The other side of sadness: What the new science of bereavement tells us about life after loss.* Basic Books.

Bonanno, G.A., Boerner, K. & Wortman, C.B. (2008). Trajectories of grieving. In M.S. Stroebe, R.O. Hansson, H. Schut & W Stroebe (Eds.), *Handbook of bereavement research and practice: Advances in theory and intervention* (pp.287–307). American Psychological Association.

Bonanno, G.A., Wortman, C.B., Lehman, D.R., Tweed, R.G., Haring, M., Sonnega, J., Carr, D. & Nesse, R.M. (2002). Resilience to loss and chronic grief: A prospective study from preloss to 18-months postloss. *Journal of Personality and Social Psychology, 83,* 1150–1164.

Bowlby, J. & Parkes, C.M. (1970). Separation and loss within the family. In: E.J. Anthony & C. Koupernik (Eds.), *The child and his family* (pp.197–216). Wiley.

Burke, L.A. & Neimeyer, R.A. (2013). Prospective risk factors for complicated grief: A review of the empirical literature. In: M.S. Stroebe, H. Schut & J. van den Bout (Eds.), *Complicated grief: Scientific foundations for health care professionals* (pp.145–161). Routledge.

Chaplin, D., Kerslake, D., Chalmers, A., Frazer, D.J., Betley, C. & Dudwala, Y. (2014). *Bereavement care service standards 2014.* Cruse Bereavement Support/Bereavement Services Association. http://bsauk.org/uploads/593853480.pdf

Clukey, L. (2007). 'Just be there': Hospice caregivers' anticipatory mourning experience. *Journal of Hospice and Palliative Nursing, 9,* 151–158.

Faulkner, A. & Wallbank, S. (Eds.). (1998). *Bereavement counselling: A 60 hour introductory training course.* Cruse Bereavement Care/Help the Hospices.

Fortner, B.V. & Neimeyer, R.A. (1999). Paper presented at the annual meeting of the Association for Death Education and Counseling 1999, San Antonio, Texas.

Freed, P.J. & Mann, J.J. (2007). Sadness and loss: Toward a neurobiopsychosocial model. *American Journal of Psychiatry, 164,* 28–34.

Freud, S. (1917/1957). *Mourning and melancholia.* Hogarth Press.

Furnham, A. & Swami, V. (2008). Patient preferences for psychological counsellors: Evidence of a similarity effect. *Counselling Psychology Quarterly, 21*(4), 361–370.

Graves, D. (2012). *Setting up and facilitating bereavement support groups: A practical guide.* Jessica Kingsley.

Klass, D. (2006). Continuing conversation about continuing bonds. *Death Studies, 30,* 843–859.

Klass, D., Silverman, P.R. & Nickman, S.L. (1996). *Continuing bonds: New understandings of grief.* Taylor & Francis.

Kubler-Ross, E. (1969). *On death and dying.* Macmillan.

Neimeyer, R.A., Burke, L.A., Mackay, M.M. & Van Dyke Stringer, J.G. (2010). Grief therapy and the reconstruction of meaning: From principles to practice. *Journal of Contemporary Psychotherapy, 40,* 73–83.

NICE. (2004). *Improving supportive and palliative care for adults with cancer.* National Institute for Clinical Excellence. https://www.nice.org.uk/guidance/csg4

O'Connor, M. (2022). *The grieving brain: The surprising science of how we learn from love and loss.* HarperOne.

Parkes, C.M. (1971). Psychosocial transitions: A field for study. *Social Science and Medicine, 5,* 101–115.

Parkes, C.M. (1981). Evaluation of a bereavement service. *Journal of Preventive Psychiatry, 1,* 179–188.

Parkes, C.M. (2002). Grief: Lessons from the past, visions for the future. *Death Studies, 26,* 367–385.

Parkes, C.M. (2009). *Love and loss: The roots of grief and its complications.* Routledge.

Parkes, C.M. (2013). Elisabeth Kübler-Ross, On Death and Dying: a reappraisal. *Mortality, 18,* 94–97.

Prigerson, H.G., Maciejewski, P.K., Reynolds, C.F., Bierhals, A.J., Newson, J.T., Fasiczka, A., Frank, E., Doman, J. & Miller, M. (1995). Inventory of complicated grief: A scale to measure maladaptive symptoms of loss. *Psychiatry Research, 59,* 65–79.

Saunders, C. (1984). Pain and impending Death. In P. Wall & R. Melzak (Eds.), *Texbook of pain* (pp.472–478). Churchill Livingstone.

Schut, H., Stroebe, M.S., Van Den Bout, J. & Terheggen, M. (2001). The efficacy of bereavement interventions: Determining who benefits. In: M.S. Stroebe, R.O. Hansson, W. Stroebe, & H. Schut (Eds.), *Handbook of bereavement research: Consequences, coping and care* (pp.705–737). American Psychological Association.

Stroebe, M.S. & Schut, H. (1999). The dual process model of coping with bereavement: Rationale and desciption. *Death Studies, 23,* 197–224.

Stroebe, M.S. & Schut, H. (2002). Meaning making in the dual process model of coping with bereavement. In: R.A. Neimeyer (Ed.), *Meaning reconstruction and the experience of loss* (pp.55–73). American Psychological Association.

Stroebe, M. & Stroebe, W. (1991). Does 'grief work' work? *Journal of Consulting and Clinical Psychology, 59,* 479.

Stroebe, M., Schut, H. & Boerner, K. (2017). Cautioning health-care professionals. *Omega (Westport), 74,* 455–473.

Stroebe, M.S., Schut, H. & van den Bout, J. (Eds.). (2013). *Complicated grief: Scientific foundations for health care professionals.* Routledge.

Tonkin, L. (2007). *Certificate in grief support: Extending your skills in working with grieving adults.* Port Hills Press.

Wilson, J. (2013). *Supporting people through loss and grief: An introduction for counsellors and other caring practitioners.* Jessica Kingsley.

Wilson, J. (2017). *Moments of assimilation and accommodation in the bereavement counselling process.* PhD dissertation. University of Leeds.

Wilson, J. (2020). *The plain guide to grief.* Nielsen.

Wilson, J., Gabriel, L. & James, H. (2016). Making sense of loss and grief: The value of in-depth assessments. *Bereavement Care, 35.*

Wilson, J.F., Gabriel, L. & Stiles, W.B. (2021). Assimilation in bereavement: Charting the process of grief recovery in the case of Sophie. *British Journal of Guidance & Counselling, 51*(3), 367–380.

Wortman, C.B. & Silver, R.C. (1989). The myths of coping with loss. *Journal of Counselling and Clinical Psychology, 57,* 349–357.

Wortman, C.B. & Silver, R.C. (2001). The myths of coping with loss revisited. In: M.S. Stroebe, R.O. Hansson, W. Stroebe, & H. Schut (Eds.), *Handbook of bereavement research: Consequences, coping and care* (pp.405–430). American Psychological Association.

Chapter 9

Counselling children, young people and families

Sarah Watson
with Sarah Houghton, Alison Roy, Lorna Birrell and Rhona Kenny

In this chapter, I will be drawing on my experience as a counsellor specialising in work with children, young people and families (CYPF) over many years, and on my current role as a CYPF ethics consultant. I want to start by briefly sharing my career pathway and why I love working with young people, so you'll get an idea of how your counselling journey might evolve. Then I'll focus on the competences required of a CYPF counsellor, as there are important training requirements if you're wanting to practise in this sector. There are many different employment opportunities available to qualified CYPF counsellors, and I'm really grateful to Sarah, Alison, Lorna and Rhona for their insights into their work areas. Finally, I offer some considerations to help you assess whether practising as a CYPF counsellor is right for you.

My career pathway
I experienced counselling for the first time as a 17-year-old A-level psychology student referred into my college counselling service. It wasn't a great experience, with an opinionated, judgemental therapist, but it was ground-breaking for me and shaped my life. I knew then that I wanted to become a counsellor so I could help teenagers and young people like me, but to do it better than the counsellor I had just experienced. I started out on an adult counselling training route and switched to specialise in work with children, young people and families, where

I have stayed for more than 20 years and achieved my accreditation with BACP as a senior practitioner.

It was an interest in the mind, behaviour and mental health that led me to A-level psychology and then a degree in psychology. I enjoyed working with children and families on placement when doing the degree. I began my basic level training in counselling and also completed a counselling CYP qualification (the 'families' element in CYPF emerged several years later). These studies led me into numerous counselling placements and to a master's in counselling. I qualified as a post-16 years lecturer alongside these studies and found that lecturing paid enough to subsidise my studies. I continued my studies in counselling, set up my private practice, trained to be a supervisor, clocked up my counselling hours on placements and picked up numerous paid contracts in my area, often travelling 60-plus miles in a day to see clients. Much of my work was unpaid, and to counter this I had to juggle numerous paid jobs and small contracts so that I could gain the experience I needed in different settings.

I have always worked with young people. My first placement was with a service offering counselling to CYPF, and I have dedicated my career to this sector. I love working with young people and at every opportunity have sought out CYPF CPD and further qualifications. For me, it's important to keep up to date with developments and best practice. I truly believe that, if a counsellor has the skills and ability to connect with CYPF, then they will find working with adults easy. In my experience, it takes effort, dedication, enthusiasm and humour to gel with our CYPF clients, and these skills will always come in handy in any counselling work.

Training and continuing professional development

As an employee and member of BACP, much of my experience relates to that organisation, although there are several other equally worthwhile professional bodies for people in our profession (see Appendix for more details).

My work is governed by the BACP *Ethical Framework for the Counselling Professions* (BACP, 2018), which requires me to work within my competence. BACP has also produced a CYP competence framework (BACP, 2022a) and curriculum to help me ensure my skills and abilities are in line with best practice. The National Counselling & Psychotherapy Society (NCPS) has its own CYPF competence framework to guide its members and ensure they are suitably qualified before beginning work with children and young people (NCPS, 2023).

Most counselling providers will expect applicants for CYPF roles to be suitably qualified and experienced. The BACP CYPF competence framework is detailed and covers the key areas in which we should be able to demonstrate competency, from child development to skills. I definitely recommend looking at the framework for guidance when you start your journey in this field.

As a CYPF counsellor, we need to have specialist skills and to be able to adapt our work to meet the needs of children aged anywhere between three years and 25. We need to be aware of child development models and safeguarding rules and procedures, and have a thorough understanding of the complex issues that are likely to crop up frequently.

The necessary training and development are covered in Stage 1 of the *BACP Counselling Children and Young People (14–18 years) Training Curriculum* (BACP, 2020a), which gives counsellors the competences required to begin working with children and/or young people in a placement setting. This introduction to counselling children and/or young people is for trainee counsellors on adult-focused, counselling/psychotherapy core training courses who wish to undertake some of their practice hours in a placement working face-to-face with children and/or young people. It is also designed for counsellors already qualified to work with adults who want to extend their scope of practice to counselling children and/or young people and work towards a formal award in counselling children and/or young people.

Competences

For BACP therapists, our intention is always to maintain high standards of training and ethical practice, and nowhere more than when working with this vulnerable client group. The BACP *Ethical Framework* (BACP, 2018) states:

> We must be competent to deliver the services being offered to at least fundamental professional standards or better. When we consider satisfying professional standards requires consulting others with relevant expertise, seeking second opinions, or making referrals, we will do so in ways that meet our commitments and obligations for client confidentiality and data protection. (Working to professional standards, point 13)

The framework also commits practitioners to 'working within [their] competence' (Commitment, point 2a), and says: 'We must be competent to deliver the services being offered to at least fundamental professional standards or better' (Good Practice, point 13). This could mean that you need additional specialist training. It could also mean that you need additional supervision with a supervisor who has 'adequate levels of expertise' (Good Practice, point 62), and that you may need to consult others to ensure the work you are undertaking meets professional standards. Good Practice, point 13 goes on to remind us that, when 'consulting others with relevant expertise, seeking second opinions, or making referrals, we will do so in ways that meet our commitments and obligations for client confidentiality and data protection'.

For any work with CYPF, we can use BACP's CYPF competence framework (BACP, 2022a) and training curriculum (BACP, 2020a) to guide us when assessing our skills, knowledge, experience and competences needed in respect of this client group.

BACP members may also find it helpful to read the Good Practice in Action resource *Working with Children and Young People* (GPiA 046) (BACP, 2020b). The resource aims to help practitioners considering moving into working with children and young people to equip themselves for this complex area. It covers the differences between adult and CYPF work and the relevant skills required; referral processes and the roles of other agencies in the field; the legal issues involved; self-referrals and capacity and consent, including parental/carer consent; creating a therapeutic agreement or contract; safeguarding and confidentiality issues, and safeguarding training and policy.

Other important topics include supervision, working in private practice, therapeutic boundaries, skills and competences including child development, attachment, trauma-informed support, the varying therapeutic models, issues for parents and carers, and the importance of the arts and play. The resource also considers training and support, record-keeping and data protection (GDPR) requirements. A helpful concluding section looks at 'pitfalls'.

Alongside the competence frameworks and training curricula, there are the MindEd e-learning resources.[1] MindEd is a free educational resource on children, young people, adults and older people's mental health, and is a good resource for both general CPD and specific CYPF training needs.

To conclude, we must ensure we have the basic competences that enable us to practise safely and ethically with children, young people and families, and we need to have completed the training and development required.

CYPF supervision

Your CYPF-experienced supervisor will be able to help you assess your CYPF competences to practise ethically and competently. If we work with CYPF, we need to ensure that our supervisor has sufficient knowledge and experience in this field. The benefits of having a strong CYPF supervisor will be demonstrated in the outcomes of our work with children and young people. A competent supervisor will be able to hold and guide us through the complex ethical dilemmas we are likely to encounter. All too often I speak to counsellors whose

---

1. See www.minded.org.uk

supervisors have not known what to do or failed to know basic safeguarding procedures for under-18s. I wouldn't take my dog to a non-qualified vet, and I wouldn't take my CYPF counselling work to a non-CYPF supervisor!

Particular areas of concern and presenting issues

The most common presenting issues with CYPF clients include:

- family breakdown, divorce, blended family
- loss of a grandparent
- loss of a family pet
- sleep issues and sleep hygiene
- confidence, self-esteem and self-belief
- identity, sexuality, questioning
- bullying
- obsessive compulsive disorder
- exam techniques
- relationships
- friendship issues
- worries about future, leaving home, choices, university, failure
- risk-taking behaviours
- looked after children (LAC), adoption, care system
- low mood, depression
- self-harm
- disordered eating
- unwanted, intrusive thoughts.

Safeguarding is a huge and growing concern. Another of BACP's suite of Good Practice in Action resources, *Safeguarding Children and Young People within the Counselling Professions in England and Wales* (GPiA 031) (BACP, 2022b), does a great job in covering the key areas of safeguarding in our work with CYPF. Its contents list captures the range of complexities a CYPF specialist practitioner is likely to encounter.

It looks at legal definitions relevant to children and young people, court processes and legal orders, children in need of services, children in need of care and protection, and the rights of the child.

It includes the welfare checklist from the Children Act 1989 Section 1(3). It also covers mental capacity and consent for children and young people, and what's known as 'Gillick competency' – assessing the capacity of children under 16 to make their own decisions about their health and care needs.

It covers parental responsibility, data collection, storage and protection (UK-GDPR), children and consent, confidentiality, contractual agreements with children and young people, information sharing, case records, managing risk, the therapist's duty of care and confidentiality.

There's also guidance on referrals and disclosures, disclosure and barring services for all four UK nations, professional regulation, ethical dilemmas in safeguarding, pre-trial therapy for children as witnesses in safeguarding cases, law and government guidance on female genital mutilation, disclosures and referrals.

Since the Covid pandemic, we have seen rates of safeguarding issues increase in CYPF, and lockdown was hard for many children. CYPF and school counsellors are still working with this now. Stress, anxiety and panic attacks are very common issues in the counselling room, especially among SAT and exam-year groups. We frequently see CYPF clients with low mood, self-harm and suicidal ideation. Issues around food and eating have increased since lockdown ended.

Sector idiosyncrasies

For me, CYPF work is amazing and rewarding. We may do sensory play, finger-painting, using puppets or sand-tray work with younger ones in our playroom, on our hands and knees or on the floor. Then, with the next client, we can be doing Gestalt 'empty chair' work with a teenager, perhaps helping them say what they need to say to an estranged parent and working in a very adult and cognitive way.

I particularly enjoy the idiosyncrasies of working with teenagers. I find that many staff and adults see, for example, the adult-like body of a six-foot, year-12 student who drives himself to school and may be holding down a part-time job, and cannot see the child within that body. On the outside, the young person may look like an adult, but in the safety of the counselling room and our relationship/journey together, they are able to be themself – a youngster grappling with an ever-more complex world. I ground myself in the developmental stages and know that these young people are still learning and growing and making sense of the world they are beginning to encounter outside their family and school, and also making sense of themselves.

After more than two decades of working in this sector, I am aware that there's an increased appreciation of the importance of good mental health among CYPF, and a growing acceptability around accessing mental health support. The majority of young people I have worked with in recent years have been open and confident about telling their friends they are having counselling. Not all young people will feel like this but, with mental health issues featuring so strongly across all social media, it feels like any stigma around counselling and supporting mental health is being broken down further.

Children and young people and their families

Working with children and young people also involves working with or dealing with families. With younger clients, it is an everyday part of the role – for example, if we work in private practice, we are likely to get a referral from a child's parents, or we may need to seek consent from their carer if we are counselling a young child. However, as clients get older, we may feel we need to have less and less to do with their parents or family. Some CYP counsellors offer family counselling or family systems work.

If we are working with children who meet the Gillick-competence threshold, we may only deal with parents or carers for practicalities such as payment, bookings and, in private practice, paperwork. In organisations, it may only be when we have serious safeguarding issues that we need to communicate with parents/carers, to fulfil our duty of care to prevent harm to our client.

Stressors in the sector

As in most counselling contexts, you may be under pressure from your employing organisation to see as many clients per day as possible. Or you may be asked to see more clients for less than the 'therapeutic hour' or to include more group work, for example, in order to reduce waiting lists.

And there's always the likelihood of needing to respond and attend to safeguarding issues that arise from the client work. There's also paperwork to complete and referrals to follow through, as well as writing up your clinical notes. It can therefore be a heavy workload with heavy emotional content. Safeguarding issues can weigh on our minds long after the working day has ended.

My tips to CYPF counsellors are:

- Hold firm boundaries.
- Take time between clients for a comfort break and refreshment.
- Schedule time for writing up notes and updating records.
- If you have a gap between clients, go outside and get some fresh air before the next client.
- Bring plenty of food and drink with you – you may not get a chance to leave the building!

One of my sadnesses in the work is that, as in most counselling contexts, we often don't get to know the end of the client's story or journey. If our work is time-limited, we may just dip in and then out of a client's life. We may never hear the end of a safeguarding situation or court case. However, our role is to trust the process and have confidence that what we do can make a huge difference to the course of that client's life.

The feedback, smiles and journeys we witness in our role are a great privilege and honour. Sometimes we see clients at their lowest moments and points in life. We often hear things from a client that they have never told anyone before. Our work is powerful, potent, heavy and hard. What sustains us has to be a deep belief in the process and knowing that our clients will get there in their own time.

Every now and again we will get feedback – maybe an email, a chance encounter or a thank-you card from a happier person embracing and living a better life. It's often blown my mind when I happen to meet an adult with a partner and family and realise that they were my client when they were a child.

But there certainly are challenges and difficult aspects to working with children and young people. The most obvious one is about content – the issues a young person might bring to counselling. The stuff that sticks in our mind and pops up when we're in the shower, or driving home, or walking the dog.

Working with CYPF means we are privileged to be invited into young people's lives, and most often it's the sad, dark, traumatic and painful parts we are asked to share.

Working with grief and pain my entire life has inevitably influenced how I view the world. I'm sure it is the same for all therapists. A supervisor once told me she thought all therapists should have outgoing, colourful hobbies and private lives that are full of fun, and I would encourage you to follow this advice. I can no longer watch crime, murder or grim TV films or distressing media content, as they are the stuff of my day job. I've set boundaries in place in my head. My work is filled with this darker side of life and I need a complete break from all of that when I am not at work.

We need to hold our boundaries firmly. We need amazing friends, family, pets, support networks and so on – whatever grounds you. We need to self-care and have healthy, functional lives and routines. We need an amazing clinical supervisor (like mine!). Having great colleagues and teams around us can also help us lighten the darkness of our role. In my current role, we regularly debrief and check in together – I appreciate this very much.

Employment opportunities

The employment opportunities for CYPF practitioners are various. Here we hear from several practitioners who work in different CYPF environments.

Counselling in schools

Sarah Houghton is Director of Mental Health Workforce Development with Place2Be, an independent provider of mental wellbeing support in schools. Here she gives us a snapshot of the work.

The actual physical environment varies from school to school. Some schools will convert empty cupboards, abandoned bathrooms and any accessible space into counselling rooms, while others will custom-build amazing new spaces. Working days are generally around school hours and term-time only. This can particularly suit counsellors who have their own children as it allows them to be around for them during school holidays.

Support and management can vary. In most cases in a school, your manager will be from the education sector – a member of the senior leadership team, such as a deputy head of school. They are often teachers who have achieved seniority through longevity and have completed a basic safeguarding training course. Support is often readily available but not particularly expert in terms of children's mental wellbeing needs.

All service providers have slightly different approaches and models. At Place2Be, we offer an embedded whole-school service. We work closely with schools to make sure they have the model that is both right for their school and aligns with our approach and ethos. One of the benefits of working as part of an organisation like Place2Be is the support available via your line manager, internally provided qualified clinical supervisor, and a specialist safeguarding team, IT, human resources and ongoing professional development opportunities.

As a growing provider, we are always recruiting for school-based staff. Our two main clinical roles are a school project manager (SPM) and mental health practitioner (MHP). Both require a qualification in counselling or psychotherapy, and both work directly with children and young people, teachers, school leaders and parents and carers to provide a relational and systemic approach to supporting their mental health.

A placement is a good way to get to know the organisation. Many of our school-based staff started on placement with us as trainee counsellors, either from adult-focused trainings or the growing number of child-focused qualifications. You will need to check with your training provider how many children hours can contribute to your log as this varies depending on your accrediting organisation's requirements.

Place2Be provides comprehensive training prior to placement. Counsellors on Placement (CoPs) attend our two-day introductory workshop and a day on safeguarding before starting in school. These introduce Place2Be's therapeutic approach, using creativity, relationship and self-awareness to help children and young people tell their stories. You'll also get to practise creative ways to overcome the challenges of contracting with children and young people, how to work appropriately with disclosures, and how confidentiality is different in a school setting. It's a great opportunity to get comfortable with the verbal and non-verbal nature of working with children, using finger paints, puppets and sand trays, which are all part of the experience, while continually being supported by experienced practitioners at every level of the organisation from the front-line service to the most senior levels of management.

We have a large library of learning resources that you have access to while you are on placement with us via our CoP Learning Platform.

There is a clear route for trainees on placement at Place2Be schools to move into paid roles as mental health practitioners and school project managers once they qualify.

A typical day might start with a parent meeting to go through the Strengths and Difficulties Questionnaire (SDQs) for their child, followed by a meeting with the same child's teacher to go through the SDQs with them. You may choose to spend some time observing that child at playtime to understand more about their interactions and relationships.

After break, you will log your assessments on the Place2Be system. At the children's lunchtime, you will be available for our student-requested drop-in service of 15-minute sessions, which are open to all to book. You have probably spent the hour beforehand prioritising the requests and letting the children and young people know what time to come.

In the afternoon you may do one-to-one client work or run a groupwork intervention with seven or eight children or young people. Once a fortnight you will have supervision and a separate conversation with your line manager. You might end the day providing a 45–60-minute supervision session to the counsellors on placement. In addition, our school-based staff often have informal but important and meaningful conversations with the school's senior managers and staff that help them reflect on their own mental health and the needs of the staff, children and young people with whom they work.

Once in post, the opportunities to develop continue. In addition to our role-specific training programmes, we offer regular free CPD in specialist areas and significant subsidies on certificated CPD courses.

As much of the work is part-time, you could choose to work in more than one school, or to keep days clear for private practice or other work. For some people, delivering training sits alongside their main role at Place2Be.

We have a clear career pathway at Place2Be. The traditional route is from mental health practitioner through school project manager to clinical supervisor, maybe on to regional clinical lead and – who knows? – eventually to clinical director.

Child and adolescent mental health services (CAMHS)

Alison Roy is a consultant child and adolescent psychotherapist. Here she discusses the challenges and opportunities of working as a psychotherapist in an NHS Child and Adolescent Mental Health Service (CAMHS), particularly in today's changeable political climate.

For those wanting to work in NHS Child and Adolescent Mental Health Services (CAMHS) there are a number of key considerations to be aware of, which I will attempt to summarise briefly. The main and most frequently reported experience from those working in CAMHS is that it is a highly challenging and constantly changing environment, where staff and resources are both stressed and stretched.

As someone who until recently was a consultant psychotherapist in a CAMHS team and the clinical lead for a specialist adoption service, I have experienced these changes first hand. The most significant of these for me, which I realise deeply affected my practice and my sense of myself within a wider team, was the scarcity (or lack) of opportunities to come together as a whole team, or even in smaller teams, for clinical discussion, emotional processing and/or reflection. This I think is due in part to the pandemic – clinicians had to work more in isolation and from their own homes, and those corridor conversations and natural, 'easy' opportunities to come together were removed. Even though many people have returned to their offices and workplaces for some if not all of their work, these spaces and therefore opportunities haven't really returned.

In addition to this, the level of risk and complexity has increased, coupled with high demand for a service that used to be part of a much wider community CAMHS, resulting in there being much more pressure on services to meet waiting-time targets and signpost on.

There has, as a result, been a marked shift away from relationship-based interventions where establishing a meaningful connection or therapeutic alliance is key and helps to reduce the risk. Adversely, the focus is much more likely to be about managing the risk or crisis and referring individuals on through a 'treatment' pathway (emphasis on the pathway), previously understood as a 'stepped care' model. 'Treatment' may be offered to those who meet the threshold, but this in reality is likely to mean that the referred child or young person will receive an initial assessment and then be placed on a waiting list for a specialist neurodevelopmental assessment – for which there is likely to be a very long wait. My experience is that there are now numerous neurodevelopment specialist teams and pathways and very little focus on getting to know the child or young person as an individual, holistically.

The bigger-picture context and the story of CAMHS are that there are now few generic support services for children and their families in the community and the ones that do exist are usually poorly resourced. In reality, most have closed, due to lack of governmental support and statutory funding. Sure Start, family centres, youth services and centres offering young people activities and outreach programmes – places where babies, children, young people and/or their parents might have been seen, noticed and offered early support by professionals well before they hit crisis point – just don't exist anymore, and CAMHS has been left to pick up the pieces.

Consequently, parents or carers referred to CAMHS are likely to have waited a long time for their child or young person to be seen and they may well be disappointed when they are. They will be seeking answers, a diagnosis, or at the very least some useful strategies that give them hope and something to 'do' in the face of overwhelming difficulties and distress. In response to this, services, their managers and commissioners have responded to the pressure to provide a service that 'does' something, has measurable tools, or at least sounds convincing. So, the child or young person at the centre of the difficulty (if they make it through the front door) will be triaged, assessed, signposted or referred on if at all possible. Those with less neurodiverse difficulties, such as anxiety, may be offered behavioural techniques or short-term group therapy.

So, what does this mean for counsellors applying for posts in CAMHS services? In my experience, there are very few counselling posts in CAMHS. Even as an NHS-trained psychotherapist and a qualified counsellor, I have found I need to be quite evangelical about advocating psychotherapeutic interventions, relationship-based interventions and talking therapies. In most NHS mental health services, training placements are restricted to specific professional disciplines, which don't include counsellors.

Counsellors could consider taking additional qualifications in order to find a place in the wider CAMHS team, such as child psychotherapy training, one of the NHS Talking Therapies trainings or a CBT qualification, in addition to your core counselling training. The other option is to consider applying for generic posts where your counselling skills will be relevant and there may be on-the-job training, such as in outreach services linked to CAMHS or a Single Point of Access (SPoA), where mental health referrals for children and young people are screened initially.

There are now also mental health liaison services in hospitals, where applicants with a range of mental health trainings may be considered, but my understanding is that it is very difficult to get into these posts without a core NHS mental health training. The implementation of mental health support teams in schools – a joint initiative between the Department of Health and Social Care and the Department for Education (2018) intended to deliver the NHS Long Term Plan – might seem to offer opportunities for counsellors wishing to work with young people. A number of schools were given funding to train a member of the school staff to be a senior mental health lead who would be supervised and supported by a CAMHS clinician and ensure that NHS and education support services and pathways were joined up. In addition, a new role of educational mental health support practitioner has been created to offer cognitive behavioural support to pupils with mild-to-moderate anxiety and depression, and this too might seem an obvious role for counsellors. However, in reality, the interpretation and application of these initiatives varies widely between schools and areas, and some school counsellors who were doing a very good job in a local school have been pushed out of the picture.

There are more generic mental health practitioner roles and posts that come up in inpatient settings and are sometimes open to counsellors, but you are likely to be competing with art therapists, play therapists and mental health nurses, whose qualifications and roles will be more familiar to the interviewers.

So, you need to be able to demonstrate your transferable skills convincingly and clearly, and evidence that you have solid, longstanding experience of handling risk and pressure, as well as an understanding of the challenges you may face in these settings. You will also need resilience and to be ready and willing to roll up your sleeves, take on whatever task is thrown at you, and learn on the job.

In my view, understanding the CAMHS journey and the story so far is important when working out whether you want to become part of the CAMHS professional family. I also believe that understanding our own story and what draws us to this work or motivates us to become part of the child and adolescent mental health workforce is the first important step in finding a good fit and is the best preparation for managing the many challenges you will face there.

Counselling young people in the community

Lorna Birrell is Therapeutic Services Development Manager with the Young Persons Advisory Service (YPAS)[1], a youth information, advice and counselling service (YIACS) based in Liverpool.

I qualified as a counsellor 14 years ago and have worked in the third sector for the entirety of my qualified status. I joined YPAS seven years ago as a children's psychological therapist, in the 'Seedlings Service', delivering therapies to children in several Liverpool primary schools. I am proud of my professional journey as I am now the YIAC Therapeutic Services Development Manager, responsible for the management, development and representation of all YPAS's therapy services.

Established in 1966, YPAS is a mental health charity based in the north,

---

1. www.ypas.org.uk

south and city centre of Liverpool and serving a Merseyside population of more than 150,000 children and young people aged five to 25 years. YPAS's core business is to address the mental health and emotional wellbeing difficulties of children, young people and families in settings that are free as far as possible from the stigma often associated with psychiatric and mental health services.

Our offer includes open access drop-in provision and targeted support delivered in three community hubs, 96 primary schools, 33 secondary schools, numerous GP practices and many other community settings.

YPAS is a significant delivery partner of the Liverpool CAMHS partnership and represents the third sector on a wide range of strategic boards, networks, expert reference groups and collaboratives that have come together to deliver the strategic priorities of improved access to psychological therapies. Our aim is to develop the referral pathways, access, triage, assessment and treatment that will ensure our clients receive the right treatment, at the right time, in the right service, in the right place, and from the right practitioner, underpinned by the community-based 'no wrong door' approach.

YPAS's delivery model is strengthened by the nationally governed youth information, advice and counselling service (YIACS) model: services 'under one roof', self-referral and open access, offering wrap-around support for families with complex needs, community-based access and extended opening times (see the YIACS website for more information, at www.youthaccess.org.uk).

Since 2005, YPAS has been the main third sector delivery partner of the Liverpool comprehensive CAMHS pathway and has extensive experience of working with the diverse presentations and experiences of CYPF. These include adverse childhood experiences (ACEs), trauma, violence, domestic abuse, sexual abuse, bereavement, poverty, disability and neurodiversity.

YPAS uses an early intervention and prevention model of delivery that includes working with children and young people in primary school (the Seedlings Service), secondary school (wellbeing clinics) and up to 25 years, as well as working with parents/carers and families.

YPAS offers many recruitment opportunities for newly qualified counsellors and psychotherapists, and supports students on their professional journeys through to full-time employment. Vacancies are advertised via YPAS's website, social media platforms, BACP and university portals.

YPAS is passionate about its links with local training providers and its BACP-accredited therapy service offers a student placement scheme for 10 students per year to complete their required supervised clinical hours with young people (11–25 years). We offer students on placement a robust governance and support system, supported by a dedicated placement lead providing operational and supervisory oversight.

Our interview process includes young people and professionals panels, with an emphasis on personal and professional values and ethos.

There is no minimum requirement of post-qualification experience at the point of application as YPAS has a vision of a thriving, dynamic, therapeutic service that supports the next generation of counsellors and psychotherapists to enter community third-sector services.

In 2023 we were pleased and proud to be nominated for the Edge Hill University Graduate Employer of the Year award.

My top tips for working as a counsellor/psychotherapist in the third sector are:

- Apply for the role, interview and take the risk!
- Gain as much experience as possible working with children and young people before embarking on counselling training.
- Be confident in the depth of knowledge, skills and intuition you possess.
- Balance CPD with client experience, allowing yourself time to organically navigate your own and others' expectations of you as a counsellor.
- Embrace the diversity of the sector. Ride the wave of change and you will reap the rewards!
- And when you get into a management role, get used to the words 'fixed-term contract'.

Working with a voluntary counselling service

Rhona Kenny is Head of Therapeutic Services at Croydon Drop In (CDI). She explains how CDI provides an invaluable local resource and counselling service for young people in its community.

Probably the best way to describe the Croydon Drop In offer is that we are a wrap-around service offering a wide variety of free and confidential help and support to children, young people aged 11–25 and their families. Over our 45 years as a front-line community service, we have been listening to what local people tell us they need and delivering services to meet those needs.

Our diverse workforce reflects Croydon's population, and the charity is rooted in a symbiotic relationship with local people and, in particular, with volunteers. In fact, for most of our existence, the counselling provision has been entirely voluntary, recruited from counsellors in their final year of training on practice placements. A rigorous selection process ensures that the successful candidates are a best fit for us, and us for them. The new recruits are welcomed into the agency and are given a thorough induction in preparation to meet the young people, who self-refer to us and receive an initial assessment. We ask for a minimum commitment of a year from trainees and an agreement that they will complete their training during their time with us.

Volunteers are line-managed, clinically supervised (individually and in groups) and invited to participate in all the charity's training and development activities, fundraising, presentations to local organisations and partnership events within the borough.

Many volunteers have stayed with us post-qualification, and it is testament to the success of this scheme that most of our current staff are both former volunteers and former beneficiaries of the charity.

We believe that young people's participation is at the heart of everything we do, and our Young People's Team (YPT) is a central part of our services. The teams are formed from members aged 16+, who come together to represent the youth voice within the service for two to three years. As these participants fledge, a new group usually emerges. Each YPT has its own distinctive focus (to cite one example, working with local NHS commissioners on establishing a borough-wide young people's participation group), and those involved can also choose what they want to focus on. We work to help them understand the responsibility of representing young people and that the collective voice is a powerful voice. We help nurture this sense of responsibility and engagement by inviting them to sit on our recruitment panels, get involved in policymaking and business plan writing, and have a seat on our Board of Trustees.

Conclusion – is the CYPF sector for you?

Over the years I have met many an applicant or trainee counsellor who, on deeper thought and self-reflection, decided that working with children and young people wasn't for them. I recall offering a paid position to an excellent therapist who had come for interview, and they turned down our offer. Having heard what the work involved, they decided it wasn't what they were looking for. I will also never forget the placement applicant who, mid-interview, got up and left after we talked about safeguarding children and the complexities involved. They said that was too complicated for them, thanked us for our time and asked what the quickest way to their car was.

However, I've met far more counsellors and students who know that their passion is to work with young people – or at least they fancy giving it a try. I have to honestly say, it's a hard road to take. I can recall vividly every challenging session I've ever had with a young person, where I've had to work so hard in the room, find my best skills and try to use them in a way that might work well for that young person. Often, I worry that I only have one chance to get it right (the client might choose not to return), and desperately hope I can gel with my young client and that our relationship will work, grow and prosper.

I have literally sweated – sometimes, at the end of a five-to-six client day, I have felt too exhausted to do anything but take a long walk with the dog, or a long shower, to re-energise and re-charge my batteries.

I rarely find myself sweating or struggling in my adult work. But honestly, for me, CYPF work is the most rewarding and also what I am most proud of.

My core belief is in the value of even just a moment of support for a young person who otherwise might not have anyone else they could talk to about a particular issue. I hold the hope that my counselling work might help a young person in distress make a better or safer choice than if they had no one to talk to. The right support at a crucial moment could make a lifetime of difference for a young person. I know it is what I needed when I was 17 but failed to find.

I like the idea of thinking outside of the box. I have always been ready to consider other creative options and ideas that may bring about positive change that perhaps a school or family has been unable to provide, to help that young person reach their goal or bring about positive change.

Every day is different in CYPF work – the hours fly by; we are always busy, and we must always expect the unexpected. Safeguarding issues always come up at the busiest and worst times in our diary, and the 'Aha' moments will come out of the blue but will be amazing to witness. They fill me with a renewed sense of energy and commitment to this amazing sector.

Above all, keep your mind open and alert –there is always something to learn when you're working therapeutically with young people. And good luck in your CYPF journey!

Acknowledgements

With grateful thanks to Jo Holmes, BACP Children, Young People and Families Lead, for feedback, and to Lorna Birrell, Sarah Houghton, Rhona Kenny and Alison Roy for their contributions from the frontline.

Further reading

The following documents helpfully outline the wider policy context for children's mental health services and the roles within them:

Agenda For Change (Department of Health, 2004). https://webarchive.nationalarchives.gov.uk/ukgwa/20100407031625/http://dh.gov.uk/en/managingyourorganisation/workforce/paypensionsandbenefits/agendaforchange/index.htm

Every Child Matters (UK Government, 2003). https://assets.publishing.service.gov.uk/government/uploads/system/uploads/attachment_data/file/272064/5860.pdf

National Service Framework for Children, Young People and Maternity Services (Department of Health, 2004). https://assets.publishing.service.gov.uk/government/uploads/system/uploads/attachment_data/file/199952/National_Service_Framework_for_Children_Young_People_and_Maternity_Services_-_Core_Standards.pdf

The Five Year Forward View for Mental Health (Mental Health Taskforce, 2016). www.england.nhs.uk/wp-content/uploads/2016/02/Mental-Health-Taskforce-FYFV-final.pdf

The NHS Long Term Plan (NHS, 2019). www.longtermplan.nhs.uk/wp-content/uploads/2019/08/nhs-long-term-plan-version-1.2.pdf

References

BACP. (2018). *Ethical framework for the counselling professions*. BACP. www.bacp.co.uk/media/3103/bacp-ethical-framework-for-the-counselling-professions-2018.pdf

BACP. (2020a). *Counselling children and young people (4–18 years) training curriculum*. BACP. www.bacp.co.uk/media/16763/bacp-children-and-young-people-training-curriculum-jun20.pdf

BACP. (2020b). *Working with children and young people within the counselling professions*. BACP. www.bacp.co.uk/events-and-resources/ethics-and-standards/good-practice-in-action/publications/gpia046-working-with-children-and-young-people-caq (available to members only).

BACP. (2022a). *BACP CYP competence framework 2022*. BACP. www.bacp.co.uk/media/15873/bacp-cyp-competence-framework_2022.pdf

BACP. (2022b). *Safeguarding children and young people within the counselling professions in England and Wales*. BACP. www.bacp.co.uk/events-and-resources/ethics-and-standards/good-practice-in-action/publications/gpia031-safeguarding-children-and-young-people-within-the-counselling-professions-in-england-and-wales-lr (available to members only).

Department of Health and Social Care/Department for Education. (2018). *Government response to the consultation on 'Transforming children and young people's mental health provision: A green paper' and next steps*. HM Government. https://assets.publishing.service.gov.uk/government/uploads/system/uploads/attachment_data/file/728892/government-response-to-consultation-on-transforming-children-and-young-peoples-mental-health.pdf

National Counselling & Psychotherapy Society. (2023). *Competency framework for working with children and young people*. NCPS. https://nationalcounsellingsociety.org/assets/uploads/docs/cs/NCS-CYP-Compctcncy-Framework-V3.pdf.pdf

Chapter 10

Spirituality in counselling practice

Alistair Ross
with Sukhi Sian, Keith Duckett, Amy McCormack, Salma Khalid and Delroy Hall

An overview – Alistair Ross

Spirituality may seem a bit of an anomaly in this book, in that there are very few counselling opportunities (paid or unpaid) where a specific faith, religion or belief system is absolutely necessary for the role or where the counsellor will be practising within a centre or community that is specific to a particular religious faith or spiritual belief system.

There are many faith-based counselling services in the UK that were set up specifically to meet the needs of that faith group. It's a career path most suited to people who are part of that faith community. I have worked with two rebbetzin (wives of rabbis) who were motivated to train professionally as counsellors because their religious and pastoral roles brought them into contact with people whom they felt counselling could help. People from a particular faith community may not want to go outside that community for help and may feel they will be better understood by counsellors from within that community, with an understanding of and sympathy with their belief systems. There are also low-cost counselling services offered by some faith communities as a contribution to the wellbeing of their local community.

I have also trained students who specifically wanted to offer counselling to people from their own faith communities, and went on to set up in private practice, where they were able also to work with people from other faith traditions and spiritualities.

In my own private practice, I have seen clients who hold Spiritualist, Mormon, Taoist, Sikh, Muslim, Buddhist and Hindu beliefs, and clients who are part of what might be considered cults. They knew about my Christian background, but to them it was not important: they were simply looking for someone who would respect their religious/spiritual background and who was well qualified professionally.

There are also chaplaincy-type roles that require counselling skills. These are predominately found in schools, colleges, universities, hospitals, emergency services, and industry, commercial and sporting contexts. The people in these roles are likely to find their counselling skills very useful in their work, but generally they are not employed to practise as a therapist, even if this is something they are trained and equipped to do. There are tensions and complexities at the interfaces of pastoral care, pastoral counselling, counselling and psychotherapy, especially in relation to boundaries, which I discuss in my book *Counselling Skills for Church and Faith Community Workers* (Ross, 2003). Much has happened in the two decades since that book was published, with the professionalisation of counselling, a greater awareness of power dynamics, and the challenging nature of managing dual relationships. Nowadays a chaplain is viewed as just a chaplain, not a therapist as well.

Religion versus spirituality

The first hurdle that needs to be overcome is to tease out the differences between religion and spirituality. They are popularly depicted in binary opposition, like two heavyweight boxers preparing to slug it out, hoping to win by a knockout rather than a points decision, so they can be declared the undisputed champion. There is a growing distinction between religion and spirituality in Western culture. So rather than 'Religion vs Spirituality', it will always be more productive to embrace 'Religion and Spirituality'. A great example of this can be found in the work of American Franciscan priest and writer Richard Rohr and his colleagues at their Center for Action and Contemplation.[1]

Defining religion

Religions are hugely varied, with histories that stretch back over many centuries. Yet what they have in common is an organised system of beliefs, practices, rituals, symbols and traditions. These are designed to enable connection with a sacred or transcendent being or presence variously described as God(s),

---

1. https://cac.org

deities, higher power or ultimate truth/reality. These are also designed to facilitate being in community with others – understanding one's relationship and responsibility to others in living ethically and worshipping together. Yet adherents of every religious tradition want to claim theirs is distinctive and has a unique revelation to offer. As part of the Christian tradition, I understand and experience that. But it does not mean that wisdom cannot be found by listening, dialoguing, agreeing and disagreeing with other traditions. So, each religion has a clear definition of what it is and does. Religions offer an identity and a certainty that broader conceptions of spirituality lack.

Defining spirituality

There are myriad definitions of spirituality. Those rooted in religious traditions have defined boundaries, clear lines of demarcation, and practices honed through the centuries that offer something substantial. Those rooted in the self have less clear-cut boundaries and lines of inclusivity and multiple, ever-evolving practices offering something new. In the interests of clear communication as to what spirituality is, we need to begin with a definition. Any such definition needs to encompass three over-lapping areas of distinctive meaning.

The first locates spirituality in the devotional practices, religious observances and meditative and mystical states found in various religious traditions. The outcomes of these practices are to take the person and community closer to their God, gods or universe. In this form, there is a close and reciprocal bond between religion and spirituality. The second locates spirituality within the thinking, reflexive and existential nature of being human. The deep questions of life emerge: 'Who am I?', 'Why do I exist?', 'What gives life meaning?', 'Do I have a destiny?' This form of spirituality involves the exploration of the ultimate concerns for self and society. In this form, there is no close and reciprocal bond between religion and spirituality. Spirituality can be both secular and sacred.

The third locates spirituality in aesthetic experiences and ethical sensitivities to the self and the world. This can incorporate the wonders of nature; the awe of a starry sky and the universe beyond, and the artistic appeals of art, architecture, sculpture, music, literature and poetry. In this form, there is a paradoxical bond with religion and spirituality.

Having set out the over-lapping areas, one valuable over-arching definition of spirituality captures many aspects:

> Spirituality is a distinctive, potentially creative and universal dimension of human experience arising both within the inner subjective awareness of individuals and within communities, social groups and traditions. It

may be experienced as relationship with that which is intimately 'inner', immanent and personal, within the self and others, and/or as relationship with that which is wholly 'other', transcendent and beyond the self. It is experienced as being of fundamental or ultimate importance and is thus concerned with matters of meaning and purpose in life, truth and values. (Cook, 2004, p.548)

Experts in translation

In many parts of the world other than the UK, religion and spirituality are accepted as an intrinsic part of the national culture, with no secular divide and no assumption that religion and spirituality are forms of pathology or relics of a world that is long gone. North America has its own rich context of writing and research on issues of therapy, religion and spirituality (Sandage & Strawn, 2022), but these do not always cross the Atlantic well. The contributors to this chapter all live and work in the UK, with its unique four nations identity. There is much of value we can learn from other countries and cultures, but it needs translating, as our own contexts and the expectations and those of the people we see are so very different.

So, one of the key skills counsellors and therapists develop when they own a faith and/or a spirituality is to become an expert in translation. They turn the language of one way of understanding the world and our place in it into another language to aid communication. Thankfully these languages overlap as we become multi-lingual. For example, I could see a client from a different religious tradition from my own and I don't need to know the details of that religious tradition, but I do need to be able to identify the psychological struggles they might be having in the context of their faith tradition. Or it may be as simple as letting the client know this is safe space where nothing is off limits, and that this may include their emerging spirituality. It is also important to acknowledge the context of spiritual and religious abuse that therapists can encounter when working with spirituality and religion, as highlighted by our contributor Salma Khalid, who works with individuals who have experienced coercive, cultic and spiritual abuse.

Spirituality in counselling practice

There is always an authenticity to be found in the lived experience of people and their stories – in this case, counsellors and psychotherapists who own a faith tradition and or a spirituality. What is it like in their real-world contexts? This section will report a range of perspectives from five practitioners, who bring their insights and learning from practice in many settings to bear on the subject. But first, I want to explore a way of looking at spirituality in the workplace that I think may resonate with many counsellors, whether they work in that setting or not.

Workplace spirituality

In our increasingly secular world, we are starting to understand how the workplace can become a focus for the human need to find meaning and value within a larger collective whole. For many of us, feeling both that they matter to and are part of the business or organisation where they work brings a larger dimension to, or spiritually enhances, their life. They believe in what they do and what the organisation does, and this gives meaning to what (after all) they spend the majority of their days and lives doing.

It's notable that the Covid pandemic left many people feeling isolated, and especially when they were furloughed or out of work, or simply confined to working from their home – it seems people lost that sense of connection to their workplace or other centre of activity as a place of belonging. Many successfully replaced this with a close connection to their community (see, for example, some of the narratives in *Weathering the Storm*, a resonant collection of first-person stories about surviving the pandemic, collated by Liz Rothschild (2023)). Others were not able to do so, for a range of reasons, and their isolation was a cause of great suffering and distress. For me, this illustrates the importance of workplace spirituality to those who work or volunteer or are otherwise part of large groups and organisations outside traditional religious and spiritual traditions.

There are four aspects to the best workplace spirituality. It is a recognition of the significance of:

- the inner life of the spirit in each person
- occupation that offers meaning
- being part of a community where spirit and meaning are acknowledged
- making explicit the link between personal values and organisational values.

Awareness of the importance of workplace spirituality is still patchy in the UK (Rathee & Rajain, 2020). Some of the clients I see bemoan its absence in their workplace, feeling they are just being used – expected to constantly deliver by managers who are only interested in productivity, outcomes and sales figures. It is a space where the counselling profession can usefully play an influential role.

I think we would all agree that many more people are turning to therapy in search of much more than a change in their cognitions or an immediate solution to a current problem (although there is a growing need for that too).

They are seeking a safe space to explore who and what they are, which of itself embraces the potential for the discovery or renewal of a religious and spiritual dimension. And for those seeking communication with peers treading this path, BACP Spirituality (a sector-specific division within BACP) exists as a body to promote a 'community of practitioners' who share a commitment to supporting that which is authentically therapeutic, religious and spiritual.

Practitioners' voices

I am now going to hand over the narrative to five therapists – Sukhi Sian, Keith Duckett, Amy McCormack, Salma Khalid and Delroy Hall – to tell their stories about how and where spirituality features in their work. I have used a common framework of questions to structure their descriptions of their unique but diverse experiences, practices and workplaces.

I am grateful to them for being so open and courageous in letting us into their lives to help us all explore further what spirituality means in the workplace. One of the engaging aspects of working with spirituality is that there is always something we can learn that can enrich us.

1. How would you describe your religion and/or spirituality?

Sukhi. I was born into the Sikh faith, but I do not consider myself religious. The Sikh faith introduced me to a way of living through 'seva' (service to humanity), by being part of a wider community that practises mutual support through love, compassion, truth and generosity. In hindsight, these are some of the fundamental spiritual principles I later discovered when I consciously opened up to spirituality in my late 30s. Spirituality, to me, is that journey back to the self – our true essence, our soul. I believe we are spiritual beings having a physical human experience, through which we experience mental and emotional aspects of ourselves. Spirituality has given me the understanding that through suffering comes growth, and with that an acceptance that suffering is inevitable. Through acceptance and understanding of that suffering, spirituality helps us perceive our experiences as opportunities for learning. This is underpinned by a sense of faith and belief in something much greater than us – the universe, God, the divine; a sense that life is playing out for the highest and greatest good. Spirituality to me is about our growth and soul evolution. Through practices such as mindfulness, meditation, prayer and yoga, we can strengthen this connection to ourselves and therefore to God.

Keith. 'Contemplative Christianity' was probably the most appropriate label for my belief system until recently. In the last few years, I have also used 'the-Buddhist-end-of-Christianity' as an alternative when talking with people for whom 'contemplative Christianity' means little. In this I am trying to be provocative and evocative at the same time. I am wanting to connect with people, and also to get them to think and feel for themselves about their spirituality. As a result of some painful and profound experiences over this past year, I am leaning away from such labels but use the term 'non-dual' philosophy/spirituality if pushed. Until I discovered this tradition, I realise that I had been feeling a sense of a subtly unsatisfactory dualism in much of the contemporary mindfulness movement, although I could not have named it as such. So, spirituality is something that is alive and developing within me.

Amy. I have developed a nature-based, embodied spirituality that plays a key part in both my self-care and the way that I practise. The philosophies I learned in my development as a therapist have had an important influence on my evolving spirituality. I started learning Eugene Gendlin's focusing a couple of years into my career (Gendlin, 1982). This philosopher, who worked alongside Carl Rogers, described this self-care tool as a way of getting what he called the body-sense of a situation by listening within and accessing an inner form of knowing. I wanted to be more present in my body so that I could become a more responsive practitioner. This regular practice quickly transformed my capacity to be present with myself and with my clients. It also connected me with a deep sense of faith within.

Salma. As a British Asian Muslim woman, my faith and spirituality has evolved over time as I have leaned into both my own transformational journey and my development and growth as integrative therapist, clinical supervisor and poet. My approach to spirituality and faith is very much shaped by philosophical approaches to life that are embedded in understanding the soul, also known as the psyche. These include the works of Jallal ud din Rumi (Arasteh, 2013), Khalil Gibran (2020) and Ibn Arabi (the Sufi poet and philosopher). I have also over time integrated concepts of Islamic psychology into my work. I believe I touch on spirituality and faith when exploring the journey towards the self and my understanding of the meaning and purpose of life. For me, my faith and my approach to spirituality, which includes an encompassing of other faiths and philosophies and spiritualities, shapes who I am and how I work. I have a great interest in nature-based and embodied spirituality and the divine feminine, and I find exploring the interspace between the client and the therapist very fascinating.

Delroy. I struggle with the word 'religion' because I think in the West it is a despised and loaded term. I was born into an African Caribbean Pentecostal Christian household. My parents had a firm faith in God. They were part of the

Windrush generation, and their faith, I believe, helped them enormously as they made their home in the UK. At the age of 20, I made a conscious commitment of faith, a born-again experience. Spirituality is a somewhat loose term that is now in vogue and often not anchored anywhere. I recall someone once saying to me, years ago, that she was spiritual: 'I know it is a cop out, Delroy, because I am not committed to anything.' For me, my spirituality is connected to a personal relationship I have with Jesus Christ that is alive, real, present and dynamic. My religion/spirituality is not something I pick up as I walk through the church doors on a Sunday morning. It is lived daily experience.

2. Where do you practise as a therapist?

Sukhi. I work in private practice as a therapist/counsellor and clinical supervisor. I also work as a holistic therapist, offering reiki/crystal healing sessions and numerology readings. I offer a variety of courses and group work around a holistic approach to self-love. I have predominantly worked in women's or children and young people's organisations, naturally falling into leadership roles, specifically in areas of sexual violence, substance misuse and mental health. In my current role, I am a clinical supervisor for practitioners working with children aged between five and 18. I was previously head of service for an organisation supporting victims of sexual trauma.

Keith. I am lead counsellor, co-ordinator and leader of the bereavement support team within the specialist palliative care division of an NHS trust in an urban, multicultural setting, comprising both acute and community provision. We are based in a modern, purpose-built palliative care centre, surrounded by trees, well away from the main acute hospital site. Immediately before taking up this post, I was part-time specialist palliative care chaplain and centre chaplain in the same location, part of the trust's spiritual care team, while also working part-time in a local NHS Talking Therapies service.

Amy. I am an integrative counsellor working in private practice. My core training was in Petruska Clarkson's five-relationship model (Clarkson, 2003). I have since become a British Focusing Association recognised focusing practitioner and this embodied practice has become central to my approach. I initially trained in person-centred bereavement, and this remains a foundation. In addition to my therapeutic hours, I am the editor of the BACP Spirituality journal, *Thresholds*.

Salma. I currently work in private practice as a psychotherapist. More recently, I have embarked on a journey into creative arts and art for wellbeing. In addition to providing clinical supervision, I also offer supervision of reflective practice to several organisations, including Early Break, who specialise in drug and alcohol work, and VESTA, who support people impacted by domestic violence and modern slavery. I also provide psychotherapy services for the Rory Peck Trust, which supports freelance journalists and their families worldwide, and I work in a school-based setting, offering talking therapy to children and young people. As a creative writer and poet, I am a 'creative health practitioner' with Cartwheel Arts, an art-for-wellbeing project. This involves working with meditation, art and movement, often in a community-based group setting.

Delroy. I now work for myself, but much of my work as a therapist was in a secular higher educational establishment, where I was based for some 20 years. I found the work challenging, but for me, if faith is unable to meet the demands of daily living, it does not make any sense. I worked for a while for the NHS in Leicester and at Leicester University, where I trained as a psychotherapist.

3. How does spirituality enhance your work as a therapist?

Sukhi. Spirituality features in my work as a therapist in my commitment to increasing my reflective practice and prioritising my own healing, through introspection, meditation, journalling, spiritual practices, clinical supervision and personal therapy. This helps me to identify my own blocks, blind spots and shadows, which creates the opportunity for learning, healing, self-care and growth.

Spirituality gives me a sense of inner strength that is difficult to put into words. It is something I feel from the core of my being. This helps me to feel more grounded in my own intuition, and therefore enhances trust and faith in myself, my client and the therapeutic process. Spirituality also gave me the courage to come out of what I referred to as the 'spiritual closet' within the counselling profession (Sian, 2020). It helped me to overcome my fears and step into becoming more of an authentic therapist by embracing and continuing to integrate my own power and truth.

Spirituality has helped me to become more aware of my own needs and supports me to continuously strive for a better work-life balance by recognising the benefits and challenges of experiencing ignition and being driven by my passion. The benefits of this fuel me with courage, strength and a sense of purpose in my roles as a therapist and clinical supervisor, which helps me to lead others through inspiration and empowerment by taking a very proactive approach. The challenges are that enthusiasm and saying 'yes' can lead to over-commitment, impacting on that work-life balance, and, ironically, this can distract from spiritual practices. Spirituality has made me more aware of this paradox – this potential conflict between the inner and outer worlds.

It therefore enhances my work as a therapist because it reminds me of the importance of a balance of giving and receiving, brings my attention back to my self-care, and helps me to love, honour and respect myself more, always endeavouring to 'practise what I preach' and to lead by example.

Keith. My implicit and explicit spirituality enhances my work as a therapist by shaping my approach to being and practice. My general approach to spirituality (prior to this year at least) is reflected in an article I published in 2022, 'Spirituality in Reflective Practice' (Duckett, 2022). In terms of my therapeutic practice, I am aware that I have spent a lot of time with my clinical supervisor over recent years reflecting on the notion of 'holding'. She was also my supervisor as a chaplain before we continued the relationship into my new role. The sense of holding means to me a holding open and a holding safe of broad spaciousness in which the spirituality, identity and other issues of the client can feel welcome and have room to breathe. In some cases, this is a temporary holding up of someone whose sense of stability and agency has crumbled, or a holding down of one's own roots, and an invitation to the client to de-escalate their emotional state by temporarily anchoring in the therapist's harbour. I think the mixing of metaphors is inevitable in this profession!

In tandem with this there may be a holding of oneself alongside (a being with) the client as a temporary travelling companion, when other supports might have fallen away (a 'holding of hands', if you like). Beyond this, there could be a holding together where there has been a breaking apart (perhaps initiated at first by the therapist where needed, but working towards a mutuality of holding). Then there might be a holding of tools: I imagine the assistant to the surgeon, the dentist, the carpenter, or other craftsperson handing over and taking back the tools and materials as the expert (the client) works on their task of mending, sculpting, pruning or otherwise attending to their own psycho-spiritual landscape.

Then there's the holding of possibility, where there might have been a narrowing of options, a fading of hope, a shrinking of inspiration and initiative. Alongside everything, there must be that holding firm in the face of mystery – holding firm to a trust in the life forces that counterbalance the mysteries of life that sometimes cause us fear; holding firm to a humility in the face of the mysteries of Otherness that we often colonise or oppress in our fear or ignorance; a holding firm to the evolving mysteries of faith that transcend all that we try to pin down as rigid certainties and to which we often feel mysteriously drawn.

And all this is contained within the aspiration of 'boundless holding' (Totton, 2021, p.229) – the holding out of the hand of generosity, even love.

This spirituality of holding has grown out of a Christian spirituality of being held (by God) and being a channel (a minister) of God's holding of the whole universe – each atom, each cell.

Amy. When I started my private practice, working from a room in my garden, I soon realised that I would need to acknowledge the beginning and end of each therapy hour in a more symbolic, deeply felt way. I wanted to create a 'container' to gently hold the hours I spend with clients each week. I was already connected with the earth, trees and animals around me, and quickly began to feel that these 'held' me and the therapeutic space. I turned to my trusted, focusing-oriented supervisor for help. She invited me to explore how I could develop a gentle ritual and sat quietly while I sensed into what that could look like. She then invited me to try this out with her in our session. Being witnessed was the sacred part. It created a sense of supervision as 'the vessel through which the spiritual is expressed' (Shohet & Shohet, 2021, pp.22–25). This session, and many others like it, have gifted me with an embodied experience of supervision as the container I was looking to create for myself and my clients.

I have come to visualise these layers of holding as circles within circles. Of course, there are days when it all goes out of the window: I am flustered, shaken by life circumstances, hormones or a bad night's sleep. But I do know these circles are there to come back to. I was delighted to discover Nancy Falls' description of creating a 'precious container' to hold clients' experiences by visualising an ironwood bowl (Speyer & Yaphe, 2020, p.38). It has also been enriching to study polyvagal theory and to understand the neuroscience behind the deep, wordless, embodied knowing that comes with focusing practice. This state of peace and wellbeing is known as ventral vagal energy – the good feeling that comes from a nervous system that is at rest.

Salma. My ongoing personal journey back to self and the transformational soul work I engage in keeps me spiritually anchored both as a person and as a therapist. Part of my value base on cultivating self-awareness and soul work is embedded in the Sufi tradition, and its concept of 'To know thyself is to know thy lord'. In my personal journey and practice, Lord can mean God, the cosmos, nature, the universe or whatever it is that helps us to connect with our self.

At a personal level, my clients can show up in my reflective, meditative, contemplative and prayer space and this leads to me finding inspiration and reflection in how I might work and be present with them. I also believe that my work is part of my calling in my search for purpose and meaning and, to quote Khalil Gibran, 'Work is love made visible.' Being open to spirituality and faith also creates space for me and my clients to work with the shadow side of self.

Delroy. My understanding is, when I sit in the company of another human being in the therapy room, I believe Jesus is with me, and the human being I am present with is a fellow human being, created in the image of God, who I consider to be sacred, whether they have a faith perspective or not.

When I was a student counsellor, I was never too concerned whether the student was destined for a first-class honours degree or not. I was interested in helping them to make sense of the world and their life in it. If they were suicidal, I was clear that part of my role as a counsellor and Christian was to preserve life, where possible, with the full understanding that, if a person ended their life by suicide, it was finally, and ultimately, their decision.

I also see my engagement with another human being as an act of worship. Pentecostal worship is mediated through songs, extemporised prayers and expressive music. However, for me, God's presence is not limited to a building and my worship to him as a therapist is how I treat the client who is with me.

4. How do you integrate spirituality into your work?

Sukhi. The more I integrate my own spirituality, the more I integrate spirituality into my work. The biggest shift for me has been around becoming and continuing to be the therapist who is aligned with my authentic self, which is of course constantly evolving. I have found it important to explicitly advertise the spiritual aspect of my therapeutic work to the public through my website and social media presence so that clients know that I welcome spirituality. I often get feedback from clients and supervisees that this is what drew them to me, and knowing that I also practise reiki, crystal healing and numerology gives them permission to bring their spiritual beliefs into the room. Even if clients never speak about their faith, religion or belief, they often tell me that knowing they could gave them permission to bring their whole self into the relationship. When and if I integrate holistic approaches with counselling, I take into account ethical considerations such as contracting, ensuring informed consent, managing dual roles, and considering the client's best interest. I explored this further in an article, 'Integrating Holistic Approaches', published in *Thresholds* journal (Sian, 2021).

In my previous workplace, I was able to find funding for several body/spirit-related therapies, including reiki and trauma-sensitive yoga. This complemented the existing talking therapies and, given that many of the issues were related to trauma, proved effective. In my current role as clinical supervisor, I am starting a spirituality-with-children special interest group, as other colleagues are discovering this is an important but overlooked area. In both these contexts, it was important for me to find the right supervisor – someone who was rooted in the psychodynamic modality I was initially trained in and who also integrated spirituality into their practice. I feel I can take my whole true self to supervision, without having to hide my spirituality and or keep it separate. My supervisor has supported me in my clinical and ethical thinking around developing and integrating spirituality into therapeutic practice, which I also wrote about in my *Thresholds* article (Sian, 2021).

Keith. My recent experiences have led to the opening up of a subtle re-orientation in my approach. This has been greatly helped by my therapist pointing me in the direction of Martin Wells' *Sitting in the Stillness* (Wells, 2019). Reading other people's stories has enabled me to put therapeutic flesh on the spiritual bones of non-dual enlightenment and then led me to the wider discoveries in that world. In therapeutic encounters, I am aware at times of being drawn towards a sense of sitting within and being mutually held by the spaciousness of 'non-dual being' or 'pure consciousness' rather than me doing the holding. Of course, there are many occasions when this flips or slips back round the other way, into a more dualistic mentality. Nevertheless, at any point on this rotation, integration is perhaps a misleading concept, for the spirituality of the frame, the frame of holding, has an elastic quality to it, whether it is the 'being held' of non-dual being or my dualistic intentional holding. And within that infinite space, the spirituality and spiritual issues of the client find a hospitality. Eventually even elastic can snap, and that's been the journey for me. When the elastic snaps, you can discover there's still space outside the elastic.

Amy. As the editor of *Thresholds,* BACP's journal for therapists with an interest in spirituality, belief or pastoral care, I have drawn inspiration from the many authors who bring a transpersonal dimension to their work. In this role, I have also been called to better understand the professional complexities of providing counselling with a spiritual component. Every piece of writing in the journal reflects a practitioner's unique spiritual outlook and way of working. Having considered many articles through an ethical lens, I have come to understand the importance of transparency. I've tried to get as curious as I can about my own spirituality. It's not always easy, but self-reflection, therapy, supervision and creativity have helped me to explore where my own edges are. Spirituality in counselling and psychotherapy is a vibrant field. There are endless permutations. I feel so grateful that I get to work with so many practitioners who are exploring what this means to them in writing. I learn from them all. It is a discussion that always feels fresh. In fact, sometimes it feels brand new. Talking about religious or spiritual belief can be taboo in counselling – which is perhaps a reflection of our largely secular society. But this is reductive, because people have always turned to religion for solace and meaning and a person's faith can significantly increase their resilience. There are countless articles in *Thresholds* and elsewhere that attest to that. Going forward, it seems important that the profession more openly acknowledges that experiences can sit at both ends of the spectrum, and anywhere in between.

In terms of my private practice, I do not present it on my website as spiritual in nature. I am a focusing practitioner, so I will offer to 'teach' focusing to support self-care, but I do not usually talk about my personal spiritual experience in relation to that. I am very open to clients exploring their own spirituality and I am inspired by Speyer's idea that therapy can be a 'search for sources of wholeness' (Speyer & Yaphe, 2020, p.2). I watch carefully for times where I may be at risk of imposing my worldview, because I have observed this to be the common denominator in most ethically intricate scenarios involving faith and belief.

Salma. Many of my clients choose to work with me because my approach is inclusive of spirituality, from those who hold atheist and agnostic values to those who are from an established faith background or from new and emerging faiths. Many therapists feel that they need to tread carefully when positioning spirituality and belief in their therapeutic work, fearing an imposition of values and ideologies. This has not been my experience, and I believe accessing conversations about the psycho-spiritual is as simple as exploring the concepts of meaning, purpose or hope in life.

As a creative health practitioner, this can also be achieved through the media of art, drama, music, poetry, dance and movement, and so much more.

Some of my work involves working with the dark side of spirituality and belief, and over the years I have worked with clients who have experienced coercive, cultic and spiritual abuse. I refer to the work of Jenkinson (2008), who is a pioneer in this arena. Any trauma can injure and interrupt the development and growth of the psyche, or the soul, so often what I endeavour to work towards in my practice is realigning this by exploring the psychospiritual.

Delroy. I do not think I integrate spirituality consciously as I have God with me all the time. To think of spirituality in compartmental terms is to have dualistic thinking, which I do not find helpful. Just as an important aside, while I worked as a therapist, I was also a pastor, and later became an ordained bishop within the church organisation I was affiliated to at the time.

My work as a minister and therapist were integrated and both disciplines informed each other in how I helped people. There have been times in therapy when I have had insights that have baffled both me and the client; on other occasions, as I patiently listen, I have quietly prayed to God to help me understand what is happening to the client. At yet other times, I have prayed with quiet desperation, almost, for guidance because I did not have a clue what was happening to the client in the session.

I have always been sensitive around raising issues of faith/religion/spirituality within secular organisations, as I have not wanted to be seen as proselytising, given my active faith. However, over the many years, I have many interesting conversations with young people about faith and spirituality.

5. What have been the biggest changes you have seen in the last 10 years?
Sukhi. Holistic therapies such as reiki have become much more mainstream, in the same way as meditation and mindfulness. Therapies in the NHS have an underpinning of a spiritual quality such as compassion, as seen in compassion-focused therapy. Mindfulness has its roots in Buddhist traditions, such as being grounded in the present moment, being grateful in everyday life, and bringing our awareness to our five senses of touch, smell, taste, sound and sight. I have noticed that more and more people are questioning life, searching for something deeper and meaningful, and are looking for spiritual direction. With much more access to a variety of books with spiritual context, as well as audio versions, podcasts, documentaries and channels focused specifically on spiritual growth, people are increasingly open to approaches that go beyond the psyche. In a similar vein, counselling and therapy have become much more aware of the complex nature of trauma and there is increasing research into trauma and how people can be best helped holistically through a mind, body and soul connection (van der Kolk, 2015).

Keith. The biggest change for me has been moving full-time into counselling work. I am now a counsellor within the same field (healthcare) and the same organisation where I once worked as a spiritual care specialist practitioner (or 'chaplain'). As counsellor, I have experienced more opportunities for direct and open engagement with a wide breadth of religious and other spiritualities than I ever did as a chaplain. In the 15 years I spent in the chaplain role, I experienced the label as a barrier to access and engagement as often as it was a key and an entry point to being with and exploring being (or 'spirituality') with patients and staff. As a Church of England priest working as a chaplain, I never wore my clerical collar in the palliative care centre for my four years there, but still felt its imputed presence. Of course, this may say as much about me as about the context. Nevertheless, by the application of relational skills and the nurturing of relationality within my personal/spiritual development, I was able to gain invitation to enough situations to make me suspect that there was scope for a lot more 'spiritual care' among patients, relatives and staff, if only I could just 'be there' more. Of course, there are some people for whom the labels 'counselling' and 'psychological support' are just as much barriers as 'spiritual care' or 'chaplain' are for others. However, without having any data to hand, I can assure you that, for me at least, spirituality is very much present in my current work. You might expect that existential concerns would more naturally surface within a bereavement setting anyway, but I am also aware how easily spiritual dimensions can be shut down, and particularly how the system can water down the spiritual flavours that are everywhere if we have the eyes to see and ears to hear.

Amy. Talking about religious or spiritual belief can be a taboo in counselling – which is perhaps a reflection of a largely secular society. I've noticed that this is slowly changing and that there is a move towards approaching a person's spiritual beliefs in a more integrative way. This feels important as a person's spirituality doesn't sit in a separate box in a counselling session. I have come across many writers making this point. For instance, Philip Evans, who is lead chaplain at St Andrew's Hospital, Northampton, developed an outcomes measure in recognition of what he describes as 'the central question of whether faith and spirituality amount only to a separate piece of human activity or observance, or whether they contribute substantively to someone's health' (Evans, 2021, p.24). In the eight years since I qualified, embodied ways of working seem to have become more prevalent. This may also play a part in faith and spirituality becoming more integrated. When something is felt at a bodily level, it is generally less likely to be considered as being 'separate from' (Cornell, 2013, p.215). The increasing use of polyvagal theory in counselling practice means both counsellors and clients have new tools at their disposal to create a calmer, more grounded foundation for therapeutic work. This too can have a spiritual component (Dana, 2021, p.137).

Salma. The catalyst for my journey towards integrating faith and spirituality into my work was my quest to understand and make sense of the word 'psyche' that is often used in our overarching reference to psychological therapies. The irony is that 'psychology' is based on the Greek word 'psyche', meaning soul or spirit (Khalid, 2007). Psychology is therefore literally the study of the soul. Over the past 10 years, it has been incredibly exciting to see the soul increasingly emerging in research and training and becoming more integrated into the practice of psychotherapists and counsellors. However, there is still much work to be done, as spirituality and belief continue to sit under the headings of equality and diversity. The lack of training and self-awareness with regards to understanding spirituality and belief can mean practitioners 'miss out' on opportunities for growth and transformation, to the detriment not only of themselves as practitioners but also of their clients. This can lead to misunderstandings and pathologising, and even discrimination, as the significance of religion and belief can be further lost when there is a lack of understanding around differences along the dimensions of race, class, gender, sexuality and disability.

My journey and hope for the future with regards to addressing spirituality and belief are embedded in this poem:

Embracing the psyche

I am the psyche who has been confined within the walls of intellect,
and lost in the abyss of secularism.
I am the psyche who has been intoxicated by medicine and lost in the synaptic void,
where only cranial activity can be defined as truth.
I am the psyche that has been fragmented into cognitive thoughts and behaviours.
I am the psyche that transcends time and space.
I am an existential entity roaming the universe since the beginning of time.

I am the psyche that holds eternal truth.
You can l find me in the interspace between the I and thou.
You can find me through the stillness of time.
You can find me in the wilderness of nature, in the depths of the ocean and in the moonlit sky.
You can hear me through the cosmos and through the voice of ancestors.

I am the breath, I am the heartbeat, I am the music, I am the song.
I am the creator, I am Goddess, I am God.
I am me; I am you.
I am here to be embraced.
I am here to heal and find peace.
I am here I am purpose I am meaning,
I am life's calling.

Delroy. Some of the biggest changes I have seen in the last 10 years involve the transition of counselling services into wellbeing centres and how, in many institutions, what is taking place in helping people is simply symptom management. I am aware of financial restraints and demands on services and people, but I cannot help but wonder, given our complexities as human beings, if we are really helping people enough.

A huge point of sadness for me is the increased incidence of students suffering with depression or anxiety, and in some cases both. When I started training as a psychotherapist in the early 1990s, I rarely worked with a student who had depression, but over the past 10 years the number has grown significantly. Another area of huge sadness and pain for me is the increasing number of young people who succumb to taking their own life. When I was leaving the university, the numbers of high-risk students were taking a toll on my colleagues.

Finally, my sense is, if one has an active spiritual life (a subjective comment that cannot be explored sufficiently here), is it a means of making meaningful connection with another person, whether they are spiritual, religious or neither?

Reflections – Alistair Ross

Engaging with the five contributors and reflecting on my 40-year involvement with religion, spirituality, faith, theology, counselling, psychotherapy, psychoanalysis, psychiatry and ethics, key themes emerge for further exploration. Spirituality is clearly alive and well in counsellors' workplaces, despite the dominant secular cultural narratives that continually decry religion.

Theme 1. Religion and spirituality are part of a wider challenge to address issues of difference and diversity in our society at so many levels. These challenges are so worth fighting for and need to be addressed again and again. The hope is that a time will come soon when therapists feel safe enough to come out of the spirituality closet. At the same time, religious and spiritual traditions need to address their own issues in terms of difference and diversity, especially around gender and sexuality. In a follow-up conversation, Keith comments: 'Perhaps the biggest challenge is simply honing our ability to embrace the great opportunity that lies ahead, as the equality, diversity and inclusion agenda opens up further the vistas of space in which spiritualities could be more freely and easily seen and heard (both in client and in therapist, we should note).'

Theme 2. All therapy trainings need to adapt to or adopt issues of religion and spirituality as a demonstration of their inclusivity. I still think this is a vital step if we are to address the dearth of knowledge and awareness in counselling trainees. At least alerting them to what they don't know gives them the opportunity to decide what they need for themselves and their clients.

Keith offers a different perspective: 'Some get very concerned that there is not enough training for counsellors in spirituality. However, as I wrote in my *Thresholds* article (Duckett, 2022), I think the skills, attitudes and orientations needed are more those of curiosity and wonder, which should be generic skills anyway (wondering what/how, wondering at and wondering if). There are many issues and themes that can come up in counselling work; I have certainly not had detailed awareness training in all of them. There is always the chance I may need to refer on to someone else who has; but often, with a trusting rapport forming, I just need to stay with that person in curiosity and wonder, rather than know lots about some particular subject matter. So, I am not sure we need to worry too much about training courses squeezing in yet another module (on spirituality) as such; more on the nurturing of curiosity and wonder, and their application to a greater range of experiences, issues and beliefs. We might also want to become aware that when the avalanche/landslide/nosedive happens and we fall off the cliff of duality into the ocean depths and swirl below, inviting an awakening to non-dual being, it may well be painful as well as disorientating, but it will ultimately be a gift to an expansiveness that gives more room to our clients.'

Theme 3. Finding the right supervision. All five contributors have evidenced the vital importance of supervision as a space where they feel safe to bring their inner most feelings, often located around spirituality. Thinking about my own clinical practice, I have 11 supervisees, eight of whom have come to me precisely because they can raise religious or spiritual matters in their therapeutic practice. This does not mean spirituality emerges in every session of supervision, but they feel safe to do so if and when they wish. As one supervisee said recently, 'It feels as if the whole of me can be in the supervision space.'

Theme 4. Continual attention needs to be paid to the complex balancing act that faith and therapy bring, with inevitable and enriching overlaps and boundaries. This is even more so in some counselling settings where there may be organisational limitations about what can, or cannot, be explored. Most counselling organisations would view any form of proselytising as unethical, especially given the power imbalance common in therapeutic relations. Yet clients can set the agenda and raise whatever matters are of importance to them, including issues of spirituality.

Theme 5. It is important to recognise that religion or spirituality, in and outside the counselling setting, can be toxic. We also need to avoid dualistic and reductive views of religions as all bad and spirituality as all good. Not everything that is done in the name of religion or spirituality always helps people. As ethically aware practitioners, we should have a commitment to the wellbeing of the client, whatever their background, and this ethical core should be at the heart of all religious and spiritual traditions and practices.

A final word. The sheer enthusiasm and creativity that emerge from the words of Sukhi, Keith, Amy, Salma and Delroy as they tell their stories reveal that spirituality plays a vital and vibrant role in our culture. Society will be impoverished if such voices are never heard.

References

Arasteh, A.R. (2013). *Rumi the Persian, the Sufi.* Routledge.

Clarkson, P. (2003). *The therapeutic relationship* (2nd ed.). Wiley-Blackwell.

Cook, C. (2004). Addiction and spirituality, *Addictions, 99,* 539–551.

Cornell, A.W. (2013). *Focusing in clinical practice: The essence of change.* W.W. Norton.

Dana, D. (2021). *Anchored.* Sounds True.

Duckett, K. (2022). Spirituality in reflective practice. *Thresholds,* (January), 16.

Evans, P. (2021). Can the impact of faith and spirituality be measured? *Thresholds,* (July), 24–27.

Gendlin, E. (1982). *Focusing.* Bantam Books.

Gibran, K. (2020). *The prophet.* Alma Classics.

Jenkinson, G. (2008). An investigation into cult pseudo-personality: what is it and how does it form? *Cultic Studies Review, 1*(3), 199–244.

Khalid, S. (2007). Counselling from an Islamic perspective. *Therapy Today, 18*(2), 34–37.

Rathee, R., & Rajain, P. (2020). Workplace spirituality: A comparative study of various models. *Jindal Journal of Business Research, 9*(1), 27–40. https://doi.org/10.1177/2278682120908554

Ross, A. (2003). *Counselling skills for church and faith community workers.* Open University Press.

Rothschild, L. (Ed.). (2023). *Weathering the storm: Stories of love, life, loss and discovery in the time of Covid.* PCCS Books.

Sandage, S. & Strawn, B. (Eds.). (2022). *Spiritual diversity in psychotherapy: Engaging the sacred in clinical practice.* American Psychological Association.

Shohet, R. & Shohet, J. (2021). Supervision as spiritual practice. *Thresholds,* (January), 22–25.

Sian, S. (2020). Coming out of the closet. *Thresholds,* (April), 20–22.

Sian, S. (2021). Integrating holistic approaches. *Thresholds,* (July), 10–14.

Speyer, C. & Yaphe J. (Eds.). (2020). *Applications of a psychospiritual model in the helping professions: Principles of InnerView Guidance.* Routledge.

Totton, N. (2021). *Wild therapy: Rewilding our inner and outer worlds* (2nd ed.). PCCS Books.

Van der Kolk, B. (2015). *The body keeps the score: Mind, brain and body in the transformation of trauma.* Penguin Books.

Wells, M. (2019). *Sitting in the stillness.* Mantra Books.

About the contributors

Jeremy Bacon joined BACP in 2017 as Older People Lead and is now Third Sector Lead in its policy team, heading up BACP's work to lobby and campaign for increased provision of third sector counselling services. After completing degrees in politics and social work at Hull University, Jeremy has worked in the third sector since 1997, in roles with local and national charities delivering support services and advocacy. Jeremy is also the Special Interest Lead for the BACP Coaching executive committee.

Vianna Boring Renaud is the current chair of BACP Workplace and a person-centred counsellor based in Dorset. Originally from Northern California, she completed her counselling studies at Queen's University Belfast, and is a case manager at Mind Matters Counselling. She has worked in various EAP organisations alongside her private practice with young people and adults. She has also worked in various higher and further education institutions across the south east of the UK and is currently completing her doctorate of education at Bournemouth University.

Eleanor Brown is a BACP accredited counsellor who qualified with a masters in integrative counselling in 2011 and gained qualifications in telephone and online counselling in 2015. Eleanor has also recently completed an advanced certificate in online supervision. She has worked in the Cardiff University student support counselling service since 2014. Supporting students through their university and young-adult journeys, hearing their stories and witnessing their growth is her passion. Eleanor also takes a special interest in loss and bereavement, running a therapeutic support group for students regularly throughout the academic year. She also very much enjoys nurturing new counsellors, relishing the privilege and challenge of managing the placement scheme whereby trainee counsellors can accrue qualifying hours.

Desmond Channer is a BACP registered counsellor. He currently works in the sixth-form college sector as a student counsellor and also works as a counsellor in private practice (www.choosecounselling.co.uk). Previously, Desmond worked as an honorary counsellor at Barts NHS Trust, and before that in the IT sector for 17 years. He has a BSc (Hons) in psychology and a postgraduate diploma in person-centred therapeutic counselling.

Keith Duckett is white British and works as a psychotherapeutic counsellor, team leader and service co-ordinator in the bereavement support team of a specialist palliative care centre in a multi-ethnic urban area. His integrative approach has thus far been shaped primarily by Gestalt therapy, intercultural pastoral counselling and mindfulness. His spiritual and therapeutic practice is increasingly informed by non-dual awareness and Iyengar yoga. He was ordained priest in the Church of England in 1998. These days he assists in a small way in the parish where his wife is vicar, having been a healthcare chaplain for many years. He has been a cricket fan since about six years of age and has in the past enjoyed voluntary and paid work as a junior cricket coach.

Géraldine Dufour is an expert in matters related to university wellbeing and mental health, working directly with individuals and organisations across the sector through her consultancy, Therapeutic Consultations. Previously head of counselling at the University of Cambridge, chair of national executive committees for student mental health and counselling and founding member of national research groups in student mental health, Géraldine has wide-ranging experience nationally and internationally, with a visiting professorship at Fudan University. She is an associate in the European Association for International Education (EAIE) Expert Community Guidance and Counselling. A psychotherapist with senior registered accredited membership of BACP, Géraldine was the editor of BACP's best practice guidance for the universities and colleges sector, authored the chapter on assessment in *Short-term Counselling in Higher Education* (Dufour, 2016) and was a contributor and reviewer for BACP's *Competences Required to Deliver Effective Counselling in Further and Higher Education* (2016). www.geraldinedufour.com

Dufour, G. (2016). Assessment. In D. Mair (Ed.), *Short-term counselling in higher education: Context, theory and practice*. Routledge.

Eugene Farrell is a respected leader in mental health and wellbeing, with more than 30 years' experience. Qualified in psychology, radiotherapy and health economics, he is a graduate member of the British Psychological Society and board member of the UK Employee Assistance Professionals Association (EAPA). Twice chair of UK EAPA, he has been awarded emeritus status by UK EAPA for services to the EAP industry. He has striven over the past 20 years to promote workplace EAPs, mental health and the removal of mental health stigma. He has consulted on the management of work and personal mental health and wellbeing with many of the UK's largest companies, as well as smaller organisations, mental health providers, professional bodies, the World Health Organization, The Council for Work and Health, charities and government. He has also worked extensively on organisational crisis and critical incident support in situations ranging from bank raids to terrorist attacks.

Ellie Fretwell has been a qualified counsellor since 2011 and a qualified online therapist since 2013. She has worked for Stockport NHS Adult Community Eating Disorder Service since 2012. She is a senior accredited member of BACP. One of her recent special interests has been working with clients with neurodiversity who are experiencing eating disorders. She is currently studying for a diploma in CBT for eating disorders with Sheffield University. She loves to take non-conventional approaches and has run many creative therapy groups as well as exploring how, personally and professionally, imagination and open-mindedness can enhance her life and the lives of others. She has been running her own care team for about 20 years and continues to explore how the obstacles of her disability can be managed, accepted and confronted in a courageous, radical and fully authentic way.

Mark Fudge was head of counselling and mental health support at Keele University and has worked in HE for more than 20 years. He was chair of BACP Universities and Colleges and a member of SCORE (Student Counselling Outcome Research and Evaluation) research group. Previously he worked in the NHS. Mark currently works as a freelance therapist and trainer.

Delroy Hall is a trained counsellor of more than 30 years' experience, wellbeing practitioner, ordained minister, trainer, independent scholar and author of *A Redemption Song: Black British pastoral theology and culture* (2021). He has coordinated mental health projects and has worked with Birmingham Community Health Care Trust (BCHC) facilitating the inclusive leadership component on their Inspire Leadership Programme. He is coordinator for a black male suicide prevention programme under the auspices of Sheffield

Health and Social Care (SCHC). Since April 2020, he has hosted live wellbeing sessions on Facebook, LinkedIn, X and YouTube. He now serves as the chaplain for Sheffield United Football Club. He is also a former 400-metre hurdler, ranked No.2 in Great Britain in 1979 in the under-20 age group. He keeps fit and is presently training for various aqua bike events in the UK.

Hall, D. (2021). *A redemption song: Illuminations on Black British pastoral theology and culture*. SCM Press.

Jennifer A. Hamilton is a clinical supervisor and psychotherapist/counsellor accredited with IACP and BACP. She has a higher diploma in biodynamic and integrative psychotherapy, a postgraduate diploma in expressive arts therapy and post-traumatic stress disorder, and a BA honours degree in psychology. Jennifer originally trained as a life and business coach with the Irish Life Coach Institute and then became a clinical hypnotherapist and a certified practitioner of neuro-linguistic programming (NLP). She has a certificate in training and development from the Irish Institute of Training and Development (IITD) and a postgraduate diploma in advanced cognitive behavioural therapy. Jennifer adopts a humanistic person-centred approach with a body-mind perspective, which emphasises the importance of the body and 'bodywork' in achieving holding and maintaining emotional mental physical and spiritual well-being. She is especially interested in assisting people to overcome trauma by means of body orientated psychotherapy and trauma work.

Jane Harris is the head of counselling at the University of Oxford, and previously was head of student counselling and wellbeing at the University of Leeds. Jane has also held a variety of roles in the voluntary sector, particularly in areas relating to social and economic disadvantage, homelessness, substance misuse and mental health difficulties. Jane is a UKCP accredited psychodynamic counsellor, reflective practice group facilitator, chair of HUCS (Heads of University Counselling Services) and a co-chair of the Wellbeing in Higher Education Expert Group hosted by Advance HE.

Julie Hughes is co-director and senior case manager at Mind Matters Counselling LLP, and a BACP-accredited counsellor, supervisor and EMDR-accredited practitioner. She has written a number of articles for *BACP Workplace* journal covering contracting, supervision and report-writing. Julie has served for more than 10 years on the BACP Workplace executive committee and was chair of the BACP Workplace division from 2019 to 2022.

Rick Hughes is currently editor of *BACP University & College Counselling* journal, having also been editor of *BACP Workplace* journal. Latterly, he was Head of Service at the University of Aberdeen Counselling Service, after eight years as BACP's Lead Advisor: Workplace. He completed his initial counselling training at the University of Strathclyde in the 1990s, under Professor Dave Mearns. His portfolio counselling career has predominantly involved self-employment in a range of private practice contexts, including several years running Edinburgh Coaching & Counselling, then as co-director of PCT Glasgow. As well as working as an affiliate counsellor for several EAP providers, he has also been the nominated lead counsellor, in a privately contracted capacity, for a host of organisations, including regional counsellor for a global pharmaceutical corporation.

Yvonne Inglis is a dual practitioner with decades of career expertise in corporate environments. She has spent the last few years coaching, mentoring and guiding executive leaders on gaining competitive edge, identifying value differentiators and accelerating career growth. As a founder of a private practice, accredited executive coach and supervisor, Yvonne specialises in supporting clients to develop and grow by building strong relationships that are sustainable, reliable and transparent. Yvonne is passionate about empowering personal growth. Having come through some challenging times in both her personal and professional life, she understands how difficult it can be to identify and make the changes required to achieve your full potential. Yvonne's blend of coaching and psychotherapy experience means she can offer tailored solutions at a deeper, more holistic level. www.yvonneinglis.com

Catherine Jackson is a journalist and editor who has specialised in mental health and counselling for more than 30 years, in a variety of editorial roles, including editor of *Mental Health Today* and *Therapy Today* magazines and commissioning editor with PCCS Books.

Salma Khalid is a psychotherapist, clinical supervisor and creative health practitioner. She has worked in the field of mental health and wellbeing for more than 25 years and has a varied range of experience in the NHS, the private sector and the voluntary sector. She was formerly lead advisor for spirituality and belief with BACP. She currently works in private practice and with several organisations, including Cartwheel Arts, Early Break (drug and alcohol service for children and young people), The Rory Peck Trust (supporting freelance journalists worldwide), FD Consultants (psychosocial support and trauma specialist services) and VESTA (specialist family support service).

Andrew Kinder is a chartered counselling and chartered occupational psychologist, a registered coach and a registered practitioner psychologist with the HCPC. He is a senior accredited practitioner with BACP, a fellow of BACP and an EMDR practitioner. He has more than 25 years' experience and frequently speaks at conferences in the UK and overseas. He has published many books and articles. His latest book, *Occupational Health and Wellbeing; Challenges and opportunities in theory and practice* (2023), is co-edited with Rick Hughes and Professor Sir Cary Cooper. Andrew is currently the professional head of mental health services at Optima Health. He is on the board of UK EAPA and in 2018 was awarded emeritus status in recognition of his long-standing work in the employee assistance industry.

Kinder, A., Hughes, R. & Cooper, C.L. *(2023). Occupational health and wellbeing: Challenges and opportunities in theory and practice.* Routledge.

Rachael Klug works in private practice with a range of ages, from children up to adults. She has trained to work with neurodiverse clients and has both personal and professional experience of neurodiversity. She works with clients with autism, ADHD, dyslexia and dyspraxia to provide a supportive and relational space that focuses on the strengths that each client brings and what adjustments they may need in their environment, without seeing neurodiversity as a 'disorder'. Many of her clients have a history of trauma, which led her to train in EMDR. She is adapting the EMDR approaches to her online setting and integrates it with her training in trauma-informed mindfulness interventions. She has counselling diploma and certificate courses, ACTO levels 1, 2 and 3, and created the Level 2 Children and Young People training programme with a colleague (and friend) Basi. Rachael is director for children and young people at the Association for Counselling and Therapy Online (ACTO) and responsible for establishing the ACTO network of children and young people therapists with Lesley Simpson-Gray and Basi.

Veronica Lysaght is the founder of Leading with Humanity (https://leadingwithhumanity.org). She has 20+ years' experience in coaching (individuals and groups) as well as extensive international management and leadership experience. She has a unique commercial, political and media background, including leading the International Coaching Federation's team across Europe, the Middle East and Africa. Veronica describes herself as a humanitarian, in that she actively works with people to promote joy, strength and compassion in herself and others. She is co-founder of the Novara One Planet project and, with her husband Nigel, is working with coastal communities to promote and encourage climate change adaptation. This project is based around their boat, Novara – a 60ft, high-latitude sailing yacht. She has lived and worked in several countries and considers herself an international citizen.

Amy McCormack is an integrative counsellor working in private practice. She started as a person-centred bereavement worker and her core training was in Petruska Clarkson's five-relationship model. She is a British Focusing Association-recognised focusing practitioner and this is central to her therapeutic work. In addition to her counselling practice, she is the editor of the BACP Spirituality journal, *Thresholds*. She began her working life as a newspaper journalist, then moved into communications roles for voluntary and community sector organisations, including health, mental health and social care advocacy. She sometimes works as a French-to-English translator and is interested in the impact of language and culture on a person's sense of self.

Dominic McLoughlin is counselling service manager at the University of Westminster. Trained at Birkbeck, University of London in psychodynamic counselling, Dominic has a special interest in how individual creativity intersects with emotional and psychological health in students. He has published articles on this broad theme, including 'Making and finding creativity in student counselling' for *BACP University & College Counselling* journal (McLoughlin, 2023), and book reviews and papers for *Psychodynamic Practice*. Before taking up his current role, he was manager of student support for a specialist institution of the University of London.

McLoughlin, D. (2023). Making and finding creativity in student counselling. *University & College Counselling, 11*(1), 17–21.

Carolyn Mumby is a coach who integrates aspects of therapeutic work in her practice. She offers supervision, mentoring and thinking sessions for practitioners who are interested in integrating the practices of counselling and coaching. She is a licensed Time to Think facilitator, coach, teacher and consultant, providing leadership training and teaching foundation and Thinking Partnership courses. She is a founder member of Coaching for Social Impact and was a member of the BACP Coaching executive for five years, three as chair. Carolyn writes for *Coaching Today* and other magazines, primarily on aspects of integration. Recently Carolyn has become particularly interested in coaching for the third act of life. www.carolynmumby.com/www.workingtitlesleadership.com/www.coaching4socialimpact.com

Lucy Myers is a psychotherapist, executive coach (accredited senior practitioner EMCC), systemic team coach, leadership consultant and coaching supervisor, specialising in therapeutic coaching with individuals and teams in private practice and within organisations. Lucy has a master's degree (distinction) in integrative psychotherapy from the University of Roehampton. Her collaborative, creative and solutions-focused approach to working with clients is underpinned by the psychological principles of enhancing self-awareness and self-acceptance to enable authentic and sustainable change to be achieved. Lucy draws on humanistic, psychodynamic and CBT modalities, along with an understanding of business leadership challenges, to tailor her approach to the unique background, experiences and objectives of each client. As chair of BACP Coaching, Lucy contributes regular articles and columns to *Coaching Today*, and is happiest connecting with and learning from colleagues and peers and exploring new personal and professional adventures. www.therapeuticcoachingconsultancy.co.uk

Vicki Palmer is a senior accredited counsellor with BACP and has been a member of the BACP Health Executive for eight years. She has trained counsellors and counselling supervisors and has set up and run a variety of counselling services, including Oasis-Talk CIC, where she was chief executive officer for eight years. She now works as a counsellor and supervisor and runs a small therapy centre in Wiltshire.

Cloie Parfitt is an integrative psychotherapist who works with both adults and young people online and in-person from her office in Norwich. She holds a doctorate in counselling and psychotherapy from the University of Edinburgh and trained with the Academy for Online Therapy in 2020. Her research at the University of Edinburgh examines the intersection between autism, trauma and therapeutic practice, and this research informs her work with clients. Cloie has worked in the mental health field for more than eight years in a variety of roles and settings – including as a mental health nurse, peer support worker and support group facilitator. Within her private practice, Cloie specialises in working with neurodivergent individuals. She takes a trauma-informed, collaborative and compassionate approach to her therapeutic work in an effort to foster connection, healing, and personal growth.

Paul Parsons is the adult bereavement co-ordinator for St Christopher's Hospice. He retrained to become a counsellor and qualified more than 20 years ago, having had a very successful career in sales. He has specialised in bereavement counselling for more than 10 years, gaining an additional diploma in trauma and PTSD. Paul is an accomplished trainer, offering workshops locally and internationally on bereavement and loss, especially during Covid times. Paul became a member of the Association of Bereavement Co-ordinators (ABSCo) soon after joining the hospice and found the meetings supportive, informative and friendly. So much so that he currently holds the post of vice chair and has been part of the executive committee for more than five years. Self-care is very important to Paul and outside of work he has a supportive family and manages to find time to be a football referee, which brings its own challenges!

Alistair Ross is a minster of religion (Baptist) and a psychodynamic therapist, supervisor and trainer with a life-long interest in how religion, spirituality and therapy relate. This has been the focus of much of his academic work, his various publications and his practice as a practical theologian. He is also a regular contributor on real-world spirituality to the BACP spirituality journal *Thresholds*. He is an associate professor of psychotherapy and director of psychodynamic studies at Oxford University. His favourite place to be is in the mountains of Scotland, the land of his birth, where his spirit can soar.

Allie Scott works as the mental health and counselling manager at the University of the Highlands and Islands and teaches counselling skills at Perth College, UHI. She is the chair of the Heads of University Counselling Services Scotland (HUCSS), executive committee member of the Heads of University Counselling Services (HUCS) and co-chair of the Mental Wellbeing in Higher Education Group and the College Counselling Network Scotland Group. Allie is accredited as a BACP pluralistic counsellor and trainer for COSCA Counselling Skills, Scottish Mental Health First Aid and ASIST. She is a qualified supervisor for both face-to-face and online work. Her original academic training was in psychology and then community education.

Sukhi Sian is a British Asian woman. She trained as a psychodynamic counsellor after studying psychology at university as she was interested in the unconscious influence of our past on our present. Since qualifying around 20 years ago, she has predominantly worked in women's or children and young people's organisations, naturally falling into leadership roles, specifically in areas of sexual violence, substance misuse and mental health. In recent years as part of her own journey, she trained in some holistic, energy-based therapies and has since been developing a spiritually integrated therapeutic practice and clinical supervision.

Stella Sookun is a BACP registered integrative child and young adult counsellor. She works at the University of Arts London as a student counsellor and also in schools and private practice, and runs creative workshops supporting wellbeing outcomes. Stella's original clinical training was in integrative child and adolescent psychotherapy and counselling, with a central underpinning of attachment theory, child development, use of creative arts, body based (somatic) processing, and neuroscience, focusing on safety systems and self-regulation. Since qualification, she is incorporating these interests within and outside the therapy room, including being a forest bathing practitioner. Stella currently has a growing interest in functional medicine, a holistic, systems-based scientific approach to treating health diseases through the ancient wisdom of food as medicine.

Sarah Watson is a BACP senior accredited CYPF psychotherapist, a cognitive behavioural therapist and BACP CYP ethics consultant. She is also a clinical supervisor and has specialisms in CYPF, safeguarding, ethics, solution-focused therapy, transactional analysis, Gestalt and couples work. Sarah has a private practice working mostly with trauma and police/NHS referrals. Her background is in lecturing psychology and counselling. Sarah has also worked in education and schools throughout her career. Before joining BACP, she was clinical lead and set up the counselling service for a large multi-academy trust in Northumberland. Sarah now offers consultancy to senior leaders in schools in the north east of England to help set up and support schools-based counselling services. She is a member of the BACP school and college counselling expert reference group.

John Wilson has specialised in bereavement counselling for 22 years. From 2000 to 2017 he worked at Saint Catherine's Hospice Scarborough, as a trainer and counsellor working with clients bereaved from any cause. In 2017 he completed a PhD and, in the same year, retired from Saint Catherine's Hospice. He was awarded a visiting fellowship of York St John University and was appointed director of the bereavement service at the University's Communities Centre. This a voluntary but very active role, which includes training and research. John is the author of two books, *Supporting People through Loss and Grief* (2013) and *The Plain Guide to Grief* (2020). He is a national and international trainer, and his research has been published in academic journals. John lives in Ryedale, North Yorkshire, with his wife and two cats.

Wilson, J. (2013). *Supporting people through loss and grief: An introduction for counsellors and other caring practitioners.* Jessica Kingsley.

Wilson, J. (2020). *The plain guide to grief.* Nielsen.

Stefan Wilson is a BACP accredited psychodynamic counsellor/psychotherapist and a BPC accredited DIT practitioner. He works as a student counsellor at Birmingham City University and has an online private practice. Stef's original academic training was in analytic philosophy – mainly in the philosophy of mind (especially artificial intelligence), language and logic. He also has an interest in ethics and metaphysics and is a lifelong martial artist.

Joanne Wright has more than 25 years' experience of developing leaders and supporting people through tough times at work. She works in a very person-centred way to help solve the most stressful, challenging workplace issues. Joanne has held many senior positions in the corporate, NHS and charitable sectors, and has headed up large, UK-wide organisational development departments and award-winning training teams. She runs her own private practice and specialises in therapeutic coaching, having been a coach and a counsellor for more than 10 years. Joanne sits on the executive committee of BACP Coaching and works as an Associate for Insightful Exchange and the Therapeutic Coaching Consultancy. She has also had several articles published in *Coaching Today* journal. She is a registered member of BACP, a senior accredited practitioner of EMCC, a Fellow of the Learning and Performance Institute and is an MBTI and strengthscope practitioner and an ACAS-trained mediator. www.wrightinsight.co.uk

Nick Wood is senior wellbeing adviser at Gloucestershire County Council's occupational health service and an accredited counsellor. He has previously served on the BACP's Workplace executive committee and is a co-author of BACP's *Workplace Counselling Competence Framework*. His areas of specialist interest include tackling work-related stress and improving access to work for neurodivergent employees, as well as increasing access to health and wellbeing programmes in the workplace. Inspired by Geldard and Geldard's model of 'counselling skills in everyday life' (Geldard & Geldard, 2002), he coordinates a peer-to-peer scheme offering support for people who experience bullying or harassment at work.

Geldard K. & Geldard D. (2002). *Counselling skills in everyday life*. Red Globe Press.

Sarah Worley-James is a BACP senior accredited counsellor, supervisor and trainer with 25 years' experience in the public, private and third sectors. She is former chair of ACTO and interim Counselling Service Manager at Cardiff University. Sarah is passionate about online counselling, setting up the online service at Cardiff University in 2011 and contributing to the BACP's initial response to the Covid-19 pandemic in 2020. She has had a regular column about online counselling, 'Cyberwork', in the *BACP Workplace* journal since 2016 and published a series of articles about the process of setting up a university online counselling service in the *BACP University and College Counselling* journal in 2017. She is the author of *Online Counselling: An essential guide* (2022).

Worley-James, S. (2022). *Online Counselling: An essential guide.* PCCS Books.

Appendix

Professional membership bodies

Addiction Professionals (AP) – formerly Federation of Drug and Alcohol Professionals (FDAP)

Suite 277
8 Shoplatch
Shrewsbury
Shropshire SY1 1HF

Contact: Via online form
Website: www.addictionprofessionals.org.uk

AP is a voluntary registration body and network for the addictions sector. It has a growing and diverse membership of practitioners working in the addictions sector, including behavioural addictions.

Association of Child Psychotherapists (ACP)

CAN Borough
7-14 Great Dover Street
London SE1 4YR

Telephone: 020 7922 7751
Website: www.childpsychotherapy.org.uk

ACP is the main professional body and accredited register for child and adolescent psychotherapists in the UK. It is responsible for regulating the training and practice standards of child and adolescent psychotherapy across the public and private sectors.

Association of Christians in Counselling (ACC)

PO Box 6901
Coventry CV3 9SG

Telephone: 024 7644 9694
Website: www.acc-uk.org

ACC is the only Christian UK-wide counselling organisation holding an accredited register with the Professional Standards Authority. It offers membership to individual counsellors and psychotherapists; organisations, agencies and churches concerned with counselling/psychotherapy or related activities, and pastoral carers.

Association for Coaching (AC)

Golden Cross House
8 Duncannon Street
London WC2N 4JF

Telephone: 0333 006 2676
Website: www.associationforcoaching.com

AC is an independent, not-for-profit professional body dedicated to promoting best practice and raising the awareness and standards of coaching worldwide.

British Association of Art Therapists (BAAT)

24-27 White Lion Street
London N1 9PD

Telephone: 020 7686 4216
Website: https://baat.org

BAAT is the professional organisation for art therapists in the UK. It is regulated by the Health and Care Professions Council.

British Association for Behavioural and Cognitive Psychotherapies (BABCP)

Imperial House
Hornby Street
Bury
Lancashire BL9 5BN

Telephone: 0330 320 0851
Website: www.babcp.com

BABCP is a leading organisation for cognitive behavioural therapists in the UK and Ireland. It promotes, improves and upholds standards of CBT practice, supervision and training.

British Association for Counselling and Psychotherapy (BACP)

> BACP House
> 15 St John's Business Park
> Lutterworth
> Leicestershire LE17 4HB
>
> Telephone: 01455 883300
> Website: www.bacp.co.uk

BACP is the main professional association for members of the counselling professions in the UK. It promotes and provides education and training for counsellors and psychotherapists, maintains a members' register, which is accredited with the Professional Standards Authority, publishes a suite of therapy journals, campaigns for improved access to therapy, and informs and educates the public about counselling and psychotherapy.

British Infertility Counselling Association (BICA)

> Rookdale
> Malton Road
> York YO31 9LT
>
> Contact: www.bica.net/contact-us
> Website: www.bica.net

BICA is a registered charity and the only professional infertility counselling association recognised by the Human Fertilisation and Embryology Authority and the British Fertility Society in the UK.

British Psychoanalytic Council (BPC)

> Suite 7
> 19-23 Wedmore Street
> London N19 4RU
>
> Telephone: 020 7561 9240
> Website: www.bpc.org.uk

BPC is the UK's leading professional association and accredited public register for psychoanalytic psychotherapy. It responsible for setting the standards required of the profession and considering concerns raised against its registrants. BPC is an association of institutions, made up of psychoanalysts, analytical psychologists, psychoanalytic psychotherapists and child psychotherapists. Its register is accredited by the Professional Standards Authority.

British Psychological Society (BPS)
> St Andrews House
> 48 Princess Road East
> Leicester LE1 7DR
>
> Telephone: 0116 254 9568
> Website: www.bps.org.uk

BPS is the representative association for psychology and the professional membership body for psychologists in the UK. It champions psychology, psychologists and the wider psychological professions by conducting research, providing continual professional development and hosting psychology-related events. It does not hold an accredited register for counselling psychologists as they are required to register with the statutory Health and Care Professions Council.

College of Sexual and Relationship Therapists (COSRT)
> 10 Queen Street Place
> London EC4R 1BE
>
> Telephone: 020 8106 9635
> Website: www.cosrt.org.uk

COSRT is the UK's only professional body for practitioners in psychosexual and relationship therapies. Its charitable objectives are to set and monitor professional standards, provide and support training, and promote research.

Counselling and Psychotherapy in Scotland (COSCA)
> 16 Melville Terrace
> Stirling FK8 2NE
>
> Telephone: 01786 475140
> Website: www.cosca.org.uk

COSCA seeks to advance and support all forms of counselling, psychotherapy and the use of counselling skills in Scotland, and to promote high quality counselling supervision and continuing professional development for all individuals and agencies delivering counselling services and education.

Counsellors Together UK (also known as UK Counsellors)

Contact: info@ukcounsellors.co.uk
Website: https://ukcounsellors.co.uk

This is the UK's largest campaign organisation for counsellors, with more than 9000 members. It was founded in 2017 as a Facebook group to discuss the issue of counsellors working unpaid. Its aims are to challenge the culture and prevalence of unpaid work within the counselling profession; to ensure counselling training and ongoing personal and professional development is accessible for all, and to encourage organisations to embed the authentic application of equality, diversity and inclusion in everyday practice. Its website provides a platform to report news on its current campaigns and for counsellors, other professionals and the general public to raise and join in relevant discussions about current polices and issues affecting the profession.

Health and Care Professions Council (HCPC)

184-186 Kennington Park Road
London SE11 4BU

Telephone: 020 7582 5460
Website: www.hcpc-uk.org

HCPC protects the public by regulating 15 health and care professions in the UK. It sets standards for these professionals' education and training and practice; approves programmes that they must complete to register with it; keeps a register of professionals who meet its standards, and takes action if professionals on its register do not meet its standards. The professions on its register include art therapists, speech and language therapists, occupational therapists and practitioner psychologists (including clinical and counselling psychologists).

International Coaching Federation (ICF)

2365 Harrodsburg Road
Suite A325
Lexington
KY 40504
USA

Contact: Through support link at https://coachingfederation.org/support
Website: https://coachingfederation.org

Formed in 1995, ICF is the world's largest organisation of professionally trained coaches, and the leading voice for the global coaching community.

Irish Association for Counselling and Psychotherapy (IACP)
>First Floor
>Marina House
>11-13 Clarence Street
>Dun Laoghaire
>Co Dublin
>Ireland

>Telephone: 00 353 1 2303536
>Website: https://iacp.ie

The largest counselling and psychotherapy association in Ireland, IACP develops and maintains professional standards of excellence in counselling and psychotherapy. It links practitioners with potential clients, and sets and maintains training and practice standards through its code of ethics and practice.

National Counselling & Psychotherapy Society (NCPS)
>19 Grafton Road
>Worthing
>West Sussex BN11 1QT

>Telephone: 01903 200 666
>Website: https://nationalcounsellingsociety.org

Formerly the National Counselling Society (NCS), this UK-based, not-for-profit membership association operates a national register for counsellors and psychotherapists that is accredited by the Professional Standards Authority. It accredits individual counsellors and training courses. NCPS works to be the voice of its membership under the original founding principle of counselling as a vocation, not just a profession.

UK Association of Humanistic Psychology Practitioners (UKAHPP)
>PO Box BCM AHPP
>27 Old Gloucester Street
>London WC1N 3XX

>Telephone: 0843 2895907
>Website: https://ahpp.org.uk

UKAHPP is the professional association for all those who apply the theories of humanistic psychology in their practice. It works to advance the diversity of practices and theories of humanistic psychology.

UK Council for Psychotherapy (UKCP)
   2 America Square
   London EC3N 2LU

   Telephone: 020 7014 9955
   Website: www.psychotherapy.org.uk

UKCP is the leading UK organisation for psychotherapists and psychotherapeutic counsellors. It offers professional support for its members, regulates the profession, and promotes access to psychotherapy for all. Its national register is accredited by the Professional Standards Authority. It is an umbrella organisation for several colleges representing particular schools of practice. Its members are also accredited by the individual college to which they belong, which include the Psychotherapeutic Counselling and Intersubjective Psychotherapy College, the Humanistic and Integrative Psychotherapy College, the College for Sexual and Relationship Psychotherapy, the College for Child and Adolescent Psychotherapies and the College of Family, Couple and Systemic Psychotherapy, among others.

Name index

A

Academy of Executive Coaching (AoEC) 109
Age UK 134
Aisling Centre 137
American Psychiatric Association (APA) 156
Arabi, I. 193
Arasteh, A.R. 192
Arthur, A. 6, 43–45
Association of Bereavement Service Coordinators (ABSCo) 162
Association for Coaching (AC) 7, 91, 109
Association for Counselling and Therapy Online (ACTO) 52, 53, 63, 65
Association of Genetic Nurses and Counsellors (AGNC) 5
Attenborough, D. 103
Attig, T. 154
Auerbach, R. 114

B

Bachkirova, T. 94
Bacon, J. 8
Bailey, S. 8, 140–143, 145
Barden, N. 114
Barkham, M. 12, 117
Barnardo's 131, 139
Bedfordshire Open Door 8, 140, 141, 142–143
Bell, E. 113, 116
Bell, G. 135
Bereavement Care Service Standard 161
Bereavement Services Association 161
Berglas, S. 91, 92
Berman, W.H. 92
Bignall, T. 135
Binstead, C. 29, 30
Bion, W.R. 119
Birmingham City University 113
Birrell, L. 9, 168, 180–182
Bishop, H. 103
Bluckert, P. 93
Bonanno, G.A. 150, 151, 153, 156
Boring Renaud, V. 7
Bowlby, J. 152, 154
Bradt, G. 92
British Association for Counselling and Psychotherapy (BACP) xi, 3–4, 5, 6, 7, 8, 9, 24, 29, 36, 39, 47, 49, 54, 72, 73, 82, 83, 87–88, 92, 93, 95, 96, 97–98, 99, 100, 103, 108, 109, 114, 116, 131, 136, 139, 140, 144, 169, 170, 171, 172, 181, 184, 191, 193, 198
British Focusing Association 193
British Infertility Counselling Association (BICA) 5
British Psychological Society (BPS) 109
Brocklehurst, R. 135
Broglia, E. 118, 122
Brown, E. 6, 50, 55, 57, 66, 68
Brown, S. 36
Buchanan, L. 2
Buckeridge, S. 6, 26
Burke, L.A. 150

C

Caleb, R. 114
Calm Zone, The 62–63
Carroll, M. 90
Carslake, P. 6, 45–47
Cartwheel Arts 194

Center for Action and Contemplation 187
Center Collegiate for Mental Health 117
Channer, D. 8, 114, 120–121, 123
Chaplin, D. 161
Clarkson, P. 193
Cliff, G. 135
Clukey, L. 158
Companies House 34
Cook, C. 188–189
Cooper, M. 53, 106
Coren, A. 119
Cornell, A.W. 201
Cox, E. 94
Craig, D. 133
Critchley, B. 93
Croydon Drop In (CDI) 182–183
Cruse Bereavement Support 161

D

Dana, D. 201
de Haan, E. 91, 94
Department for Education (DfE) 121, 179
Department of Health 184–185
Department of Health and Social Care 179
Dr Julian 64
Dryden, W. 121
Duckett, K. 9, 191–192, 193, 195–196, 198, 200–201, 203
Dufour, G. 7, 114, 116, 124

E

EAPA 64, 72, 76, 77, 79
Early Break 194
Edge Hill University 182
Essex University 97
ETherapy 64
European Mentoring & Coaching Council (EMCC) 91, 92, 93, 100, 109
Evans, J. 53
Evans, P. 201

F

Fahy, M. 99
Farrell, E. 7, 71
Faulkner, A. 151
Finlay, L. 90
Fortner, B.V. 151
Freas, A. 91
Freed, P.J. 154

Fretwell, E. 6, 49–50, 55, 58, 66, 67
Freud, S. ix, 94, 152
Fudge, M. 8, 117–118
Furnham, A. 150

G

Gardner, L. 6, 41–43
Gendlin, E. 192
George, H. 136–317
Gibbard, T. 6, 19–21
Gibran, K. 192, 196
Gloucestershire County Council 82, 83
Grant, A.M. 91
Graves, D. 158
Green, R.M. 91
Guide Dogs for the Blind Scotland 2
Gyllensten, K. 93

H

Hall, D. 9, 192–193, 194, 197, 199–200, 202–203
Hamilton, J. 6, 54, 65, 67
Harris, J. 8, 114–115, 123–124
Harwood, H. 14
HCPC 73
Health Education England 22
Holmes, J. 9, 184
Hospice UK 162
Houghton, S. 9, 168, 176–177
HSE 88
Hughes, G. 114
Hughes, J. 7, 72
Hughes, R. 2, 33, 36

I

IACP 54
Inglis, Y. 7, 100–103
Insightful Exchange 95
Institute of Leadership and Management (ILM) 102, 104
International Coaching Federation (ICF) 7, 91, 92, 97, 99, 109

J

Jenkinson, G. 199
Jeung ix

K

Keele University 118

Kenny, R. 9, 168, 182–183
Kewell, H. 135
Khalid, S. 9, 192, 193–194, 196–197, 199, 201–202
Kilburg, R.R. 92, 94
Kinder, A. 7, 36, 71
Klass, D. 155
Klug, R. 6, 52, 55–56, 63, 68
Kooth 64
Kubler-Ross, E. 152

L

Leavesley, M. 6, 18–19
Leicester University 194
Lemisiou, M.A. 93
Lenadoon Community Counselling Service 138
Lightfoot, L. 114
Living Life to the Full 63
Loughborough University 103
Ludlow, L. 47
Lysaght, V. 7, 97–100

M

Macmillan 5
Mair, D. 127
Malan, D. 127
Mann, J.J. 154
Marie Curie 5
Maxwell, A. 91, 92
McCormack, A. 9, 192, 193, 196, 198–199, 201
McLoughlin, D. 8, 118–120
Mearns, D. 106
Mental Health Taskforce 185
MindEd 171
Mind Matters Counselling 86
MindOut 133
Mintz, R. 121
Moukam, R. 136
Mumby, C. 7, 107–109, 110
Myers, L. 7, 103–107
My Therapist Online 64

N

National Counselling & Psychotherapy Society (NCPS) 73, 169
Neimeyer, R.A. 150, 151, 153
NCVO 132

Newsome, A. 118
NHS xi, 4, 5, 6, 11–28, 50, 73, 81, 96, 123, 131, 132, 133, 136, 137, 179, 180, 183, 185, 193, 194, 200
NHS Child and Adolescent Mental Health Services (CAHMS) 178–180, 181
NHS Digital 134
NICE 14, 15, 16, 151
Norcross, J.C. 93
Novara One Planet 98

O

O'Connor, M.-F. 154, 156
O'Donnell, J. 135
Office of the Race Relations Conciliator (New Zealand) 99

P

Palmer, S. 93
Palmer, V. 6
Parfitt, C. 6, 50–52, 56, 59, 63, 67
Parkes, C.M. 148, 151 152, 153–154
Parsons, P. 162–164
Pattigift Therapy 136–137
Place2Be 176–177
Prigerson, H.G. 156
Professional Standards Authority xi
Pybis, J. 132

R

Rajain, P. 190
Rathee, R. 190
Reeves, A. 40, 121
Refugee Council 139
R-evolution for Good 131, 138
Reynolds, D.J. Jnr, 52
Rhead, R. 14
Rogers, C. R. 92, 142, 143, 192
Rogers J. 91
Rohr, R. 187
Rory Peck Trust 194
Ross, A. 9, 187
Rothschild, L. 190
Roy, A. 9, 168, 178–180
Royal Society for Public Health (RSPH) 134
Rumi, J. 100, 192

S

Samaritans 62

Sandage, S. 189
Saunders, C. 159
Schut, H. 151, 152, 153, 154
Scott, A. 8, 114, 120–121, 123
Scottish Government 138
Seaton, N. 14
Shackle, S. 124
Sheffield Mind 134–135
Sherman, S. 91
Shohet, J. 196
Shohet, R. 196
Sian, S. 9, 191, 193, 194–195, 197–198, 200
Side by Side 62
Silver, R.C. 152
Simpson, S. 49
Sky 103
Sookun, S. 8, 121–122, 123
Spanner, L. 114
Speyer, C. 196, 199
St Andrew's Hospital, Northampton 201
St Christopher's Hospice 148, 162–164
Strathclyde University 96
Strawn, B. 189
Stroebe, M.S. 152, 153, 154, 156
Stroebe, W. 152
Sue Ryder Online Bereavement Counselling 64
Suler, J. 49, 53, 60
Sunderland Counselling Service 144
Sure Start 179
Survivors Manchester 133
Swami, V. 150
Sweet, T. 144

T

Therapeutic Coaching Consultancy 95, 103, 105
Togetherall 62
Tonkin, L. 155
Totton, N. 195

U

UK Government 184
United Kingdom Council for Psychotherapy (UKCP) 3–4, 6, 73
University of Cambridge 7, 113
University of Roehampson 104

V

van der Kolk, B. 200
VESTA 194

W

Wallace, P. 121
Wallbank, S. 151
Watson, S. 8–9
Wells, M. 198
Weir, D. 139
Western, S. 92,
Whitmore, Sir J. 97
Wilson, J. 8, 137, 148, 150, 151, 153, 155–156, 157
Wilson, S. 8, 125–127
Wood, N. 7, 71–72
World Health Organization (WHO) 51
Worley-James, S. 6, 31, 35, 55, 64, 121
Wortman, C.B. 152
Wright Insight Ltd 95
Wright, J. 7, 95–97

Y

Yaphe, J. 196, 199
York St John University Counselling and Mental Health Clinic 8
Young Persons Advisory Service (YPAS) 180–182

Subject index

A

accreditation 21, 40, 85, 127, 144, 150, 163
   for coach-therapists 107
administration 80, 121, 163
anonymity (in online counselling) 49, 52, 60, 62
applications/interviews
   for EAP/workplace roles 84–86
   for further and higher education roles 114–116
   for hospice roles 149, 152, 156
   for NHS Talking Therapies 22–24
   preparation for, 115
   for working with CYPF 181–182, 183
Asian 52
assessment (*see also* risk)
   in bereavement counselling 151, 156–157, 161
   in coach-therapy practice 108–109
   in CYPF counselling 178, 181, 182
   free, in private practice 32, 46
   in job applications 115
   in PWP role 15, 16
   in workplace counselling 87
Assimilation of Grief Experiences Scale (AGES) 157
attachment theory 105, 119, 154, 171

B

BACP Coaching Competence Framework 7, 92
BACP Coaching Training Curriculum 109
BACP CYPF Competence Framework 169–170, 171
BACP Workplace Counselling Competence Framework 83, 87, 89
BACP Ethical Framework for the Counselling professions 169, 170

Black (*see also* racially minoritised, racialised) 14, 52, 136, 142
Black Lives Matter 90–91
boundaries
   in coaching 91, 100, 102
   of confidentiality,
      in EAP work 76, 80–81, 88
      in higher and further education settings 120, 121
   in CYPF work 171, 174, 175
   in faith settings 187, 204
   in higher and further education settings 122
   in hospice counselling 157, 160
   in online therapy 59, 61
   in private practice 30, 31, 32, 40, 42
business
   management skills 96, 105, 107
   model in higher education 118, 122

C

case management/ers
   in EAP work 72, 74, 75, 77
child and adolescent mental health services (CAMHS)
   counselling in, 178–180
Clinical Outcomes in Routine Evaluation (CORE) 12, 118
cognitive behavioural therapy (CBT)
   in CAMHS contexts 179
   in dual coaching-therapy 105
   in EAP work 73
   in NHS Talking Therapies 13, 14, 15,
      computerised 16
   effectiveness of, 133
   high-intensity 18, 20, 21

low-intensity 17, 21
  in Northern Ireland 27
  in Scotland 25
  training in, 21, 25
 online, 50, 58
competence(s)
 accreditation as marker of, 40
 in coaching 93, 109
 in counselling CYPF 170–171
 in further and higher education 116–117,
 Gillick-, 173, 174
 limits to, 3, 18, 141, 169
 in online therapy 67
 in private practice 38
 in self-care 54
 workplace, 87, 88
complaints/complaints policy 88
 in hospice work 161
confidentiality (*see also* boundaries, risk)
 in CYPF settings 170, 171, 173, 177
 in EAP/workplace settings 75, 76, 88
 in hospice settings 148, 157, 160
 in online counselling 59
 in primary care settings 62
 in private practice 39
conflicts of interest
 in EAP work 75, 87, 89
consent, informed
 in CYPF settings 171, 172, 173, 174
 in EAP work 74, 77
 in hospice settings 160
 in spiritual/faith contexts 197
continuing bonds (bereavement) 155
continuing professional development (CPD)
 for CYPF work 171, 177, 182
 in higher and further education settings
  125–126
 in hospice settings 148, 149, 160
 personal and, 92, 115, 119, 140, 141
 in primary care settings 13, 17, 24
 in private practice 40
 in third-sector settings 139–140, 142
 in workplace/EAP settings 84–85
contract(s)/ing
 in coaching-therapy practice 96, 98, 108
 in CYPF work 176–177
 in higher and further education settings
  123–124
 in hospice settings 160

 in NHS primary care settings 54
 in spiritual/faith contexts 197
 in third sector settings 142
core conditions (Rogers) 151
couples counselling/therapy 14, 22, 38, 39
Covid pandemic 45, 46, 90, 101, 190
 long Covid 18–19
 and online working 6, 30, 42, 48, 49, 53,
  55, 56, 65, 70, 143
 and safeguarding 173
creative/creativity
 arts in therapy 193
 coaching as, 92
 in CYPF work 173
 in hospice work 164
 in online counselling 55, 57–58
curriculum (training)
 coaching, 109
 CYPF, 169, 170, 171

D

data collection/measurement
 in CYPF work 173
 in EAP/workplace settings 79
 in higher and further education settings
  117–118
 in hospice settings 157
 in primary care settings 12, 23, 25
 in private practice 36
 in the third sector 133, 134
*Diagnostic and Statistical Manual of Mental
  Disorders (DSM-5)* 156
dialectical behaviour therapy (DBT) 18, 73
did not attend (DNA) 41
disclosure/personal disclosure
 client, in online therapy, 49
 therapist/counsellor, 115
Disclosure Barring Service (DBS) 64, 78,
  173
dual-process model (bereavement) 152, 154,
  155
dual-trained/dual practitioner (coach-
  therapist) 90, 92, 94, 95, 105, 107,
  108
duty of care 39, 75, 76, 121, 173, 174
dynamic interpersonal therapy (DIT) 14, 18,
  22

E

embedded counselling services x, 71, 81–86, 121, 125, 176, 192
Employee Assistance Programme (EAP)
    affiliate 31, 32, 64, 70, 71, 72–81, 87
    provider 70
employment opportunities/finding paid work
    in CYPF services 174–183
    as EAP/workplace counsellor 3, 70–71, 79–80, 82–83, 83–86
    in faith/spiritual contexts 186–187, 193–194, 200–201
    in higher and further education settings 114–116
    in hospices 149–150
    in NHS primary care 11, 16–17, 18–19, 22–24
    in online practice 58
    in private practice 63–65, 71
    in the third sector 133, 143–145
equality, inclusion and diversity 22–23, 126, 133–134, 201, 203
ethical frameworks (*see also* BACP Ethical Framework) 59, 103, 160
ethical practice/ethics 36, 65, 103,
    codes of, 72, 160
evaluation (*see also* CORE, data collection) 12, 13–14, 162
eye movement desensitisation and reprocessing (EMDR) 18, 19, 21, 59, 73

F

facilitator/facilitating 70
    bereavement groups 158
faith-based counselling services 186–187
fees (client) 30, 33–34, 42, 44, 45–46, 83, 103
    competitive pricing 140
    corporate, 106

G

GDPR/data protection 30, 32, 33, 36, 64, 170, 171, 173
general practice/practitioner (GP)
    counselling services in, x, 2, 12–13, 14, 157, 160
        in Northern Ireland 27
        in Scotland 25–26
        in Wales 27

    liaison with/referral, 50, 74, 75, 123, 126, 138
    risk management 40, 62, 63, 66, 76
Gestalt 100, 173
    'coaching' 94
Good Practice in Action (GPiA) (BACP guidance)
    CYPF, 171, 172
groups/groupwork
    with CYPF 177
    in NHS Talking Therapies 16–17, 20, 25
    self-help/peer support, in hospices, 148, 158, 163

H

health and safety (*see* risk management)
high-intensity therapist/therapy (NHS Talking Therapies) 15, 16, 17–18
    CBT, 15, 17, 19–21
    counsellor 18–19
    management and supervision 24
    training 14, 21–22
    workloads 24
home visits 157–158
home-working/working from home (*see also* online working)
    in EAP services 31, 70, 78, 79
    insurance 31
    in private practice 30–31

I

Improving Access to Psychological Therapies (IAPT) (*see also* NHS Talking Therapies)
    % of counsellors in, 4
    criticisms of, 14–15
    involvement of third sector 132
    reach to older people 134
    roll-out history of, 12–14
Information Commissioner's Office (ICO) 30, 32, 64
instant messaging (IM) 6, 49, 51, 54, 57, 60, 61, 65
interpersonal skills
    in workplace settings 84, 86

L

LGBTQI+ clients/communities 133, 152
live chat 49

long-term conditions 14, 19, 21

M

marketing/promotion
   issues for dual coaching-therapy practice 105
   in private practice 34–35, 45–46
mentoring
   and coaching 102, 104
   from experienced peers 6, 29
   in higher and further education settings 127
   in hospice settings 149
   in the third sector 140
   in workplace settings 70, 88
MindEd 171
mindfulness 58, 191, 192, 200
monitoring
   apps 58
   of EAP affiliates 77
multidisciplinary working
   in further and higher education settings 123
   in hospices 160–161

N

NHS Talking Therapies 6, 11, 15, 132
   challenges of, 25
   finding work in, 22–24
   practitioner roles in, 16–21
   training in, 21–22, 179
notes/note-taking (*see* record-keeping)

O

older people 134–135
online disinhibition 49, 60, 66
online working
   benefits for clients 49–52
   benefits for counsellors 55–56
organisations/organisational (in workplace counselling)
   context/values 75–76, 79, 84, 87, 92, 190, 204
   development 95, 96
   knowledge 106
   protocols 86–87
   skills 85
overseas working (online) 63

P

palliative care 137, 147, 160,
   working in, 162–164
pay/paid work (*see also* volunteering) 12
   in EAP work 7, 79, 80
   in NHS Talking Therapies 23–24
   unpaid (students/trainees), 12–13, 139–140, 143–145
Person-Centred Experiential Counselling for Depression (PCE-CfD) 14, 18, 19, 22
person-centred therapy/practice 18, 34, 44, 45, 54, 92, 93, 96, 102, 130–131, 148, 151
placements
   in coach-therapy 97
   in CYPF settings 169, 179, 182–183
   in further and higher education settings 120, 127
   in hospice settings 149, 152
   in NHS Talking Therapies 21, 26
   in the third-sector 8, 137, 138, 139–145
   and volunteering 143–144
   in workplace contexts 82
practice management 32–33
presenting issues
   in CYPF settings 172–173
   in dual coach-counselling 95
   in further and higher education settings 117–118
   in NHS Talking Therapies 24, 25, 26
   in private practice 37
   in workplace settings 80, 88
privacy 31, 39, 51, 157
   in online work 59, 63
professional indemnity insurance
   for EAP work 78, 79
   for online work 63–64
   in private practice 30, 31, 42
psychodrama 99–100
psychodynamic psychotherapy 3, 14, 56, 58, 91, 93–94, 104, 105, 136, 197–198
psychoeducation
   in hospice settings 152, 164
   in NHS Talking Therapies 15
psychological wellbeing practitioner (PWP) 14–15, 15–17, 21, 24

Q

qualifications
  for coach-therapists 96–97, 102, 104
  for CYPF practice 169–171, 176, 179, 182
  for EAP/workplace contexts 31, 72–73, 84
  for further and higher education counselling 116, 127
  for hospice work 163
  for NHS Talking Therapies 14–15, 27
  for online therapy platforms 64

R

racially minoritised/racialised groups/communities (*see also* Black, Asian) 12, 113, 136–137
record-keeping (*see also* note-taking) 62,
  in CYPF work 171, 173, 174
  in EAP/workplace settings 76–77, 84, 85
  in online therapy 64
  in private practice 32, 33
  security of (*see* GDPR)
referrals
  into CYPF counselling 179
  into/from EAPs 74, 77, 79, 80, 82, 85
  making (CYPF), 170, 171, 173
  self- (CYPF), 171
  into the third sector 133, 138
reflective
  practice 194, 195, 196
    in coaching 108
    in NHS Talking Therapies 23, 24
  supervision 83, 117
registration
  with ICO 63–64
  professional, 40, 72–73, 107
regulation 173
  self-, 122
religion (*see also* spirituality) 9
  defining, 187–188, 192–193
  and difference/diversity 107, 202, 203
  in secular contexts 200
  as source of solace 198–199
  and spirituality 187–189
  in training 203–204
religious abuse 189, 204
research
  underpinning practice 12, 14, 91, 93, 109, 121, 134, 151, 153, 155, 200, 201

resilience
  of clients 65, 88, 92, 131, 155–156, 199
  of counsellor 122, 180
risk assessment and management (*see also* suicide, safeguarding) 6, 16, 20
  in coach-counselling 91–92
  in CYPF settings 173, 178, 180
  in further and higher education settings 121, 126, 203
  in hospice settings 156–158, 163
  in NHS Talking Therapies 16-17, 20
  online 62–63, 66
  in private practice 39–40, 41
  in workplace/EAP contexts 75, 76, 87

S

safeguarding (*see also* vulnerable adults)
  in CYPF work 170, 171, 172–173, 174–175, 176, 183, 184
  in higher and further education settings 120–121, 125, 126
  in hospice settings 163
  in NHS Talking Therapies 23, 24
  in private practice 32
safety
  client, (*see also* risk) 41, 54, 58, 62, 63, 66, 67–68, 76, 108, 173
  personal (of counsellor), 30, 37, 77, 78, 157
self-actualisation 18, 92–93, 104–105
self-care
  in bereavement work 149–150
  in CYPF work 175
  in higher and further education settings 125–126
  in online working 54, 65, 66
    of client 54
  in primary care contexts 23, 24
  in private practice 37–38
  spiritual/faith-related, 192, 194–195
  in third sector-settings 141–143
self-help
  community/peer groups 131
  digital platforms 124
  guided,
    in further and higher education settings 8
    in NHS Talking Therapies 8, 15, 16, 17, 25, 27
  in hospices 148

materials (in private practice), 40
short-term/single-session counselling
   with CYPF 179
   in EAP/workplace settings 73, 75, 82, 84–85
   in higher and further education settings 8, 121–123, 125
   in NHS Talking Therapies 21
social media *xi–xii*, 173–174
   counselling groups 155
   marketing/advertising 35, 197
   platforms 35, 36, 181
social prescribing 164
solution-focused therapy (SFT)/models 73, 84–85, 105
spirituality (*see also* religion)
   BACP division 191, 193
      Thresholds journal 193, 197, 198, 199, 203
   in counselling practice 189–191, 193–200, 201–202
   in counselling training 203
   definitions of, 188–189, 191–193
   as language 189
   as pathology 189
   and religion 187–189
   supervision and, 204
   as taboo 201
   toxicity of, 204
   'workplace', 190–191
staff counselling 81, 124
stepped care model 15, 16, 25, 27, 178
suicide/suicidal ideation (*see also* risk) 106, 138, 173, 197
supervision/supervisor 4, 17
   in CYPF settings 170, 171–172, 175, 176, 177
   in dual coach-counselling practice 100, 103, 108
   in further and higher education settings 116–117
   in primary care settings 13, 16, 17, 18, 19, 20, 21, 22, 23, 24, 26
   in private practice 30, 32, 37–38, 39–40, 43
   in spiritual/faith contexts 194, 195, 197, 198
   in third sector organisations 141
   in workplace/EAP settings 89

T

technology/information technology 49
   creative use of, 58
   glitches in, 59
   operating quality of, 63–64, 66–67, 77
training/trainees (*see also* competences, placements)
   costs/affordability 12–13, 33, 143–144
   for CYPF practice 169–171, 176–177, 179–180, 182–183
   in dual coach-therapy practice 94–95, 97, 101, 102, 104, 107, 109
   in further and higher education contexts 113, 116
   in hospice settings 148, 158, 160–161, 162, 163
   in online working 53, 54, 56, 58–59, 63, 65, 67
   in primary care/NHS settings 11, 12–13, 14, 15, 17, 18–21, 21–24, 25, 27
   in private practice 40
   in spiritual/faith-related issues 201–202, 203–204
   in third-sector contexts 139–140, 140–143
trauma/PTSD (*see also* EMDR) 18, 20, 37, 49, 52, 54, 58–59, 63, 70, 72, 84, 87, 92, 98, 122, 137, 138, 150, 160, 164, 171, 175, 181, 193, 197, 199, 200
triage
   in CYPF services 179, 181
   in hospice contexts 151
   in NHS Talking Therapies 15, 16
tripartite relationship (in EAP work) 74–75

U

UK General Data Protection Regulation (*see* GDPR)
university counselling services *x*, 122
   applying for work in, 114–116
   placements in, 126–127
unplanned endings (in private practice) 41

V

voluntary/third sector
   and advocacy 139
   community roots of, 144
   delivering NHS contracts 25, 132–133
   employment of counsellors in, *x*, 3–4

flexibility of, 137
funding of, 131–132
independence of, 133–134
and hospice work 137
and marginalised groups/communities 131, 138–139
and suicide prevention 138
volunteers/volunteering/unpaid
  debates about, 143–144
  in hospice settings 148–150, 151, 160, 161, 162–164
  as a route into paid work 21, 113, 127, 169
  in third-sector/community services 12, 182–183
vulnerable adults (*see also* older people) 23, 24, 39, 63

W

working conditions/hours
  in CYPF services 174–175, 176–177
  in further and higher education settings 118, 121, 125, 126–127
  in hospice settings 156–158
  in NHS Talking Therapies 16–17, 18–21, 23–24, 24–25, 25–26
  in online counselling 55–56
  in private practice 31, 32–33, 42–43, 43–45
  in the third sector 140–143
  in workplace/EAP settings 70, 71, 77, 78, 79, 80–81, 83–84
workloads, managing,
  in CYPF settings 174, 175
  in higher and further education settings 117
  in NHS Talking Therapies 17, 19, 20, 24
  in online work 50–51
  in private practice 37, 41
  in workplace settings 79, 80
workplace counselling 86–89
  definition of, 87–88
workplace spirituality 190–191
wounded healers 115

Y

Young Persons Advisory Service (YPAS) 180–182
Youth Information, Advice and Counselling Services (YIACS) 181